Guinness Book of
SNOOKER
CLIVE EVERTON

GUINNESS SUPERLATIVES LIMITED
2 CECIL COURT, LONDON ROAD, ENFIELD, MIDDLESEX

Editor: Anne Marshall

© Clive Everton and Guinness Superlatives Limited, 1981

Published in Great Britain by Guinness Superlatives Limited,
2 Cecil Court, London Road, Enfield, Middlesex

ISBN 0–85112–230–2

British Library CIP Data
Everton, Clive
Guinness book of snooker.
1. Snooker – History
I. Title
794.7'35   GV900.S6
ISBN 0–85112–230–2

Guinness is a registered trademark of Guinness Superlatives Limited

Filmset, printed and bound by W. S. Cowell Limited, Ipswich, Suffolk
Colour origination: Colour Workshop, Hertford, Hertfordshire
Layout: Roger Daniels

CONTENTS

ACKNOWLEDGEMENTS

I would like to thank Janice Hale for additional research and cross checking of the manuscript; Bert Hackett for the line drawings and table diagrams; various photographers, in particular David Muscroft and Neil Wigley; those overseas enthusiasts who helped me fill in gaps in national records - though some regrettably still remain; and the four companies in the billiard trade - Composition Billiard Ball Supply Co., Powerglide Billiard Cues, Strachan's and Thomas Padmore and Sons - for their help in our pictorial section devoted to equipment; and the BBC for permission to take pictures of the table used for *Pot Black* 1981.

SNOOKER
IN THE
TELEVISION AGE

Snooker is one of television's most popular sports and extensive coverage of the game's major events is now taken for granted. Since daily BBC coverage of the Embassy World Professional Championship was instituted in 1978, the British public has become as obsessed with snooker for a fortnight in spring as it has traditionally been with tennis for the Wimbledon fortnight in mid-summer.

Each year, new peaks have been reached in viewing figures. Audiences in 1980 ranged from never less than 1·5 m for morning sessions, ordinarily a time of day when the number of viewers is barely measurable, to 14·5 m for the climax of the final. There was an all round increase in 1981 with a peak of 15·6 m on the first night of the final.

In television's early days, the structure of snooker counted against it when it was in competition for screen time with more obviously physical or more sharply condensed activities. Snooker's World Championship, for instance, ran at various venues throughout the whole season. Matches, even in the early rounds, were rarely of fewer than the best of 37 frames, spread over three days, and 73 frames, spread over a week, was regarded as necessary to provide a true reflection of ability in the event's later stages. From 1946 to 1949 it was judged that there was sufficient public demand for the final to be extended to 145 frames spread over a fortnight.

Particularly in the days when there was little recording and editing, there could be no guarantee that the part of the match which television would be prepared to cover would be its climax or even a meaningful part of it.

A few attempts were made, in the days of black and white television, to cover other events, the first involving the use of balls which had their numerical value inscribed on them in the manner of American pool balls. Segments of matches, including some coverage of the contest for the World Professional Billiards Championship between Clark McConachy and John Barrie in 1951 which was highly praised by the *Daily Mail*'s distinguished television critic, Peter

Black, gave way to makeshift versions of the game to fill limited time slots.

The latter invariably revolved round Joe Davis, as indeed the whole professional scene did. On one occasion, another professional was deputed to open the unbroken triangle of reds as vigorously as he could in order that Joe could then make three – in the event unsuccessful – attempts to make a century break.

Inserted into *Sportsview*, the Wednesday night forerunner of *Sportsnight*, was a feature in which, from a set position, Joe attempted each week to compile as large a break as he could in two minutes. One week, the luckless referee, as if to exemplify the adage 'more haste, less speed', sabotaged his effort by scattering the balls as he went to replace a colour on its spot.

As it was with Joe that the BBC conducted all its snooker negotiations, it was hardly surprising that such BBC coverage as there was should convey the impression that Joe was the only player of any real quality. Snooker on television settled into endlessly repetitive, totally lifeless 'challenge' matches between Joe and a series of opponents he himself selected.

When BBC's Saturday afternoon programme *Grandstand* was live, snooker was found to be a useful standby if racing or some other outdoor attraction fell foul of the weather. As is the way with live television, items did not always run to their predicted length so the snooker players would frequently be informed at the commencement of a frame that it had to be completed in say, fifteen, twelve or even ten minutes. For none of these matches was there even a pretence of competitive interest.

In its early days, ITV adopted a more enterprising policy. With a mere half-dozen active professionals at the time, the professional scene as such was clearly played out so ITV, in conjunction with the amateur governing body, formulated a tournament in 1961 in which four amateurs, receiving small, face-saving handicaps, wiped the floor with four professionals.

The matches were only of the best of five frames and, live as they were, television missed some of the finishes, but at least they were genuine contests. There was live coverage too in 1964 of the Northern final of the English Amateur Championship featuring a future world professional champion, John Spencer, an international amateur tournament featuring representatives of the four home countries and, at various times, much other interesting if not particularly well planned snooker. Two amateurs, Mark Wildman (1962) and Jonathan Barron (1963), made century breaks on television before any professional did.

Tragically, genuine competition was not deemed exciting enough and the amateur governing body, desperate even for the modest television fees which at the time represented a financial lifeline, disgracefully connived to prearrange certain aspects of the matches, instructing the players to ensure that the result depended on the fifth and final frame. In the ensuing hullabaloo, snooker disappeared from ITV's screens altogether.

Since BBC's last flicker of interest in snooker had been extinguished soon after Joe Davis's retirement in 1964, there was for a while no snooker on either channel. In such travestied or corrupt forms as the game had come to be seen, this was the best thing that could have happened for when a new opportunity eventually presented itself a fresh start could be made.

With the advent of BBC-2 and colour television, the BBC were casting about for ideas which would stimulate the sale of sets which could receive colour transmissions and which would thus increase viewing figures on the infant channel. One BBC producer, Philip Lewis, who had been involved on the *Grandstand* coverage of snooker, was convinced that colour – which was after all intrinsic to the very rules of the game – would make the game much more attractive on the screen than ever it had been in the days of black and white.

From this perception, *Pot Black* was born in 1969. With Joe Davis long since retired, there was no temptation to build the programme self-destructively round one player or a few tired old permutations. Indeed, various factors amounting to little more than chance had led to three leading amateurs, Gary Owen, John Spencer and Ray Reardon, becoming the first new professionals since 1951.

Eight professionals, initially split into two round robin groups of four, took part. All matches (except

Line up of *Pot Black* 1981 contestants.

for the best of three frames finals of some series) were, and have remained, sudden death affairs of one frame, a format which the snooker world itself, brought up on 37 and 73 frame matches, would never have devised but which, with the game only just emerging from the worst depression it had ever known, it was prepared to accept.

The non-snooker public responded enthusiastically to this simple but carefully presented formula. Millions new to snooker were fascinated by the quiet delicacy and precision of the game and the cool, controlled demeanour of the players, such a contrast, as Philip Purser put it in the *Sunday Telegraph*, 'to the hysterical pooves of the football field'.

Players invariably found that appearances on *Pot Black* stimulated demand for the one-night club exhibition engagements which were then their staple income and which, even now, remain an important portion of it for most professionals. Slowly, very slowly, snooker began to attract sponsors.

John Player sponsored the World Professional Championships of 1969 and 1970 but as the event was still a season-long affair of week's matches, television understandably displayed no interest.

Gallahers, the second tobacco combine to enter snooker, employed a different strategy. Their agents, West Nally, the West End company who rapidly established themselves as the leaders in the expanding trade of servicing sports sponsorship campaigns, devised a tournament not only to capture the interest of the snooker world but to serve twin objectives: a relatively immediate merchandising return and indirect advertising by means of obtaining televison time for an event carrying a company name.

Just as cricket's Gillette Cup had been introduced on the assumption that many spectators who would not watch a segment of a three day match might be attracted to a one day contest which they could witness, result and all, in its entirety, the Park Drive £2000 offered a complete snooker match of seven frames in one evening. The four best available professionals played a triple round robin – eighteen matches in all – in prime club venues, a highly favourable situation in which to promote a particular brand of cigarettes.

None of the matches constituted an attraction strong enough for television but – so West Nally put it to the BBC – a seven frame final between the first two finishers in the league table did. BBC responded by covering all the four Park Drive £2000 finals for edited transmissions on *Grandstand*. Both Park Drive £600's, another West Nally brainchild, were recorded in their entirety by Yorkshire TV and screened as a seven week series.

The success of the Park Drive events persuaded Gallahers and West Nally that snooker had wider possibilities. Under Park Drive's sponsorship, the World Championship was telescoped into a fortnight with simultaneous play on eight tables and, for the first time, substantial television coverage of a semi-final on the first Saturday afternoon and the climax of the final, still a five day affair of 75 frames, on the following Saturday.

Eager as snooker was to encourage television, the medium's technical requirements often caused problems. In the second Park Drive £2000 final, the heat from the lights was so intense that it caused the formica on the cushion rails of the table – admittedly of new design – to curl up. So hot were the cushion rails that a player who had to rest his bridge hand on them completed his shot with a rare sense of urgency! Special television lights, unnecessary in the days of black and white but essential for colour, provided the players with problems of glare and dazzle which they coped with as best they could until the eighth session of the 1973 world final, an occasion so important to the players that they had to put their own preferences well in front of television's, brought the matter to a head.

After only a few minutes under the blinding newly installed lighting it was obvious that Eddie Charlton could see but that Ray Reardon could not. Leading 27-25, Reardon lost two frames with ludicrous ease and a third after his protests had led to two of the largest floodlights, which were in any event needed only to illuminate the crowd, being switched off. Further discussions took place at the mid-session interval during which Reardon was able to compose himself and then emerge to win four of the remaining five frames of the day. With the hiatus which had threatened to change the course of the final having passed, Reardon went on to win 38-32.

ITV covered the 1973 and 1974 Norwich Union Open finals from the Piccadilly Hotel, London, recording the 15 frame matches in their entirety on the Friday night and transmitting the highlights on their Saturday afternoon *World of Sport* programme. The BBC adopted a similar procedure for the inaugural Benson and Hedges Masters in 1975, a tournament from which television has since gradually increased its coverage.

Both Norwich Union and Benson and Hedges were clients of West Nally, thus emphasising that snooker needed someone outside the sport to look at it dispassionately and create packages which, without belittling the game itself, were acceptable to sponsors and television companies. What chiefly transpired was that a huge number of frames was not required either for the public to take a match seriously or indeed for it to constitute a fair test of skill.

Television lighting continued to vary in acceptability. The 1976 World Championship, having been played up to the semi-finals under traditional lighting with a shade over the table, switched to television lights for the final but these were hung in such a way that there was an altogether unacceptable degree of glare and dazzle from the balls. Reardon erupted, the lights were re-hung and the incident was of value in that Nick Hunter, the BBC producer whose first experience of covering snooker this was, instituted research with BBC's lighting engineers and consultation with the players to produce a lighting system acceptable both to the competitors and television itself.

Substantial improvement, followed in due course by certain refinements, led to such a good system, now adopted as standard, that players no longer feel that television lighting is in any sense a handicap in producing their best form. They have also welcomed the practice of suspending a gauze-like filter beneath the lights, not only because it reduces the glare, but because any exploding lights cannot thereby rain down on their unsuspecting heads. One such explosion at the William Hill Welsh Professional Championship in 1977 had burnt a hole in the cloth, fortunately, not while a player was at the table!

The 1976 world final provided the BBC with another problem. It was planned to record the climax of the match on Friday to transmit highlights on Saturday but Reardon obtained such a commanding lead in the best of 53 frames final against Alex Higgins that a hasty decision had to be taken to record on Thursday in order to ensure live action.

Even then, it was not plain sailing. Higgins, falling hopelessly behind in some frames, conceded them with reds still on the table in order to deny Reardon the further boost to his confidence of potting the remaining balls. In turn, when Higgins was set for victory, Reardon lost no time in throwing in the towel. In this way, frame followed frame at what some felt was excessive speed.

A clause was inserted in the playing conditions for subsequent championships to the effect that frames could not be conceded until the brown had been potted, but the players, reluctant to abrogate their right, for tactical reasons, to concede a lost cause at a moment of their own choosing, quite rightly ignored it.

Undeterred by his trying baptism, Hunter appreciated as no one in television previously had snooker's potential as a television sport. While *Pot Black*, which had attracted between one and two million viewers from its inception, was now attracting a highly respectable three to four million viewers on BBC-2, Hunter believed that bigger audiences could be obtained if the BBC developed its coverage from a glimpse of the final to a portrait of the event. The public, initially prepared to accept snooker only on a short simple basis, was now becoming familiar enough with its leading players and the game itself to accept more substantial fare.

West Nally, unappreciated by the professional game, had save for retaining its connection with the Benson and Hedges Masters pulled out of snooker in 1975. Chaos was looming when a new promoter in Mike Watterson providentially emerged to stage the 1977 World Championship.

BBC coverage was extended to the last three days, less than Hunter wanted and less indeed than could have been accommodated in the schedules but for a change of dates for the event. The viewing figures were encouraging but, even more, the BBC, the sponsors, Embassy, and the snooker world were reassured by the overall quality and efficiency of the promotion.

Thus encouraged, BBC gave the 1978 World Championship daily coverage by means of a late night 50-minute compilation, sometimes with live inserts, in addition to Saturday afternoon exposure in *Grandstand* and, a final triumph, live coverage of the final on BBC-2 on the second Thursday and Friday of the thirteen day championship and early on Saturday evening.

The very first late night compilation, edited from simultaneous recording of two matches, a total of 26 playing hours through the day, attracted a near midnight audience of four million which built to seven million by the end of the tournament. The nation stayed up late and went to work red-eyed as some 150 BBC personnel were involved in recording and editing some 300 miles of video-tape during the championship fortnight.

'Backstage at The Crucible', wrote Peter Fiddick, *The Guardian*'s television correspondent, 'there is a sense that the result scarcely matters, that something new is happening. The top professionals are very conscious of their new audience and its implications. For them, the game is at last being shown properly, at length, with all its tactics, and the fact that it could prove even more popular that way opens a whole new future even to men said to be potting £30 000 a year. "What the public are getting here", says Fred Davis, "is the feel of what it is like playing under pressure hour after hour for days on end".'

The 1979 and 1980 World Championships built on these foundations as coverage was extended – in 1980 to a staggering 70 hours – and television audiences increased.

This success bred other successes. The new United Kingdom Championship, another Mike Watterson promotion, attracted BBC's *Grandstand*'s cameras to its inaugural final in 1977 before coverage was stepped up to embrace the semi-final and final in 1978 and 1979 and to eight days, that is, from the quarter-finals onwards, in 1980. This coverage included the signif-

POT BLACK SNOOKER CHAMPIONSHIP
1969   Ray Reardon (Wal)
1970   John Spencer (Eng)
1971   John Spencer (Eng)
1972   Eddie Charlton (Aust)
1973   Eddie Charlton (Aust)
1974   Graham Miles (Eng)
1975   Graham Miles (Eng)
1976   John Spencer (Eng)
1977   Perrie Mans (SA)
1978   Doug Mountjoy (Wal)
1979   Ray Reardon (Wal)
1980   Eddie Charlton (Aust)
1981   Cliff Thorburn (Can)

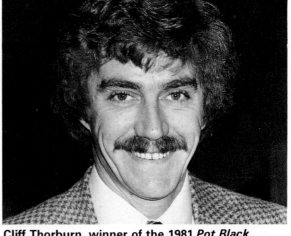

Cliff Thorburn, winner of the 1981 *Pot Black*.

icant breakthrough that most transmissions were on BBC-1, still the corporation's senior channel. A third Watterson promotion, the State Express World Cup, a new world team championship, was covered by BBC in its entirety for eight days in 1979 and nine in 1980.

Pot Black not only continued as an annual series of fifteen 25-minute programmes but in 1981 inaugurated a *Junior Pot Black* with the same format featuring young unknowns; coverage of the Benson and Hedges Masters was extended to its last four days; and BBC Wales covered the four days of the Woodpecker Welsh Professional Championship. Snooker on BBC had reached what even its most enthusiastic supporters were prepared to concede was almost saturation point.

The by-product of tournament coverage, though, is more public interest in the game's personalities, techniques and reminiscences. One demonstration of the enhanced status of the snooker professional was the prominence given to the exhibition of trick shots which the 1979 world champion, Terry Griffiths, also a subject of *This is Your Life* on ITV, gave at BBC's Sports Personality of the Year awards night. Ray Reardon, a previous *This is Your Life* subject, appeared on that barometer of public celebrity, *The Parkinson Show*. Lengthy reviews of the spring World Championships transmitted within a few days of the following Christmas proved popular. Fred Davis was the subject of an extended profile in the Maestro series.

While snooker became a mainstream sport on BBC, its position on ITV was less satisfactory, largely because of the internecine strife which is inherent in its federal structure. Nationwide network television on ITV could only be guaranteed if an item was accepted for the Saturday afternoon *World of Sport* programme but sponsors became reluctant to support tournaments from which their total television exposure might be only some 40 minutes.

The Norwich Union Open finals of 1973 and 1974, the one-off Dry Blackthorn Cup of 1977 and the one-off *Daily Mirror* Champion of Champions in 1978, all recorded Friday night for Saturday showing, provided top class snooker on this programme and Thames committed themselves to three days of 'same day' coverage from the Holsten Lager tournament at Slough in January 1979.

This project misfired through difficulties peculiar to the television industry. The hours of play in a snooker tournament are long and arduous, too long for union regulations to permit a complete day's play to be covered by one crew. A television company thus has to choose between incurring more labour costs or covering only a proportion of a day's play.

Thames, having failed to secure the agreement of other ITV companies to show the tournament nationwide, were screening it only in their own region, in itself an argument against extra expense. It opted not to cover the first three frames of the semifinal between John Spencer and Cliff Thorburn and thus missed an historic 147 break by Spencer, the first ever maximum in tournament play which would, of course, also have been the highest break ever made on television. The snooker shown was keenly competitive and of high quality but Thames's misfortune in missing the 147 led to the formation of a body of executive opinion, not confined to ITV, in favour of covering either the whole of an event or none of it. It was a possible compromise to cover the latter stages of a tournament but once coverage had started it was all or nothing.

Snooker on ITV settled back into a routine of recording events for much later showing and a few of these series saw the light of day in areas not covered by their originating companies. They were good pay days for the players but the tournaments could not and did not achieve any great status either within the game or with the general public.

Two of the smaller companies, HTV and Tyne Tees, ran annual amateur series. The HTV event, featuring the leading Welsh amateurs, provided such future professional luminaries as Terry Griffiths and Doug Mountjoy with their first television exposure, and in 1978 Tyne Tees secured a scoop when Joe Johnson, later a professional, made an official world amateur record break of 140 in their final.

ITV's coverage of snooker was fragmented and lacking in continuity. There was some agreement that snooker made good television but inter-company rivalry and lack of administrative backbone within the game left the situation untidy.

The professional governing body, as such, made no attempt to control televised snooker. Any promoter, not necessarily possessing any previous connection with the game, could approach a television company and/or a sponsor and concoct a deal to put to the players. Confusion and squabbling were common.

Ironically, the only snooker to be nationally if not simultaneously networked was Yorkshire's annual Pro-Celebrity tournament which the snooker world regarded as a travesty of the game but which achieved audiences the television companies deemed satisfactory.

The Wilsons Classic (Granada 1980, 1981), the Padmore Super Crystalate International (ATV 1980) and the Tolly Cobbold Classic (Anglia 1980, 1981) were well enough received in their regions but it was not until March 1981 that 'same day' network coverage of a major tournament was achieved with the Yamaha International from Derby. Mike Watterson had established himself so clearly as the leader in his field that he was again the promoter.

It was not only in its federal structure that ITV continued at a disadvantage to the BBC. Its programme times could not be so flexible and the availability of only one channel restricted the time which could be devoted to one event.

The advent of the fourth channel should certainly give ITV more elbow room in covering sports events at length. For snooker this could mean more tournaments, more sponsorship and possibly an eventual attempt by ITV to outbid BBC for the championships which are at present in the company's contractual portfolio.

Britain has remained very much the centre of the professional game and snooker has not achieved a comparably high status as a television sport abroad.

New Zealand, like Australia, buy *Pot Black* and some edited World Championship coverage from the BBC. Some tournaments with visiting professionals have been staged especially for television and there has been coverage of the World Amateur Billiards Championships of 1975 (in Auckland) and 1977 (in Melbourne) and the 1980 World Amateur Snooker (in Launceston). There has been some televised snooker in South Africa (including the 1976 World Amateur) and some studio snooker in Canada prior to its first snooker outside broadcast from the final of the Canadian Open in 1980. On Britain's doorstep, Radio Telefis Eireann covered the World Amateur Snooker in Dublin in 1974 and the Benson and Hedges Irish Masters professional tournament annually since 1975.

No doubt some enterprising international entrepreneur of the eighties will attempt to shape this often wasteful miscellany in a Grand Prix series of international tournaments similar to the tennis circuit with coverage of each country's respective television companies, particular sponsors for each tournament and a multi-national sponsor for a cumulative points table, the top finishers in which would contest a Grand Prix Masters, another plum for television.

That such a scheme can ever be seriously contemplated is a commentary on the progress snooker has made in the last decade. Snooker has always been a great game but, held back by administrations variously weak, autocratic or out of touch, it has taken outside influences, of which television is the chief, to bring this home to the public at large.

ELEMENTS
OF THE
GAME

Snooker has achieved its current status through an erratic process of evolution which can be traced back through its parent game, billiards, and, further still, to a recognisable form of billiards which was played, like croquet, on a lawn.

Although the Greeks and Romans played many games with balls and sticks, it was not until the 1340s that a game in which an arch and pin, common features of early table billiards, were placed on a lawn and in which maces, the precursors of cues, were used to propel the wooden balls.

Louis XI of France (1461-83) is believed to have been the first to transfer the game to a table, and billiard tables became quite a common item of furni-

ture among the French and then the English nobility.

Although the lawn version survived into the 1600s, billiards was by this time played almost exclusively on tables.

Mary Queen of Scots, only months before she was beheaded, complained bitterly that her 'table de billiard' had been taken away by her captors who were later to rip the cloth off the table and half cover her decapitated corpse with it.

By the Elizabethan Age tables were common in the taverns of London and the cafes of Paris and billiards had come to be one of those games of skill and chance at which it was the done thing for gentry and aspiring gentry to gamble.

Louis XIV playing billiards.

0·1·2·3·4·5·6·7·8·9·10·11·12·13·14·15·16·17·18·19
9876543210
NEWS OF THE WORLD
BILLIARDS
TOURNAMENT
FINAL
At THURSTON'S
(LEICESTER SQUARE, W.1)
ON
FRIDAY
PLAY

CUE

Around 1670 the thin end of the mace started to be used not merely when the cue-ball was under the cushion rail – originally designed, of course, merely to prevent the balls dropping off the table – but for other shots as a matter of preference. The complete change from mace to cue – the word deriving from the French *queue* meaning 'a tail' – took until about 1800.

Since then the design of the cue has altered very little, though the last five years have seen a rapid increase in the number of players using two-piece cues, that is, those with either a wooden or metal joint in the middle. John Spencer was the first player to win the World Professional Championship with such a cue in 1977.

In November 1938, Alec Brown, a London professional, was the central figure in an incident which lead the governing body to stipulate that a cue 'must be at least 3 ft in length and conform to the accepted shape and design'. With the cue ball marooned in the middle of a pack of reds, Brown produced from his pocket a tiny ebony cue, complete with tip, which his father had made. He duly chalked the tip and played his shot but his opponent protested. Thurston's resident referee, Charlie Chambers, sensing no doubt that the use of this implement was outside the spirit if not the letter of the law, awarded a foul – and the rule was changed.

Charles Chambers, the resident referee at Thurston's between the wars, who was recognised as supreme in his profession *(left)*. Bartley's famous billiard room at Bath, 1798 *(below)*.

TIP

Before tips were invented, players tried to strike the cue-ball as centrally as possible to avoid a miscue. Striking low (to bring the cue-ball back from the object-ball) or high (to make it follow through) were two skills current only in a limited way before the invention of tips by a French infantry captain, Mingaud, in 1807.

Languishing in a Paris prison for debt, Mingaud devoted his ample leisure to a study of billiards, experimenting successfully with a leather tip and astounding all and sundry with his cuemanship on his release.

Mingaud also discovered that by raising the cue almost vertically – in fact into the position in which the mace was used – extraordinary spin effects could be obtained by striking a sharp downwards glancing blow to the left or right across the cue-ball. This type of stroke is called a *massé* – French for mace.

CHALK

In pre-tip days it was common for players to twist the points of their cues in a wall or ceiling so that the chalk-like deposit was at least partial insurance against a miscue. Ordinary chalk also came to be used but the first marketing was done by John Carr, a marker in John Bartley's Billiard Rooms at Bath.

Between 1818 and 1823 either Bartley, who subsequently showed Carr, or Carr himself discovered the positive uses of side spin (or 'side' as it has come to be known). If the cue-ball was struck to the right or left of centre, it was discovered that the spin thus

After importing specially dried and selected squares of Canadian maple or South American hardwoods like ebony and rosewood, the basic preparation of the butt square—sawing and shaping—begins (1). A wedge piece is removed to produce the shape of the splice.

Specially dyed decorative veneers are selected (2) and glued to the front splice of the butt. The picture also shows four shafts which have been rounded from their original squares by a previous process. The rounded butt is sawn spliced to accept the milled end of the shaft (3) and the butt and shaft assembled and glued (4).

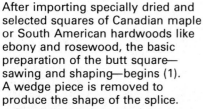

One of several tapering operations is carried out on custom-built machinery. Only a third of the original butt and shaft remains after the final tapering.

In the case of two-piece cues (5) the shaft is sawn and the joint inserted. Joints consist of nine components employing specially turned aluminium parts, basically of the screw and washer type, designed to give maximum strength to the joint and provide perfect alignment.

The cue is weighted and balanced (6). The lead weight (see left hand) is pushed up the shaft and secured by the dowel (see right hand) which is then driven and glued into the central boring. The end of the shaft is sealed and fitted with a rubber buffer. The tip end of the cue is prepared and shaped (7) ready to accept its threaded brass ferrule. The ferrule is fitted and a tip

affixed (8). The ferrule, incidentally, guards the wood against erosion when it is necessary to sandpaper down a new tip.

Cues are horizontally sanded (9) to produce a fine finish and final overall shape, and dipped into a sealing compound (10). The compound has the effect of sealing the natural grain of the timber in order to prevent any loss of moisture content from the wood, thus minimising warpage and ensuring maximum stability.

The butt end is polished (11). What appear to be bricks lying on the bench are in fact blocks of polishing compound.

Finished cues are checked for weight, straightness, balance and visual effect (12) and the name plate implanted.

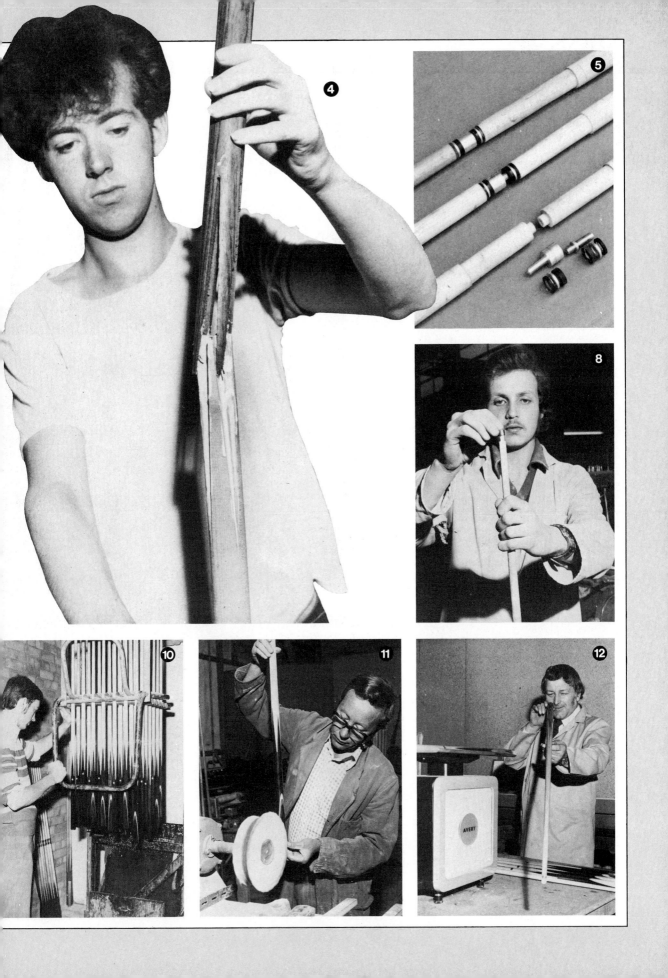

A billiard table is a complex construction which requires many kinds of highly specialised workmanship to produce its individual components. Contrary to a widely held belief, tables are never transported in their constructed state but are always assembled and reassembled as need be. The table installed in BBC's Birmingham studios for the 1981 *Pot Black* series was for many years in the home of Joe Davis. It was made by Thurston and Co. in 1907 and was installed (as shown in the sequence of photographs) for *Pot Black* by Thomas Padmore and Sons of Birmingham, a member of the Clare-Thurston-Padmore group.

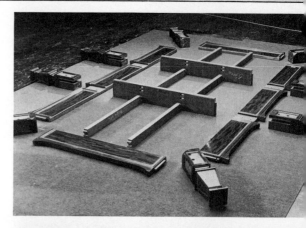

The components of the table are laid out in a pattern roughly corresponding to the way they fit together (1).

A pair of legs to which the end rail has been joined is attached to the rest of the frame (2). The upper surfaces of the frame are planed level if necessary (3).

The five slates, each weighing between 4 and 4½ cwt and between $1\frac{3}{4}$ and 2in thick, are set on the frame (4). They are held in place by means of gravity. The wood lining strips are screwed to the underside of the slate around its edges and shaped to the pocket openings (5). These strips are necessary to hold the tacks which secure the cloth.

A spirit level is placed on every area of the table and if the playing surface is not perfectly level the table is jacked up and discs of masonite or veneer of varying thicknesses are placed under the appropriate leg (7). Beer mats or any other material which can be compacted or absorb water are unsuitable for this purpose.

The bed cloth is stretched as tightly as possible and tacked to the wood lining strips (8). Enough tacks to fill a 1oz tobacco tin will be necessary to complete this operation.

After the spots, baulk line and 'D' have been marked on the table, the cloth is ironed (9), always with the nap which runs from the 'D' towards the black spot end of the table.

The cushions are bolted into place with the aid of a brace (10), and as each pocket is completed, the pocket openings are measured with the official templates (11).

Ready for play.

Billiard cloths are manufactured from fine merino wool imported from Queensland, Australia. 180 000 gallons of softened water per day is used during the manufacturing process at the Lodgemore Mills, Stroud, home of the twin West of England cloth companies, Strachan's and Hunt and Winterbotham's.

Washed wool is blended and made into threads. The wool is taken out of bales, drawn through a fan into a mixing machine, through a vortex and sprayed with emulsion of oil and water before going to the blending chambers. It is then packed into bales ready for carding. The best way of obtaining uniformity is to use different types of wool, sometimes as many as four in a blend. The best quality wool has high elasticity and natural crimping.

The blended wool from the previous process is fed into a hopper, combed out on a series of wire covered rollers and condensed into threads (2). The fibres are presented at right angles to other fibres on a second machine to produce a multi-directional effect in the yarn (3). Without this random direction the cloth would not be as dense. Eventually the web is split into separate threads.

After carding, the thread still has no strength. The object of the machine in picture 4 is to insert twists before these threads are re-wound on to cones.

The finished thread is then put onto the warping machine (5) which lays the warped threads to the required width on a roller which can then be fitted to the loom.

The cloth is woven wet to enable the threads to be packed more tightly and make the cloth more dense. The warp thread is the down thread, the weft thread the cross thread (6). The cloth is well washed to remove any grease or impurities and is then put through a process where the wool is impregnated with soap and squeezed under very heavy rollers in a shrinking process which can take between eight hours and two days (7).

A cloth which was 134" wide on the loom and 120" wide after scouring can shrink to 74" after milling. This process markedly increases the density of the cloth.

The cloth, sewn into a loop, as it was for scouring and milling, is passed on a large roller type machine over a wide teazle which raises a pile. It is then layered with a wire brush to give the nap direction and the pile which has been raised trimmed with a rotating cutter like a lawn mower (8).

This process is repeated on another machine using natural teazles which are grown in Somerset as a crop. The teazles (9) are fitted into a rod (9a) in which they are set as flat as possible. The cloth is started on worn teazles and upgraded to new ones. The natural teazle process uses water this adds lustre to the cloth.

The cloth is dyed in a dye vesse (10) in which it is boiled for one and half hours.

A continuous wet dressing proce takes place on a West of England g in which one roller feeds cloth on another. The cloth is thoroughly w and is passed over a rapidly rotati brush. Again the water is necessa to give lustre to the cloth.

The green cloth is now raised a dressed (as in picture 8) to ensure th it has the length of nap required (1

The cloth is inspected both horizontally and vertically and pressed to consolidate it and make level surface.

Throughout the process, it is inspected for broken threads whic are repaired by hand using needle with ball points so that the needle goes between the threads. Any kno also have to be removed. There c be up to 3000 knots per 60 yard length.

Various chemicals are reacted together for two days in large resin kettles. Dye is also added at this stage so that each batch will produce all red, all white or all blue balls (1).

This mixture, the consistency of thick glue, is poured into glass light bulbs (without the filaments of course) (2).

These light bulbs are baked in an oven for many hours until they are hard (3) and then left to cool for several days (4).

The glass is smashed to leave a neck where the resin has overflowed the round part of the light bulb. This neck is sawn off roughly with a slitting saw (5).

The balls are roughly turned to remove the remainder of the neck (6) and ground for the first time to make the ball quite round (7).

Spot white billiard balls at this stage are drilled with two small holes and filled with black resin to provide the 'spots'.

The balls are again heat treated to stabilise them and to make their outside surface more durable.

The balls are then ground again to correct any distortion that may have been created during the heat treatment (8).

A micrometer checks their diameter (9).

The balls are polished and finely ground using a polishing compound (10) and are checked and given a final wipe with a duster.

In the case of the matched billiard sets, the balls are weighed (11) allowing a difference in weight of not more than 0.2 grams. These balls are packed in sealed boxes (12) so that sets cannot be mixed up prior to sale. Even the non-matched sets of billiard balls should not differ by more than one gram.

imparted would affect the angle at which it rebounded from the cushion. In some cases, too, side could be used to help the cue-ball into the pocket when playing an in-off.

Carr attributed the strange new affects he was producing to a special brand of 'twisting chalk' which he sold in small boxes though it was, of course, merely ordinary chalk.

Today's leading players use American chalk manufactured in such a way as to give maximum adhesion between tip and cue-ball.

TABLE

The demand for tables and equipment was first met by furniture makers, carpenters and the like, some of whom, like John Thurston (established 1799) went over entirely to this new specialist trade (1814).

Thurston was responsible for many of the improvements which were to bring the manufacture of tables almost to perfection. Table beds were originally of wood but Thurston began experimenting with slate in 1826 and by 1840 slate, naturally found in flat layers which make it ideal for the permanently flat surface necessary for the game, was generally accepted.

Early cushions were layered strips of felt but after trying hair, list, Russian duck, white swan-skin and other substances, rubber was introduced in 1835.

This innovation was not without its problems. Cold weather caused the rubber to lose all its elasticity, a contingency which Thurston's met temporarily with cushion warmers – metal pans or tubes to hold hot water. But the real breakthrough was the development of the vulcanising process, raising the temperature of the natural rubber and combining it with sulphur to produce a substance more resistant to temperature changes. In 1845, Queen Victoria received the first set of these new cushions.

In essence, the modern table was in existence though there were subsequent refinements. Strip rubber was replaced by block rubber and the highest degree of predictability in the angle of rebound from cushions was obtained with the advent of steel blocks, which were used as backing for the rubber.

Pockets changed, not so much in size as in shape. Initially, the cushion rubbers were shaped as squarely at the entrance to the pockets as they were elsewhere but this meant that a ball could not enter a pocket unless it did not touch the sides or at any rate brushed a jaw by the merest fraction.

Easier access was promoted by cutting away the underside of the rectangular shape of the rubber in such a way that the ball was turned towards the pocket rather than allowed to bounce off the cushion at the usual angle.

The extent and angle of this cut-away of the under-

side of the rubber has a crucial influence on the ease of pocket entry. The greater the undercut, the more it is possible for the rounded surface of the ball to tuck underneath it and thus enter the pocket.

The simple mathematics are that the top of the nose of the cushion is $1^1/_2$ inches from the bed of the table. A ball is $2^1/_{16}$ inches in diameter or, as the Irish would say, $1^1/_{32}$ inches at its fattest point. Therefore, if the cushion nose at the pocket entrance starts $1^1/_{32}$ inches or less from the bed of the table, the ball cannot tuck underneath the cushion and the pocket will reject it.

The Billiards and Snooker Control Council's (B & SCC), formerly the Billiards Association and Control Council, official templates, adopted in 1892 were of limited value in that they measured only the width of the pockets and took no account of the undercut. Thus, the templates could fit either a pocket which players found very easy or one which they found nearly impossible. The ease or difficulty of pockets on championship tables thus became largely a matter of custom or preference with a general tendency, after snooker superseded billiards as the most popular game, towards ease.

After decades of petty wrangling among the trade firms, who of course had to produce tables incorporating any new official specifications, a sub-committee of the International Billiards and Snooker Federation (IBSF) was entrusted with the design of a new template specifying the degree of undercut and ensuring that the pocket did not narrow beyond the edge of the playing surface. Pockets which had not incorporated the latter stipulation tended to reject even accurately struck balls if played at speed from narrow angles – that is positions in which players could not aim at the full width of the pocket opening.

The new template, designed by Norman Clare, was accepted by the IBSF and B & SCC in 1980.

CLOTH

Early tables were covered with green cloth to simulate the grass on which the parent outdoor version of the game was played. Cloth also deadened the noise which the balls would otherwise have made on a polished wooden table and made control a little easier.

Initially, cloths were coarse and heavy but once improving technology had made it possible to mow the previously long nap very short, cloths were developed specifically for billiards.

Some grades sold on cheapness and durability, chiefly to public rooms where tables could expect heavy and prolonged usage, but the very best grades were of the smooth, superfine texture which led to them being adopted for championship play.

Two West of England firms, Strachans and Hunt and Winterbotham's, later amalgamated, led the way with billiard table cloth, though in recent years two

Yorkshire companies, Hainsworth's and Booth's, have obtained a substantial share of the market. The Belgium company, Iwan Simonis, who dominate the market in the European pocketless games, have also become increasingly interested in the billiards and snooker scene in recent years.

A Manchester firm, Reddaways, introduced a cotton napless cloth, the Janus, in the 1930s and contracted the leading professionals to play on it. Some large breaks were made but despite rather than because of the quality of the surface. 'Like playing on a shirt', was Joe Davis's succinct description.

The venture ended in bankruptcy and West of England cloth resumed its reign as the championship surface, a status which today it shares more or less equally with Hainsworth's.

The chief selling point of the Janus cloth – that both sides provided an equally good surface – was actually its greatest disadvantage for serious players. Through the elimination of any 'nap', players were not only deprived of an important degree of control but had to cope with 'side' having the opposite effect to that which it had on a woollen cloth.

As on velvet, the nap of a billiard table feels smooth when stroked in one direction – in the case of a table from the baulk end, where the 'D' is situated, towards the top where, in snooker, the black is spotted – and rough in the other.

Even on the best tables, a ball will run more truly with the nap than against it or, sometimes, across it. For example, even on championship tables, a ball played slowly from the pink spot area towards a middle pocket will curl towards the near jaw. Against the nap, too, any right-hand side imparted to the cue-ball will cause it to drift to the left rather than to the right, as it would if played with the nap.

These apparent disadvantages carry numerous compensations in the ways players may use the nap to help them control various spins.

In recent years, some championship cloths have had shorter naps than ever before. Balls tend to run straighter against these naps than they would against the naps of other cloths but a degree of control is often lost because the cue-ball (like a golf ball flighted to a parched glassy green) has nothing to 'bite' on.

Cloths are kept in condition by regular brushing (always with the nap) and ironing. The heat of the room and the frequency and temperature at which the iron is used tends to affect the speed of the table.

BALLS

The earliest and most primitive balls were of wood but even in the early 19th century ivory was the accepted material.

Balls were generally of $1^7/8$ inches diameter until Thurston began to supply 2-inch balls with all his tables in 1830, one advantage of which was that the cue-ball was easier to strike when it lay against a cushion. Ever since the games's earliest official rules, the standard size has been $2^1/16$ inches.

Apparently, only a female elephant tusk was suitable for billiard ball manufacture and even this had to be of such a size that as little of its exterior as possible had to be pared away. Even the best ivories were somewhat unpredictable and the worst, lacking interior consistency, were unplayable, but the distinctive click they produced was, at least in Britain, considered as vital to the character and tradition of the game as the sound of leather on willow in cricket.

Ivory, which had to be ground regularly in order to keep the balls round, was also extremely expensive so composition balls were introduced as cheap substitutes before it was recognised that they were also very much more reliable.

In 1868, John Wesley Hyatt, a New York inventor, discovered that collodion (nitro-cellulose, camphor and alcohol), which printers brushed on their fingers to protect them from cuts and grazes, hardened when it was dry and could be made into balls. Hyatt and his brother Isaac patented their process in 1870 under the trade name of celluloid, the world's first commercial synthetic plastic. As it was also used to make piano keys and false teeth it was perhaps appropriate that the new ball should have some teething problems: celluloid was highly flammable and, if struck too hard, a ball could explode! Nevertheless, this initial discovery led directly to the cast resin and cast phenolic balls which are used today.

RULES

Before John Roberts Snr and William Cook met for the championship at St. James's Hall in 1870 in front of the Prince of Wales the leading players and trade representatives of the day met to draw up championship rules. In February 1885 the situation was formalised when a similar gathering founded the Billiards Association. Only one further meeting was necessary to approve a universal set of rules. In essence, the rule changes that have taken place since then reflect the need to curb various repetitious scoring methods in the wider interests of the game.

The spot stroke was the first such method to be so limited. Before organised competition, when champions were determined by public opinion on the results of challenge matches for money, Jonathan Kentfield, the first recognised champion, made a break of 196 which included 57 consecutive pot reds off the spot. As cushions were not then made of rubber this was no mean feat as position had to be maintained by screwing straight back (see Diagram 1) or rolling through at just the right angle (see Diagram 2). Their lack of bounce made it extremely difficult to utilise the cush-

The first contest for the billiards championship at St. James's Hall between John Roberts (Snr) and William Cook (Jnr) on 11 February 1870. The Prince of Wales witnessed the match.

ions for position. Even rubber cushions, which dated from 1935, needed many refinements before they could be considered consistent and reliable.

By 1870 the best tables were good enough for the spot stroke to be a formidable weapon. Cook was a spot stroke specialist so Roberts, who had the better all-round game, pressed for the pocket openings to be reduced to 3 inches (as against the usual and present day $3^1/_2$ inches) and for the red spot to be placed $12^1/_2$ inches from the top cushion instead of the usual $13^1/_4$ inches or the present day $12^3/_4$ inches.

Regardless of the disadvantage at which this put him, Cook won anyway but when Roberts's son, John Roberts Jnr, defeated Cook comfortably for the title two months later, Cook belatedly realised how his greatest asset had been negated. He also realised, at a

time when leading players were starting to derive income from admission charges as well as side-stakes, that billiards would be more attractive to the public if it could be presented as a varied three ball game rather than a repetitive potting contest. Accordingly, he introduced the 'spot barred' game which stipulated that the red could not be potted twice in succession from its own spot.

It was not until 1898 that this was incorporated, as an amendment, into the Billiards Association rules. It was a move which led to the championship being contested again in 1899 after lapsing since 1885, much of the intervening period having been spent in squabbles between those who preferred spot barred and those who favoured all in.

Several players could make thousand breaks with the aid of the spot stroke. W. J. Peall, the spot stroke king, made the first recorded two thousand break – 2413 in 1886 – and went on to make a 3304 in 1890. Roberts, who assiduously developed the top of the

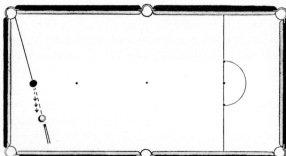

Diagram 1

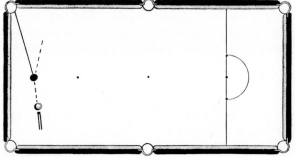

Diagram 2

table game based on cleverly maintained sequences of pot reds and cannons with the object-white near the red spot, made the first public spot barred thousand – 1392 – in 1894. But Peall had no chance with Roberts at spot barred and Roberts, the game's dominant personality and impressario, had no chance with Peall at all in. The Billiards Association unavailingly tried to end the deadlock by awarding cups for both codes.

The revival of the official championship on a spot barred basis in 1899, however, effectively killed the spot stroke, not before time. This key rule remained in force until 1964 when the Billiards Association, in a desperate but not very clearly thought out attempt to halt the decline in the popularity of billiards, permitted 15 consecutive pots and/or in-offs, the reference to consecutive pots off the spot being deleted. This limited restoration of the spot stroke destroyed much of the game's essential character. It meant, in effect, that players who potted the red from its spot the better part of 15 times then played one simple cannon

W. J. Peall v. Collins at the Royal Aquarium on the occasion of Peall's 2413 break.

before compiling another sequence of pot reds, had the advantage over players who had to exercise greater skill to control all three balls. The net result of the amendment was that it drove more players out of the game than it brought in.

Recognising their mistake, if only in part, the Billiards Association amended the rule in 1968 to stipulate that the red must be placed on the middle spot after being potted five times consecutively from its own spot.

This restored a limited degree of genuine top of the table play to the game. Interest started to pick up and standards, which had sunk very low, began to rise. When big breaks started to be made with 'five pot' the

Two spot stroke manoeuvres made easy through the advent of the rubber cushion. Stunning the cue-ball off the top cushion (3) and bouncing through off the top cushion (4).

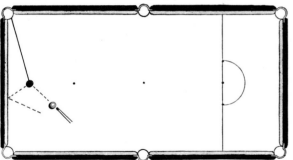
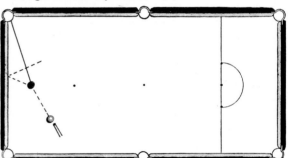

Diagram 3 & 4

tide of opinion began to run in favour of a further reduction.

The International Billiards and Snooker Federation, by now effectively the rule amending authority, although the Billiards Association (now the Billiards and Snooker Control Council) continued to claim copyright on the rules, voted to reduce consecutive pots from five to three, the amendment coming into force on 1 January 1979. Almost simultaneously, the professional governing body, the WPBSA altered the rule from 'five' to 'two', thus restoring it, for professional tournaments, to what it had been from 1898-1964.

Just as the spot stroke had to be curbed to prevent the spot red specialists from unbalancing the game so legislation became necessary to limit the exploitation of the in-off (or losing hazard) game. In the days of ivory balls, the inconsistency of reaction led to some in-offs being missed through no fault of the player. Ivories, though, were never used in Australia and with the much more consistent and controllable composition balls, mammoth breaks could be made just as easily with the in-off game as with the spot stroke.

When a 19-year-old Australian, George Gray, came to Britain for the 1910-11 season he made 23 breaks over 1000 including one of 2196. The in-off in the middle pocket – in Cardiff he made 289 in succession – was his basic shot (see Diagram 5). When the red dropped short, position was restored by a top pocket in-off which brought the red back again for middle pocket in-off position (see Diagram 6). If the red drifted towards the side of the table it was a simple matter to pot red in the middle, leave the cue-ball just past the jaws of the middle pocket and play the half ball in-off from the spotted position to restore prime position (see Diagram 7).

All these moves are still very much part of the fabric of the game but with Gray they were, until his formidable concentration flagged, the entire game. Gray's rivals were not slow to suggest various limitations on this method of scoring but his one challenge for the championship in 1914 foundered on the use of ivories with which he was only half the player that he was with composition. He lost in the first round, returned to Australia and was never the same player again.

Although the immediate threat had been dealt

George Gray

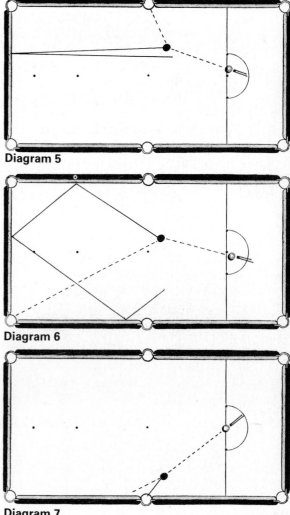

Diagram 5

Diagram 6

Diagram 7

with, the wider issues which Gray had posed were not tackled until British professionals visiting Australia were given further doses of red ball play from such players as Walter Lindrum and Clark McConachy, who both became nursery cannon specialists later. Lindrum made 7348 points out of 8000 off the red in beating H. W. Stevenson and a break of 1589 after losing the white at 292 against Claude Falkiner.

Lindrum would not at that stage come to Britain because British professionals were unwilling to surrender the advantage they felt they had in playing with ivories but the 1926 professional championship did nevertheless introduce a limit of 25 consecutive hazards (ie pots or in-offs). This limit was also applied to the English Amateur Championship in 1927 after the victory the previous year of Joe Earlam, a red ball specialist, composition balls being used in this event for the first time. In 1927, largely for commercial considerations, the professionals abandoned ivories.

With composition balls, though, even a limit of 25 hazards led to too much repetition. In 1931, the hazard limit was reduced to 15 for the English Championship and remained at that figure until 1960

when it was again increased to 25. It remained at 25 until, along with partial restoration of the spot stroke (see above), it was again reduced to its present 15 in 1964.

Whereas the curbs on potting and in-offs effectively preserved the balance and character of the game, the lack of effective limitations on cannon play not only killed billiards as a public entertainment but, with the game's apex of professional championships and tournaments removed, had serious repercussions on the amateur side.

The earliest cannon breaks where made with the two object-balls jammed in a corner pocket, none more notably than in a match for £1000 between Roberts Jnr and an American, Frank Ives, at Knightsbridge. Roberts's henchman, Tom Taylor, had played into the American's hands by agreeing to play the match on a table with pockets of 3¼ inches (smaller than usual) and with balls of 2¼ inches (larger than usual). Ives jammed the balls on the fourth evening and compiled a break of 2539 before

Tom Reece engaged in a match with his perennial opponent, Melbourne Inman.

voluntarily breaking up the position, and won by nearly half the game.

They played two return matches. In Chicago, where Ives won, a baulk line 7 inches long was drawn across each corner pocket within which only two consecutive strokes could be made. In New York, Roberts, hoping to make his all-round game tell, had the pockets widened to 3 inches. Roberts won the match but not before Ives had given, decades in advance of the Lindrum years, a classic exhibition of nursery cannons, that is 'nursing' the two object-balls along the cushion an inch or so at a time. Ives, of course, was a master of the 'cannons only' game played on the pocketless tables of Europe and the USA, parts of the world where English tables with pockets are few and far between.

Roberts himself employed runs of nurseries but only within a varied overall pattern. He was also much helped by the fact that push strokes were still permitted, at least until 1898, when he withdrew his influential opposition to a move outlawing them.

It was not until Tom Reece of Oldham came on the scene that cannons threatened to dominate billiards to anything like the extent that the respective specialities of Peall and Gray had earlier threatened. J. P. Mannock, a teaching professional, discovered the anchor cannon; W. A. Lovejoy, amateur champion in 1904, first exhibited it to the public; and Reece perfected it. The outcome was a break of 499 135 unfinished by Reece at Burroughes and Watts in 1907. With one object-ball suspended on either jaw of the top left-hand pocket (see Diagram 8) Reece proceeded to score at the rate of some 10 000 a session for five weeks. Not particularly fond of his opponent, Joe Chapman, who sat helplessly by for several sessions until he departed in disgust, Reece indulged his biting sense of humour with such witticisms at his expense as: 'How do you find the table?' or 'What sort of chalk do you use?'

The break ended, still unfinished, when the hall was required for another match. An official record certificate was refused on the grounds that press and public were not present throughout the break although the referee was. The anchor stroke was then barred.

Over the next twenty years, nursery cannons became an increasingly important part of almost every leading player's armoury. Long top of the table sequences interspersed with runs of nurseries became the norm for all the top players except Melbourne Inman and Willie Smith who relied on all-round play and top of the table. The danger signals were out as early as 1925 when, in advance of official legislation, a *News of the World* Test series between Newman and Smith specified a limit of 25 consecutive cannons – Newman being a cannon specialist – and 25 consecu-

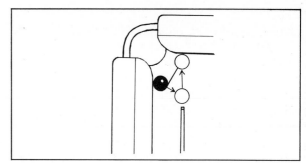
Diagram 8

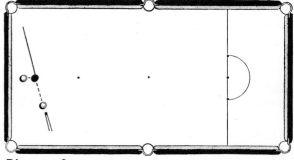
Diagram 9

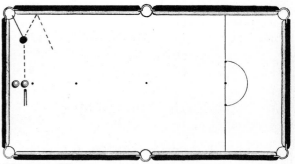
Diagram 10

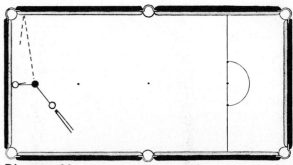
Diagram 11
The basic top of the table position with object-white near the spot. The break proceeds by means of a soft cannon, sending the red towards the pocket, followed by a pot red which in turn leaves an angle for a cannon. There are many variables within this basic pattern and the strokes which can be employed to keep the object-white near the spot offer considerable scope for artistry. In contrast to this 'floating white' technique in which the object-white is kept moving within a limited area, the 'postman's knock' sequence (see diag. 11) depends on the object-white being kept pinned on the top cushion by a full contact from the cue-ball.

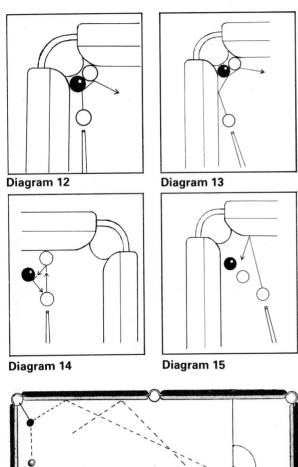

Diagram 12

Diagram 13

Diagram 14

Diagram 15

Diagram 16

Reece spent so much time trying to obtain pendulum cannon position, no easy task, that he ended on the losing side. A few weeks later while Joe Davis was contesting the world final against Newman, Reece made a pendulum break of 3964. Davis, who was trailing Newman at the time, decided after a brief morning practice session to employ the pendulum if he could. He duly obtained position and compiled a 2501 but Newman also made a pendulum 1012 and an orthodox 1073 and retained the title. It was clear, moreover, that the pendulum had to be barred.

Although it had required considerable skill to get the balls in position for the pendulum, it did not require exceptional skill or touch to compile breaks once they were. Nurseries required a great deal more skill but it was the kind of art which concealed art, for Lindrum, Davis, McConachy and Newman could play them so well that it was amazing that spectator interest lasted as long as it did.

Diagram 14 shows the 'rocker' cannon sequence which was maintained by playing, with a touch of right-hand side, full on the object-white so that the cue-ball made the finest of contacts on the red as it rebounded to its original position. Such was Lindrum's delicacy of touch that the second object-ball was grazed so thinly that it did not move.

In one of his great matches against Smith in Australia in 1929, Lindrum reached 1000 in 36 minutes by almost exclusive use of nurseries; he made a century in 95 seconds. His fastest ever thousand took only 26 minutes, his fastest century only 29 seconds. In 1932, McConachy made the then record of 297 nurseries, in which, instead of taking the balls 'round the corner' of the top pocket he turned them no less than nine times back and along the top cushion (see Diagram 15).

With the top players scoring between a third and a half of their points with nurseries it was clear that the game had become chronically unbalanced. The Billiards Association, for the 1932-33 season, tried to counteract this by introducing the '100 points baulkline' rule which insisted that the cue-ball should cross the baulkline (in a red spot to baulk direction) in every 100 points in a break of 100 or more.

McConachy made a break of 850 in the first match played under this rule for it was easy enough, for a top player, to cross the baulkline, the most favoured method being to leave a simple thin cue pot red in the top pocket so that the cue-ball could be brought round off three or four cushions to maintain top of the table position (see Diagram 16).

The rule, even if it appeared slightly artificial, did generally achieve its stated objective of breaking up long runs of nurseries but Lindrum, quite unjustifiably, thought it a threat to his supremacy. The promoters of the *News of the World* tournament gave the

tive red hazards.

Again it was Reece who forced the legislator's hand by perfecting the pendulum cannon and introducing it in his match against his arch rival Inman in the 1927 championship. Though not quite a revival of the 'jam' shot, the two object-balls were trapped, one on either jaw of a top pocket, while the cue-ball flicked across them (see Diagram 12). This was physically more arduous than the anchor cannon as the player had to walk round the corner of the table for each shot. Since the anchor cannon had been outlawed by the stipulation that no more than 25 consecutive cannons could be played without the cue-ball striking a cushion, this sequence had to be broken by achieving a cannon cushion first (see Diagram 13).

It was not quite so foolproof as the anchor but Reece nevertheless made 568 consecutive cannons with it in a break of 1151 against Inman during which he once gestured towards his hapless opponent with the words: 'Has that man paid to come in? He's a spectator.'

five entrants (Lindrum, Davis, Newman, McConachy, Smith) the option of playing under this rule or a '75 consecutive cannon' rule (after which a pot or in-off had to be played). Lindrum and Newman opted for the latter, Davis and McConachy said they did not mind and Smith withdrew.

The governing body weakened, modifying the baulkline rule to 'once every 200 points' which meant, in effect, that if the baulkline was crossed early in the break, the better part of 400 points could be made with nurseries. Lindrum was not keen even on this restriction, though he ridiculed it by taking the balls two-and-a-half times round the table with a run of 529 nurseries negotiating not only the middle pockets but the required line crossings with apparent ease. The rule was then tightened (for professionals only) to stipulate that baulkline crossings had to be made between 180 and 200 in every 200 but this amendment was too artificial and too late. The inhuman skill of the top players, the repetitive nature of the game they played, the incessant internal strife and the coming of snooker combined within a very few years to bury billiards as a public entertainment.

No world professional championship was held between 1933 and 1951 and there was a further gap from 1951 to 1968. In these 35 years, professional standards declined grievously. The top amateur game held its standards but the overall trend was to rules which made the game easier rather than more difficult. The explosion of snooker's popularity in the seventies, pulling billiards along on its coat tails, stimulated a minor but encouraging revival of interest in billiards and its skills. The baulkline rule was abolished and to encourage the preservation of nursery cannon play, a far cry from the Lindrum era, 75 consecutive cannons, direct or indirect, were in 1970 allowed instead of the limit of 35 direct cannons having then to be broken by an indirect cannon. Professionals also returned to the essence of billiards by limiting in 1978, consecutive pots from the spot to two though the amateur world at a meeting of the International Billiards and Snooker Federation in Malta that year felt that a change from five to two was too radical and compromised at three.

BILLIARDS

THE EARLY CHAMPIONSHIPS

In its early days billiards was either a gambling activity, as most games were, or a leisurely relaxation for the gentry. The twin traditions of billiards were epitomised by the country mansion and the tavern or public room. The gentry were often great patrons of the game but the best players invariably came from much lower down the social scale even though their successes were sometimes to establish them securely in the middle class.

The origins of competitive billiards are reminiscent of the prize-ring beginnings of boxing. Long before any official governing body was set there were recognised 'champions' whose titles were current on the strength of public opinion. This opinion was largely determined by a series of challenge matches for money.

Edwin Kentfield of Brighton, known as Jonathan Kentfield, was the first player to be recognised as champion, around 1820. John Carr of 'twisting chalk' fame, like Kentfield a marker, challenged him in 1827 but fell ill before the match and Kentfield remained champion until 1849 when he failed to meet a challenge from John Roberts Snr of Liverpool.

The title 'champion' meant, of course, champion of England and it was perhaps a reflection of the nation's self-confidence that this was simply assumed to be champion of the world. Incredibly, the Billiards Championship was known simply as 'The Championship' until 1933.

Roberts remained number one until he signed to play William Cook for £200 and the title on 11 February 1870. Roberts took what advantages he could from manipulating the rules and conditions (see page 24) but Cook won a battle which lasted from 8.27 p.m. to 1.38 a.m., 1200-1083.

For attractive matches – one of the attractions being heavy betting between spectators – it was not unusual to offer 500 tickets at £1 each, but demand was such on this occasion that the larger arena of St. James's Hall had all its 800 seats filled, with many spectators standing. When it leaked out that the Prince of Wales would attend, tickets rose in value with £5 changing hands for front row seats shortly before the off.

The unduly tight pockets of the championship table kept breaks small and prolonged the length of the match in an atmosphere thick with smoke. Though Roberts was only 47, years tended in those days to weigh more heavily, heavily enough for 'Bell's Life in London' to refer to him throughout their exhaustive blow-by-blow report as 'the old 'un'.

Cook, who was barely 21, has remained the youngest champion. Roberts, having trailed throughout, actually got his nose in front in the penultimate hundred but Cook finished the fresher with breaks of 26, 31 and 68 unfinished, the highest of the match, to win by 117.

His Royal Highness retired at midnight praising Cook's skill but stating that he would not watch another match on the 'championship' table but only on the tables ordinarily in use as he wanted to see some of the big breaks which the best exponents were currently recording.

Immediately after the first match, John Roberts Jnr, seeking to avenge family honour, challenged Cook for the title. In the absence of a governing body, *The Sportsman* fulfilled most of its functions, providing a referee, weighing the balls, dealing with other preliminaries . . . and holding the stake money – £100 a side, the minimum specified in the championship conditions.

The highest breaks were even smaller than in the first match, 55 by Roberts and 46 by Cook, but Roberts won very easily by 478 points in front of another capacity crowd.

The third match, held in the smaller auditorium at St. James's Hall, was a dreadful anti-climax not only in standard but in dramatic content. Alfred Bowles of Brighton was not in Roberts's class.

Seeking to enliven a predictable evening, a spectator offered 20/1 against Bowles but Roberts, in a rare display of jocularity, was the only taker! Roberts won by 241.

Roberts then lost his title to Joseph Bennett by a mere 95 points (28 November 1870) but regained it on 30 January 1871 by beating Bennett by 363. On the latter occasion, Bennett did not enjoy the best of fortune. His cue-ball was found to be light, thus causing it to bounce off the other balls at a wider than usual angle, and one of his strokes was spoiled when his cue was knocked out of his hand by a passing waiter.

On 25 May 1871, Cook regained the title, his winning margin of 15 points being likely to remain the closest finish in the history of the championship. The referee, unable to decide whether one shot was a foul or not, referred the issue to a show of hands.

Cook then fought off Bennett by 58 and Roberts twice, by 201 (making the first championship century, 116) and by 216.

On 24 May 1875 Roberts wrested the title from Cook at the Criterion Restaurant by 163 and beat him again at the St. James's Hall on 20 December 1875 by 135. When Roberts went off to tour Australia, Cook claimed the title but Roberts challenged him on his return and beat him at the Gaiety Restaurant on 28 May 1877 by 221. Roberts made a break of 118 and 'Oxford Jonathan', reported Bell's, 'marked the game with his usual accuracy'.

Roberts then went off on tour and Cook, announcing himself to be champion, accepted a challenge from Bennett. Cook led 938-864 but Bennett won by 51.

Bennett also beat Tom Taylor at St. James's Hall on 12-13 January 1881 by 90 points. Bennett made a new championship record of 125 but Bell's commented acidly on the late start and the slow play. 'Closing time was now rapidly approaching, and it was evident that unless Bennett went right away the match could not be finished before the period arrived at which a paternal Government decrees that licensed premises shall be closed. Both players, however, took their time, and though naturally desirous of finishing, did not abate one atom of their care, Bennett in particular playing as leisurely as if it had been an hour earlier.'

At 12.30 a.m., Bennett led 976-882 with Taylor in play with an additional 26. The match had to be resumed the following afternoon whereupon Taylor added only two more and Bennett ran out with 24.

Shortly afterwards, Bennett broke his arm when he was thrown out of a gig and resigned the title. Roberts billed himself as 'Champion of the World' but stated that he had no intention of ever again playing in the championship under the rules then appertaining and Cook, more or less by default, held the title for the next three years.

Roberts conceded start to all and sundry both at spot barred and spot in and the situation was – as it was to be many times in the future – that the players whom the public knew to be the best devalued the championship by not playing in it. In short, the personality of the top player was stronger than the game's administration.

Interest was centred not on the championship but on matches, often of a week's duration, between the leading players on ordinary tables. Thousand breaks utilising the spot stroke became common and, on ordinary tables, even the spot barred record rose from Cook's 309 to 322, 327 and 360, all by Roberts, in 1884.

Gradually a collective desire for proper organisation and a universally agreed set of rules led to a meeting in February 1885 at which the Billiards Association came into being and an official set of rules, after one further meeting, was agreed.

Roberts, who had been in the chair at this meeting, now decided to play for the championship again. Cook did not reply to Roberts's challenge within the stated time but immediately challenged when the cup went to Roberts. As it was clearly better to have two full houses than one, the match was scheduled for two days at the Billiard Hall, Argyll Street over the extended distance of 3000 up.

Roberts made a championship break record of 129 and won by a mere 92, a much closer margin than that which he usually achieved over Cook on ordinary tables. In fact, he conceded Cook 2000 in 12 000 shortly afterwards and beat him by 2759.

Roberts's next defence against Bennett at the Royal Aquarium, Westminster was extended to four days, 1-4 June 1885. Roberts made breaks of 147 and 155, a new championship record, and won by a resounding 1640.

Roberts had never made more than 16 consecutive spot strokes on the championship table but Peall made 128 in succession in a break of 445 in a match in which, receiving one sixth of the game in 12 000 up, he beat Roberts by 441. Ordinary tables would have given the spot stroke still greater potency so Roberts was understandably reluctant to play Peall 'all in' for the title under these conditions. Even with the 3 inch pockets of the archaic championship table the outcome would have been in doubt.

The Billiards Association tried to resolve the difficulty by awarding cups for all in and spot barred and devising a new official template which regulated the pockets to a strict $3^5/8$ inches at the fall of the slate. Peall claimed the title of 'Champion of Ordinary Billiards', and William Mitchell the 'Spot Barred' but without Roberts it was all meaningless.

Roberts so clearly was billiards that he could override the Billiards Association with impunity. He said that he could not regard 'a letter from the secretary of a moribund association as other than a gross impertinence'. He grandly offered the Association a venue, a table and a trophy for their championship – but declined to play in it.

Thus, the championship lapsed and with it the championship table for which there had never been any logical justification in the first place. The present day's only connection with this dinosaur of the game is the beautifully kept table with 3 inch pockets which is still in regular use at the Victoria Club, London.

It was not until October 1898 that the Billiards Association took action which made it possible to revive the championship, officially declaring the all in

John Roberts Jnr.

game obsolete by stipulating that the red, after being potted twice from its spot, should be placed on the middle spot.

Roberts, of course, considered himself above the championship though, after much jockeying for position, he did agree to play Charles Dawson in a fortnight's match for £100 and the whole of the gate.

By the time this took place, Dawson had overwhelmed Joe North in a week's match of 9000 up – the first time that the championship had been played over such a distance – starting on 9 January 1899 at the Gaiety Restaurant. Regrettably, the profit did not cover the cost of crockery breakages.

As matches had lengthened, sessions had come to be divided in such a way that the score of the player who was leading had to be 750 multiplied by the number of sessions played. If the trailing player rallied, that session tended to be longer than if the leader simply extended his advantage.

For instance, on the penultimate day of the Roberts *v* Dawson match, Dawson, who had led for most of the first week but had fallen 3078 behind, outpointed Roberts 1275-748 in two hours 55 minutes in the afternoon session and 1495-751 in three hours 10 minutes in the evening.

It may well have been that Roberts wanted to raise visions of a grandstand finish, thus increasing the gate, for on the final night he scored his last 750 in only 70 minutes to win 18 000-16 186.

This appears to have been the first match in which averages, obtained by dividing a player's total by the number of completed innings he has had, were officially recorded. Roberts averaged 28·04 and Dawson 25·24. More to the point, Roberts took Dawson's £100 and the whole of the then fabulous £2154 from the gate.

In addition, the dubious principle was reinforced of the 'Champion in Exile' standing out of the official championship in order to play a lucrative match with the official champion for what the public regarded as the number one position.

JOHN ROBERTS Jnr (1860-19??)
John Roberts Jnr was to billiards in the late nineteenth century what Joe Davis was to become to snooker in the middle of the twentieth: not only so universally considered the best player that he could ignore the championship as an irrelevance but so securely in control of the game's promotional and trading interests that everyone knew who was boss.

Roberts first became champion in April 1870 by beating William Cook two months after Cook had beaten Roberts Snr in the first championship match. Twice, subsequently, Roberts lost to Cook but three consecutive victories over Cook left him, in 1877, so indisputably the number one that he could concede start to everybody and opt out of the championship. He went East to set up a billiard table factory in Calcutta, transported several tables by elephant to show the Maharajah of Jaipur, a piece of enterprise which led to an annual salary of £500 with full expenses as court billiards player for life for coming to India one month a year. In all, Roberts made 11 visits to India, three to Australia, two to New Zealand, two to America and one to South Africa.

At home, Roberts took the first professional billiards circus round the provinces with short games on handicap and promoted week's matches between himself and various selected opponents at the Royal Aquarium (now the site of the Horticultural Hall, Westminster), the Argyll Street billiard hall (where the London Palladium now stands), the Egyptian Hall, Piccadilly and large provincial venues.

As a promoter he was sensitive to what the public would or would not pay to see. Seeing the spot stroke as boring and repetitive, he developed top of the table technique and an array of recovery shots, not as difficult as they appeared, for when he 'accidentally' lost position. He also developed the 'drag shot' for length of the table strokes, thus minimising the possibility of the imperfections of balls or tables (or both) causing the shot to be missed. Curiously enough, the public would have paid to see Roberts play Peall 'all in' but Roberts clearly perceived this as too great a risk to his reputation. Peall beat Roberts easily in an extraordinary contest in which at the start of each break the striker could place the balls anywhere he pleased; Peall won again in a match in which he was limited to 100 spot strokes in any one break; and, receiving 2000 in 10 000 won 441 all in on the championship table with 3-inch pockets. Peall, in fact, billed himself as 'Champion of Ordinary Billiards' after Roberts had refused an all in challenge unless there was also a second match, spot barred, with Peall receiving a third of the game in 12 000 up. Roberts, in short, was a master showman and a master negotiator, much preferring to concede start – thus leaving his reputation intact if he lost – than play level unless he felt he had a significant advantage in playing terms and conditions. His name sold cues, chalk, balls, books, cushions, even cigars and crockery. He offered the Billiards Association a venue, a table and a trophy for their championship but declined to play in it, knowing full well that in the public eye he was Billiards. He played here, there and everywhere: from ivory tables in Indian palaces – from one Indian trip he brought the game of snooker back to England – to makeshift boards in Australian mining towns. He made the first recorded thousand without the aid of specialist strokes when he compiled a 1392 against Diggle, at the time considered number two to Roberts, from whom he generally received 8000 or

9000, in Manchester in 1895, but it was his force of personality rather than statistics which accounted for his status. Once, in the early days of electric light, a bulb exploded. The table was quickly brushed and the show immediately continued with Roberts, despite burns, cuts and lingering minute pieces of glass, compiling a 400-odd break. In old age, he went through with a 1000 up match against Mitchell in Manchester when he was suffering from malarial fever and ague. He could scarcely walk but, with Mitchell within 40 of game, he ran out, with prodigious determination with 600 unfinished.

When Dawson won the championship, dormant since 1885, in 1899, his backers forced Roberts to a fortnight's match on level terms for £100 with the whole of the gate money to go to the winner. Roberts won by 1814. In 1905, a year before he retired, Roberts successfully conceded 2000 in 18 000 to the then champion Stevenson for £500 with Stevenson wagering a further £100 that he won by more than his start. Stevenson won by 1520 and the players shared a gate of £2500 for the fortnight.

The year he retired, 1906, with his eyesight failing, Roberts scored 1486 in a minute under two hours against J. Duncan in Glasgow, 23 509 in 24 hours and a break of 519 in 27 minutes.

MELBOURNE INMAN (1878-1951)

In 1891, a Twickenham marker's challenge to all and sundry was loftily taken up by W. D. Courtney, a leading amateur. 'To encourage rising talent' as he put it he offered to give 2000 start in 8000 to Inman for £25 a side. Inman won by over 4000 points and a return match level and entered the professional mainstream.

Since John Roberts's second and final retirement from championship play, there had been two champions, Charles Dawson of Huddersfield, whose book *Practical Billiards* Joe Davis confessed late in his life had been useful to him in his early days, and H. W. Stevenson of Hull. These two hated each other, none the less so when the Billiards Association declared Stevenson champion in 1901 because Dawson said the dates suggested for the title match were inconvenient. This gave Stevenson the £100 annual stipend which the Billiards Association awarded to the player it recognised as champion. When, in 1903, Dawson beat him for the title at the National Sporting Club, the customary handshake was lacking. 'So much for the Billiards Association champion', snarled Dawson as he made the winning shot.

But as Dawson's eyesight failed and Stevenson failed to endear himself to the Association by appealing in vain that the choice of tables should rest with the players, the championship lapsed from 1903-08 at which point, to get it going again, the Association

Top: Charles Dawson

Above: H. W. Stevenson

Right: Melbourne Inman

declared Inman champion. Inman defended success-fully against Albert Williams in 1909 but dissatisfaction with the Association's government of the professional game was growing and the Billiards Control Club effectively assumed control of the professional sphere by declaring Stevenson champion in 1909,

The first Stevenson *v*. Inman championship match in 1910 was abandoned three-quarters of the way through because of the death of Stevenson's wife, but Stevenson won the other two in 1910 and 1911 before he passed up the 1912 championship in favour of a lucrative domestic and overseas tour with George Gray. For three consecutive years Inman beat Reece for the championship and after the war, in 1919, beat Stevenson for what was to prove his last title.

Inman was above all a great competitor. His knack of pulling out brilliant recovery strokes when he had apparently lost position, his aggressive personality and his ability to irritate his opponents made him formidable opposition not only at his peak but long after this had passed.

His legendary rival was Reece, temperamental, artistic with a taste for close, delicate control, Inman's antithesis in almost every respect. Inman's open style tended to produce flukes more often than is usual with top players.

'How did you do that?' Reece asked acidly after one such. 'I believe you know my terms for tuition, Mr Reece', Inman replied.

There were many such verbal exchanges though Reece produced the most memorable on the night Inman clinched the 1919 championship. Lord Alverston, then president of the Billiards Association, who had earlier that week sentenced Dr Crippen to death, was just presenting Inman with the cup when Reece interjected: 'Excuse me, my Lord. But if you knew as much as I do about Inman you would have given Crippen the cup and sentenced Inman to death.'

Inman was a master of safety play and of frustrating, containing tactics. In the 1913 championship match, for instance, Inman scored 196 by misses and coups and Reece 181, the rules then allowing any number of misses or coups without other penalty than one or three away respectively. (In 1920, a player was forbidden to play two consecutive safety misses without an intervening score on pain of giving his oppo-

nent the option of playing from hand with object-white on the middle spot and red on the spot. In 1970 safety play was still further limited by making a miss or coup a foul unless the cue-ball is in hand and no object-ball out of baulk.)

The 1920 limitation on safety play was to Inman's disadvantage but as late as 1927 he was still tactically acute enough to lead the young Joe Davis by over a thousand points in their championship semi-final before Davis threw all caution to the winds, went for everything and got home by 1105 points.

No one could, of course, have reached Inman's standard without the capacity to make breaks. His 744 in 70 minutes against Reece in the 1914 final was a championship record and he had a 701 against Newman in 1923 but it was most characteristic of him to make his best break when the situation demanded, notably in the 1913 final when Reece wiped out his lead with a break of 535 only for Inman to restore it with one of 522.

WILLIE SMITH (1885-)

Willie Smith, alone among the giants of the Golden Age of Billiards, did not employ an endlessly repetitious method of scoring. His contempt for nursery cannon artists – 'cushion crawlers' in his phrase – knew no bounds and George Gray, the Australian red ball specialist, whom he sensationally defeated in 1911 when he was still a Darlington linotype operator, he dismissed as 'not a billiards player at all'.

Smith himself played the all-round game which ordinary players played in clubs and halls. He played it infinitely better and at a very fast tempo but the common man could identify with it in a way he never could with the mysterious art of nurseries. He always regarded 'the working classes' or 'average chap' as his strongest supporters and always preferred to play in large halls where there was room for cheap seats rather than at the select Thurston's which seated only 172.

His own attitude to the Establishment was coloured by being declared a professional at the age of 15 for accepting 10s 6d expenses for playing at Middlesbrough Conservative Club. The older he grew, the less inclined he was to co-operate in any scheme which he himself had not suggested. He won the champion-

Willie Smith (*left*) and Joe Davis prepare to string for break in their long awaited match at the Dorland Hall, London in January 1933. 'Stringing' is the traditional method of determining which player has choice of ball and/or playing the first shot. Both players play simultaneously from the baulk line: the player whose ball finishes nearest the baulk cushion has the choice.

Tom Newman (*left*) shakes hands with Willie Smith before their match for the billiards championship in 1923. Next to Smith is the referee, Arthur Goundrill, who despite losing an arm in the first world war, was not only acknowledged as a master referee but a good enough player to give exhibitions, including an exhibition of trick shots for King George at Buckingham Palace.

ship in 1920 at his first attempt and again in 1923 but for one reason or another – terms, dates, rules, equipment to be used – never played in it otherwise.

In part, Smith took his cue from Inman, the 1919 champion, who did not enter in 1920 but who referred to himself on the night of Smith's championship triumph as 'the undefeated champion'.

'Of course you are', said Smith. 'If you don't enter you can't be beaten'. There was an acrimonious exchange which led to a great money match at Thurston's. Inman was 10-11 and Smith allowed him to get 1000 in front. When Smith's supporters had placed all the bets they wanted, Smith sailed past him to win by over 4000.

Now no. 1 in the public eye Smith saw no need to de-

fend his title in the 1921 championship which was to be played at Thurston's and from which he could expect less financial return than from touring the provinces or arranging weeks matches on his own terms. He also stood out in 1922 when he played Tom Newman, by now the official champion, seven 'Tests' week matches. It was clear that the rewards lay in matches between the official champion and the champion in exile. Reporters commented on the regularity with which a player holding a substantial lead was caught.

Smith *v.* Newman in the 1923 championship was a true test but Smith submitted his entry for the 1924 championship two hours late. He nevertheless remained number one as far as the public was concerned, improving his consistency and breakmaking capacities until the switch from ivory balls to composition in 1928-29 saw him compile 15 breaks over 1000 during the season. His greatest effort was a break of 2743 against Newman at Manchester but he was under no illusions about his chances in Australia against their new scoring phenomenon, Walter Lindrum. Smith was as fast a scorer as any all rounder could be but it still took him between four and five minutes to compile a century. Lindrum, with his nurseries, could do so in less than half this time.

He split his first two matches with Lindrum, replying in the second to a break of 1434 by the Australian with one of 1383 and ensuring victory with a further effort of 1028 in 67 minutes. A break of 2030 against Clark McConachy involved playing through an entire session and he was playing so well that there was heavy betting on his rubber match with Lindrum, so heavy that the Sydney betting fraternity broke the cue Smith had used all his life, his beloved 'pit prop'.

The match was abandoned because of the death of Lindrum's young wife, with Lindrum leading 21 431-19 308 and the respective averages 114·6 and 102·7 but when Lindrum returned with Smith to play a British season the gulf between them widened. Neither played in the championship but their matches in Britain were regarded as being for the number one position. Lindrum's superiority was so clearcut that Smith averaged 147 for the fortnight at London's Farringdon Hall – an average no one remotely approached in the championship – and still lost by 6011. Smith, who had been instrumental in bringing Lindrum to Britain, complained that he was being used as a punchbag. Lindrum relented for a while until, in their last fortnight's match, he averaged 262 and won by no less than 21 285. Smith averaged 109.

Though Lindrum stood supreme, there were other nursery cannon specialists – Joe Davis, Newman and McConachy – who were not far behind. While these became the Big Four, Smith, cushioned by what was at the time a handsome retainer from Burroughes and Watts, drifted further and further into the wilderness, spending most of his time playing his protégé, Sidney Smith. He grew ever more cantankerous and difficult to deal with, indulging in much verbal sparring but reluctant to commit himself to real contests. One bout of sparring with Davis went on for three years until they finally met in 1933, by which time Smith's absence from the main stream had dulled his competitive edge. Davis beat him easily and that was the end of his serious competitive career.

In a way this proved to be all for the best. He and Davis became friends again and as billiards died as a public entertainment the bickering which it had stimulated died with it. He did not care much for snooker but its rising popularity made it inevitable that he played more of it and he actually reached the world final twice, in 1933 and 1935. Club exhibitions became more and more his way of life and he continued with them until well into his seventies. He accumulated a store of anecdotes, quite the most extraordinary of which was his recollection of touring as a young man with Diggle, who suffered from an obsession that someone was always following him. This caused Diggle to be always constantly looking sharply behind him and even to keep a gun beside him when he slept. One night, Smith, who was sharing a room, was just dozing off when Diggle abruptly sat up in bed. 'They're here, Willie, they're here', he shouted, fired two shots through the bedroom door and went to sleep.

TOM NEWMAN (1894-1943)

Born Tom Pratt, Tom Newman was a boy prodigy who made his first billiards century break when he was eleven and his first 500 when he was fifteen. He was given a three-year contract by the great John Roberts with whom he toured extensively.

From his world title success in 1921 to his last in 1927 – six in all – he lost in the championship only to Willie Smith in 1923. Three losses to Davis at the end of this period made up ten consecutive appearances in the final. With the elbow of his cue arm awkwardly tucked in, he lacked the cue action to excel at power strokes, at long distance or at difficult opening pots, but in cannon play and close quarter work of all kinds he was exceptionally skilful and consistent.

His match temperament, particularly against such forceful characters as Smith and Davis (once the latter

The young Tom Newman (1919).

had won his first championship in 1928) was a little suspect, partly perhaps because of his mild and easygoing nature, but his breakmaking feats included the first thousand, 1024, without the aid of push or specialist strokes in 1921, 1370 with ivories (the ivory record) in 1924, 1021, the first championship thousand in 1924 and, another championship record, 1567 in 1930, later superseded.

Newman played some of his finest billiards in the international tournament of 1930-31 held in seven cities ranging from Bradford to Plymouth. Playing level against Davis and McConachy and receiving 7000 from Lindrum, the tournament ended in a triple tie. He beat Davis, for the third time in succession, in a play-off, averaging 122·3 for the fortnight and went on to average 169·3 for the fortnight's final against Lindrum. Even with 7000 start this was not good enough for Lindrum averaged 248·1 and won by 8371.

WALTER LINDRUM (1898-1960)

Walter Lindrum mastered billiards so thoroughly, to so considerably greater a degree than any other practioner of his chosen sport, that he and his nearest rivals killed it as a public entertainment: they became so skilled, so free from error that billiards enthusiasts could no longer identify their own game with the refined, perfected version which Lindrum, Joe Davis, Tom Newman and Clark McConachy presented.

Lindrum was born to billiards. His father, Fred senior, was the 'native born' Australian title holder – an expatriate Englishman Harry Evans was the Australian champion – and his elder brother, Fred junior, became Australian champion.

As soon as he could walk, he would wander into the billiard saloons which his family owned at Donnybrook, Kalgoorlie (Walter's birth place on 29 August 1898) and Broad Arrow. As soon as he was old enough he would field out for hours as his brother practised, unconsciously absorbing the methods and sequences with which it was possible to compile big breaks.

At first, his father thought there were enough billiard players in the family and forbade him to play. When Walter stole the key to the room and crept in unobserved, his father appreciated the depth of his younger son's desire and relented, but he was to prove a hard taskmaster.

Having made his first century break at the age of 12, young Lindrum was given a daily four-hour practice schedule using only two balls. In this time, he had to practise the spot stroke and the cushion run through shot (see Diagram 17) – nothing else.

Walter Lindrum poses with Willie Smith before their match at the Farringdon Hall, London in 1930.

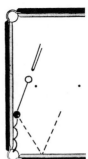

Diagram 17
The cue-ball, struck with right-hand side, strikes the red about three-quarter ball. The effect of the right-hand side is to spin the cue-ball back into the cushion and finally into the pocket even as it bounces away from it.

When he was allowed the third ball, his practice schedule was increased to two hours every morning, three every afternoon and two every night.

He was on the verge of his first double century when his father told him he was not to leave the room that day until he had made a 250: starting at 2 that afternoon he battled on until 8.30 that evening until he made it.

On and on went the backbreaking practice routine until, at 14, he went on tour with his father, who promptly carried his education a stage further by crushing him unmercifully.

Walter soon overtook his idolised elder brother but would not challenge him for the Australian title, which he was content to have remain in the family. His father backed with £200 a challenge for him to play anyone in the world with bonzoline balls but there were no takers.

In his youth, Lindrum was primarily a red ball player. He beat the former world champion H. W. Stevenson 16 000-6545 in Sydney in 1922 making a break of 1417 almost entirely off the red and at one stage scoring 7348 out of 8000 by this method. Two years later, he beat Claude Falkiner, one of the best British players never to win the championship, in two matches out of three, averaging 108 for the fortnight in the last.

Falkiner could not persuade Lindrum to visit Britain, where the British professionals insisted on playing with ivory balls as an aid to maintaining their superiority over colonial challengers, but did impart much of his knowledge of the nursery cannons which the Australian was later to display with such devastating effect.

Partly through a disinclination to play with ivories – he had played all his billiards with a composition ball – partly through, as it proved, ill-founded fears that the damp English climate would adversely affect the bronchial condition from which he suffered, Lindrum stayed in Australia for the next few years though both he and McConachy frequently recorded breaks and averages superior to those which were good enough to win the world championship. With 1380 and 1415 at Wellington, Lindrum became the

first player ever to make thousand breaks in successive days.

In the 1928-29 season, Crystalate balls were adopted for professional matches in Britain. Willie Smith, who opted out of the official championship but was still regarded as number one by the public, crushed Fred Lindrum by no less than 19 178 points, averaging 161·6 for the fortnight's match, and accepted an offer to visit Australia where he played three epic matches against Walter.

Walter won the first in Melbourne 24 234-23 147 and Smith the second in Sydney 23 446-22 317, Smith replying to a break of 1434 with one of 1383 and clinching the match with a 1028 in 67 minutes on the last day, Lindrum being in play with 701 at the close. In this match, Lindrum compiled breaks of 965 and 1090, reaching four figures in only 36 minutes and scoring exclusively with nurseries after 350.

As a prelude to the decider in Sydney, the local betting fraternity broke Smith's cue but the match was left uncompleted in tragic circumstances. Lindrum's pregnant 20-year-old wife had been knocked over by a bus and was convalescing when the match started but complications set in after a few days. Under the strain, Lindrum faltered and from 3000 in front had fallen behind by the second Thursday.

By Thursday teatime his wife had rallied. She had set her heart on the silver tea service which a Sydney newspaper had offered for the winner of the match and Lindrum was determined to win it for her. 'You've got to make a 2000 break for me', she said.

He resumed with 144 unfinished and played through all but ten minutes of the evening session to reach 2002 but returned to the dressing room to discover that his wife had suffered a relapse. She died within a few hours and the match was abandoned with Lindrum leading 21 431-19 308.

Made as it was under such severe emotional pressure, Lindrum always regarded that break as his greatest, but the whole traumatic experience created an emotionally tender area which made him more and more obsessive about billiards, harder to deal with in contracts and personal arrangements and, except when he was actually playing before the public, prone to depression and lethargy.

The immediate step he took towards recovering from his grief was to sign a contract with Burroughes and Watts and return to Britain with Smith. One of the many interminable trade and contractual wrangles of the day led to neither Lindrum nor Smith competing in the official championship but the public was shrewd enough to recognise where the number

Walter Lindrum. Note that tables of the period were lit by six conically-shaped shades before the trough-shaped shade was found to shed a more even illumination.

one position was truly being contested.

With the promise of unlimited backing from John Wren, a Melbourne sporting patron, Lindrum intended to coast for a while but without going flat out he quickly demonstrated who was boss. Ill-pleased with their first venue, a cellar in Glasgow, Lindrum nevertheless made a 910 break in his first session and a 1083 in his second. He won their first week's matches by comparatively modest margins but cut loose with six thousands in the third week, when he won by nearly 8000. With his first triple thousand, 3262, and five other thousands, Lindrum won 28 003-21 962 at the Farringdon Hall, London where Smith, who made a 1490 and averaged 147, was beaten out of sight.

Smith began to express resentment that he was being used as a punchbag and, as if by magic, won two matches by narrow margins, but Lindrum, after beating Joe Davis 29 056-26 172 in a match which eclipsed the record aggregate for a fortnight by 5500, hammered Smith 30 817-19 334. Finally, to avenge in full the drubbing Smith had given his elder brother, Lindrum averaged 262 and made eleven thousands and a 998 in beating him 36 256-14 971. Incredibly, Smith averaged 109 and lost by 21 285.

The 1930-31 British season was dominated by an international round robin tournament in which Lindrum conceded 7000 to Davis, Newman and McConachy. Against McConachy, Lindrum averaged 313 for the second week and made a new record of 3905 which spanned the whole of the afternoon session and 80 minutes of the evening. In the deciding match against Newman, Lindrum averaged 248 and made breaks of 2835 and 2583.

Against Davis in January 1932, at Thurston's, Lindrum played through most of a Tuesday afternoon and all evening to reach the close with 3151 unfinished. On Wednesday afternoon he carried this to a new record of 4137 to which Davis replied with 1247. He toured the United States and Canada rather than compete in the championship but returned for the *News of the World* tournament in the autumn by which time the BA & CC had introduced an experimental 100 point baulkline rule, a device to curb long runs of nursery cannons by making it obligatory for the cue-ball to cross the baulkline once every 100 points.

The BA & CC bowed to pressure in extending this limit to 200, which meant that if the line was crossed early in a break nearly 400 could be scored before crossing it again, but Lindrum thought this rule a threat to his superiority, an empty fear since he had compiled a run of 529 nurseries which had included the appropriate baulkline crossings.

Conceding 6000 to each opponent, Lindrum failed to win a match in the *News of the World* tournament.

His scoring power was affected but, proportionately, so was that of his chief rivals and he was still, beyond dispute, the best player.

Nevertheless, his victory in the 1933 championship at the Dorland Hall, London was anything but one-sided. Lindrum made three thousands to Davis's best of 792 but won only by a mere 694, averaging 92 to the loser's 89.

There was uproar when Lindrum declared his intention of defending the title only in Australia but the governing body could do nothing practical about it. In July 1934, Lindrum beat first McConachy and then Davis to retain the title which then remained dormant until he relinquished it in 1950.

The rule changes had come far too late to halt the decline in attendances and were in any case too trifling fundamentally to affect the all too predictable pattern of play. No doubt the championship would have been kept alive had Lindrum agreed to visit England again or to play McConachy for the title somewhere in Australia in the late forties but he was disinclined to do either. He was, everyone knew, the best player but total invulnerability was his irrational objective, hence his eccentric refusal, in his latter years, to have any kind of opponent in his exhibitions.

Tom Cleary, later world amateur champion, Lindrum's opponent in many exhibition matches, testified to a most likeable side of Lindrum's character but was never able, he revealed, to persuade him to pass on any of his knowledge of the game. Isolated to some extent by his genius but even more by an inner self buried so deep that no one could reach it, Lindrum surrounded himself with an emotional wall which accounted at least in part for his pathological reluctance to involve himself in matches that really mattered.

Free of this pressure, he scored like a machine. In 1940, he made a break of 3301 under baulkline rules against Fred Lindrum (conceding 7000 and counting only breaks over 700!) and in 1944 breaks of 3737 and 3752 in succession. His efforts for charity during the war earned him the OBE.

He died suddenly while holidaying at Surfers Paradise on 30 July 1960, aged 62. His career had included one quadruple thousand, 17 over 3000, 29 over 2000 and 711 over 1000.

CLARK McCONACHY (1895-1980)

Clark McConachy, son of a Timaru billiard hall proprietor, watched George Gray, the Australian red ball specialist, when he toured New Zealand, and set himself to practise red ball play six hours a day. When he was 17, he made a red ball break of 1983.

In 1914, he beat Bill Stevenson for the New Zea-

Clark McConachy

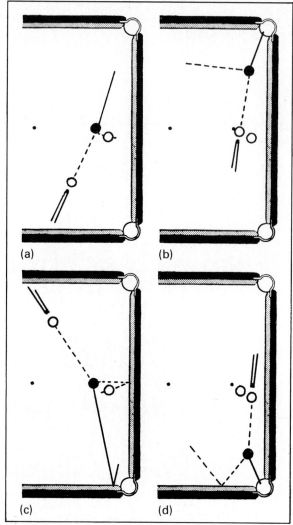

(a)   (b)

(c)   (d)

Diagram 18
(a) A soft cannon (2) leaves a pot red and moves the object-white away from the spot. (b) The red is potted (5) to leave the cue-ball at an angle to play the cannon via the top cushion. (c) The cannon (7) leaves the red over the top pocket and nudges the object-white back to its original position shown in (a). (d) The pot red (10) restores the position as it was in (a), thus completing the 'movement of ten'.

land Professional Championship and held it unchallenged for the rest of his career. He toured New Zealand, Australia, India and South Africa before coming to Britain for the 1922 championship. Playing with ivories, which 'threw' some 1½ inches narrower then the composition balls with which he had played all his life, he was well beaten by Tom Reece but later that year made a break of 985 with ivories which was then a world record.

He changed his game from red ball to top of the table, initially postman's knock but later a 'movement of ten' (see Diagram 18) which, in essence, was already in existence but which he refined into a repetitive method. By means of the latter, he made a break of 500 in 20 minutes in 1926, fast scoring for a player

whom his rivals often found disconcertingly slow. Even nurseries, which he mastered comprehensively, did not yield points at quite the rate of Lindrum, Davis or Newman. In 1932, in a then record run of 466 consecutive cannons, he revealed a new way (see page 29) of turning the balls back and along the top cushion instead of taking them round the corner.

He beat all the other members of the Big Four at one time or another in week's matches. He averaged 98 – but still lost by 5902 to Davis in the title match in 1932 and came within 1108 of beating Lindrum in the 1934 semi-final but it was something of an anti-climax when he became champion in 1951. He was past his peak but with Lindrum having relinquished the title, Davis not interested in it and Newman dead, he was still far too good for John Barrie. Even Barrie had his shot at the title only because Fred Davis, then UK champion, declined to play on the grounds that the first week in September was too early in the season.

McConachy returned to New Zealand with the title and held it unchallenged until, at the age of 73 and – incredibly – suffering from Parkinson's disease in his cue arm, he was beaten by a mere 265 points by Rex Williams. Even in his eighties he was still practising and coaching in his own private billiard room in Auckland.

Prodigious determination and self-discipline, both hallmarks of his play, led him to maintain a lifelong regimen of running and exercises. His delight in his physical fitness sometimes carried him away. Once, he picked up a chair one-handed and then responded innocently to a challenge to pick up a chair in which Lindrum, due to be his opponent, was sitting. Veins throbbing, he managed this lift as well – but was hardly in an appropriate condition for the delicacies of billiards until the session was well under way!

He was the first player ever to make two breaks over a thousand in consecutive visits to the table. His highest breaks were 1943 against Davis in 1932, and 1927, a then record under baulkine rules, in 1934. At his peak he used a 21-22 oz cue, much heavier than his contemporaries, and late in his career a monster of 30 oz.

He was awarded the MBE in 1964 and in an age when principle very frequently ran a poor second to profit, his integrity was a byword. Snooker was very much his second game though he was nevertheless good enough, with the close control his billiards mastery gave him, to record a 147 maximum at the Beaufort Club, London in 1951.

JOE DAVIS (1901-78)

Joe Davis, born in Whitwell, Derbyshire on 15 April 1901, learnt to play in his family's pub, The Queens Hotel, in Whittington Moor. Coached by a local man, Ernest Rudge, at whose house he used to practise, he

also furthered his knowledge through study of
Charles Dawson's *Practical Billiards* and made his
first century break at the age of 12.

When he won the Chesterfield and District Championship at the age of 13 it was clear that he had a fine
future in the game and Rudge, an entrepreneur,
staged exhibitions in the town featuring George Gray,
Claude Falkiner, Tom Reece and Willie Smith to give
the young Joe an opportunity to study these giants at
first hand.

After his first professional match, in which he beat
Albert Raynor by 145, receiving 1000 in 7000, at
Brampton on the outskirts of Chesterfield, Davis was
invited to play in the St. Dunstans Christmas Handicap at Thurston's, the home of professional billiards,
in Leicester Square. He made a 147 break at his first
visit to the table, reached the semi-final and made a
good enough impression to be introduced to the then
standard grind of week's matches beating Arthur

**Joe Davis *(left)* poses with Tom Newman before
the start of a session at Burroughes Hall,
Soho Square in 1924.**

Peall, son of W. J., by 588 receiving 1500 in 8000.

He was beaten by Fred Lawrence for the Midlands professional title in 1921 but won it the following year together with the Second Division Championship, beating Peall in the final, a success which entitled him to compete in the World Championship.

Well beaten by Tom Newman, he did not enter again until 1926, by which time he was enjoying a fair degree of success though he still needed a start of about a third of the game to beat Willie Smith.

Davis's first 500 break – 599 – came in the 1924 Second Division Championship. Later in that event he made a 980 at a time when the highest break under existing rules was only 1274 by Newman. His start against Newman or Smith dwindled to 1500 or 2000 in 18 000 but when it came to a second venture in the championship in 1926 Newman beat him out of sight once again.

Davis increased his best break to 992 but was again beaten, though more narrowly, by Newman in the 1927 championship final despite a break of 2501 by means of Reece's newly-invented pendulum cannon.

By this time, Davis had long since become a master of every phase of billiards: red ball, top of the table and nursery cannons. He made his first thousand, 1070, early in 1928 and took the world title from Newman later that year, retaining it with a new championship record average of 100 by the narrow margin of 781 the following year. He increased his personal best break (by orthodox methods) to 1280.

After their epic matches in Australia in 1929, Smith and Lindrum returned to Britain under contract to Burroughes and Watts, who wanted the championship played on 'nameless' tables. Thurston's were willing to give away the championship which the BA & CC had awarded to them, but John Bisset, the BA & CC's autocratic chairman, would not have its authority questioned. Consequently, neither Lindrum, Smith nor McConachy, who was also under contract to Burroughes and Watts, competed in the 1930 championship in which Davis, averaging 113·1, beat Newman by 801 in the final. During this match, Davis made the highest break of his career, 2052.

For most of this British season, Lindrum played Smith but the one fortnight's match he played against Davis produced a record aggregate of 55 288 in which Lindrum made 23 breaks over 500 and Davis twelve. Lindrum, who made four 1000 breaks won by 2884.

The following season, when Lindrum returned as a freelance, he (conceding 7000) Davis and Newman each won four matches in the nationwide international tournament. Davis lost a close finish to Newman when victory would have given him the first prize outright and lost to Newman again in a play-off.

No championship was organised in 1931 because of yet another wrangle among the leading players but

Davis successfully defended against McConachy in 1932 when he scored over 11 000 of his winning total by nursery cannons. In January of that year, Davis had immediately replied with a break of 1247 to Lindrum's record of 4137.

In the 1932-33 season, the *News of the World* tournament, played under the new baulkline rule, saw Lindrum unsuccessfully conceding a reduced start of 6000 to other members of the Big Four but it was not until the 1933 championship that it came to a test on level terms.

Davis beat McConachy comfortably – in fact he usually, though not invariably, beat both McConachy and Newman in week's or fortnight's matches – and led Lindrum for most of the final until the Australian drew away in the last two days to win by 694. When Lindrum insisted that he would defend the title only in Australia, Davis sailed out . . . only to discover that Lindrum had made no arrangements whatsoever. After a tour in which he struggled desperately to earn enough money to get home again, Davis lost the championship match to Lindrum by 875. He never beat Lindrum level. Many times, Davis was offered contracts to return to Australia but always on condition that Lindrum could be persuaded to play him for the title. He never could.

Back in London, Davis made a break of 2002 in the *Daily Mail* sealed handicap tournament, a world record under the 200 baulkline rule, and beat Newman for the new United Kingdom Professional Championship which, with Lindrum remaining in Australia and the world title thus out of circulation, became the premier event of the British season, albeit with snooker pushing billiards ever further towards the sidelines.

Davis still played billiards of high quality when there was any call for it, scoring wins in the UK final over Newman every year until the outbreak of war. His break of 1784 under the again revised baulkline rule, the crossing having to be accomplished between the 180 and 200 mark in each 200 points of a break, stood as a record from 1936 until the rules were changed, though even today, under easier rules, it has not been bettered.

After the war, Davis's billiards was limited to half-hours in exhibitions as a curtain raiser to the snooker except for an annual week's match of billiards and snooker at Leicester Square Hall with Willie Smith in which, in one session, he achieved the amazing all-round feat of a 639 break at billiards and two centuries and a 64 in three frames of snooker. Undoubtedly, he could have regained his pre-war standard or even exceeded it but with little public demand for billiards and thus no commercial end product he devoted himself almost exclusively to snooker.

WORLD PROFESSIONAL BILLIARDS CHAMPIONSHIP (1870-1920)

1870	(Feb)	W. Cook	J. Roberts Snr	1200-1083
	(Apr)	J. Roberts Jnr	W. Cook	1000- 522
	(June)	J. Roberts Jnr	A. Bowles	1000- 759
	(Nov)	J. Bennett	J. Roberts Jnr	1000- 905
1871	(Jan)	J. Roberts Jnr	J. Bennett	1000- 637
	(May)	W. Cook	J. Roberts Jnr	1000- 985
	(Nov)	W. Cook	J. Bennett	1000- 942
1872	(Mar)	W. Cook	J. Roberts Jnr	1000- 799
1874	(Feb)	W. Cook	J. Roberts Jnr	1000- 784
1875	(May)	J. Roberts Jnr	W. Cook	1000- 837
	(Dec)	J. Roberts Jnr	W. Cook	1000- 865
1877	(May)	J. Roberts Jnr	W. Cook	1000- 779
1880	(Nov)	J. Bennett	W. Cook	1000- 949
1881	(Jan)	J. Bennett	T. Taylor	1000- 910
1885	(Apr)	J. Roberts Jnr	W. Cook	3000-2908
	(June)	J. Roberts Jnr	J. Bennett	3000-1360
1899		C. Dawson	J. North	9000-4715
1900		C. Dawson	H. W. Stevenson	9000-6775
1901		H. W. Stevenson	C. Dawson	9000-6406
		C. Dawson	H. W. Stevenson	9000-5796
		H. W. Stevenson (declared champion – no contest)		
1903		C. Dawson	H. W. Stevenson	9000-8700
1908		M. Inman (declared champion – no contest)		
1909		M. Inman	A. Williams	9000-7662

Under Billiards Control Club Rules

1909	H. W. Stevenson (declared champion – no contest)		
1910	H. W. Stevenson	M. Inman (match abandoned)	13370-13212
	H. W. Stevenson	M. Inman	18000-16907
1911	H. W. Stevenson	M. Inman	18000-16914
1912	M. Inman	T. Reece	18000- 9675
1913	M. Inman	T. Reece	18000-16627
1914	M. Inman	T. Reece	18000-12826
1919	M. Inman	H. W. Stevenson	16000- 9468
1920	W. Smith	C. Falkiner	16000-14500

WORLD PROFESSIONAL BILLIARDS CHAMPIONSHIP (1921-51)

Winner (breaks)	Score (average)	Loser (breaks)	Score (average)
1921			
First round			
C. Falkiner 560	7 334 (35·3)	H. W. Stevenson	5 084 (24·3)
T. Newman 467	8 000 (54·0)	T. Tothiil	3 267 (22·0)
Semi-finals			
Newman 627, 531	8 000 (56·7)	Falkiner 587	6 627 (47·3)
T. Reece	n.r.	F. Lawrence	n.r.
Final			
Newman	16 000 (n.r.)	Reece	10 744 (n.r.)
1922			
First round			
T. Reece	8 000 (35·2)	C. McConachy	6 767 (29·9)
Semi-finals			
T. Newman 561, 512	8 000 (52·6)	J. Davis	5 181 (34·1)
C. Falkiner 391	8 000 (41·9)	Reece 455	7 289 (38·2)
Final			
Newman	16 000 (56·4)	Falkiner	15 167 (52·7)
1923			
First round			
M. Inman	16 000 (n.r.)	A. Peall	11 758 (n.r.)
C. Falkiner	16 000 (n.r.)	T. Reece	14 952 (n.r.)
Semi-finals			
T. Newman 850, 705, 500 × 4	16 000 (56·3)	Inman 701	14 506 (51·1)
W. Smith 688	16 000 (71·7)	Falkiner 782, 620	8 695 (29·2)
Final			
Smith 451, 446	16 000 (46·4)	Newman 638, 629, 575	15 180 (44·0)
1924			
First round			
T. Newman 875	16 000 (71·4)	C. McConachy 349	8 703 (38·9)
Final			
Newman 1021	16 000 (43·5)	T. Reece	14 845 (40·3)
1925			
T. Newman 957, 672	16 000 (68·4)	T. Reece 512	10 092 (43·1)
1926			
T. Newman 637, 574, 588	16 000 (82·0)	J. Davis 414	9 505 (49·0)
1927			
First round			
M. Inman 459	8 000 (n.r.)	T. Reece 1151	5 527 (n.r.)

Winner (breaks)	Score (average)	Loser (breaks)	Score (average)
Second round J. Davis 504, 588	8 000 (n.r.)	Inman	6 895
Challenge round T. Newman 787, 1073, 1012, 891	16 000 (73·0)	Davis 2501, 727	14 763 (68·0)
1928			
First round T. Carpenter	8 000 (22·4)	T. Reece	7 283 (20·5)
Second round J. Davis	8 000 (66·4)	Carpenter	5 602 (41·8)
Challenge round Davis 529, 525, 501, 425, 408, 404, 403, 400	16 000 (74·4)	T. Newman 564, 489, 467, 455, 451, 427	14 874 (69·5)
1929			
First round T. Newman 553	8 000 (74·1)	T. Carpenter 453	5 984 (55·4)
Final J. Davis 838, 609, 599	18 000 (100·0)	Newman 723, 691, 672, 647, 576	17 219 (96·2)
1930			
First round T. Newman 1567, 1047	24 001 (85·1)	M. Inman	10 104 (35·8)
J. Davis	21 975 (82·0)	C. Falkiner	19 815 (74·0)
Final Davis 2052, 500 × 9	20 918 (113·1)	Newman 500 × 12	20 117 (109·9)
1932			
J. Davis 1058, 844, 774	25 161 (112·0)	C. McConachy 1432, 916, 889	19 259 (98·0)
1933			
First round W. Lindrum 1578, 984	21 470 (n.r.)	T. Newman 877, 805	20 252 (n.r.)
J. Davis 995	20 136 (n.r.)	C. McConachy 675	16 110 (n.r.)
Final Lindrum 1492, 1272, 1013	21 815 (92·0)	Davis 792	21 121 (89·0)
1934			
First round W. Lindrum 1065, 807	21 903 (n.r.)	C. McConachy 892, 829	20 795 (n.r.)
Final Lindrum 1474, 1353	23 533 (n.r.)	J. Davis 824, 728	22 678 (n.r.)
1951			
C. McConachy 481, 438, 425, 397, 376	6 681 (60·0)	J. Barrie 367, 336	5 057 (44·8)

UNITED KINGDOM PROFESSIONAL CHAMPIONSHIP (1934-51)

Winner (breaks)	Score (average)	Loser (breaks)	Score (average)
1934			
J. Davis 537, 504	18 745	T. Newman 809, 693, 603, 547	18 301
1935			
J. Davis 609, 1264, 548, 564, 638, 1002, 545	21 733	T. Newman 848, 677, 749, 732, 598	19 919
1936			
First round W. Smith	10 373 (60·0)	S. Lee	7 212 (42·0)
Semi-finals T. Newman J. Davis	9 561 (75·0) 10 965 (93·0)	S. Smith W. Smith	7 792 (60·0) 9 566 (80·0)
Final J. Davis	21 710 (125·0)	T. Newman	19 790 (114·0)
1937			
First round S. Smith (match abandoned after nine sessions)	8 135	S. Lee	4 209
Semi-finals T. Newman J. Davis	w.o. 12 046	W. Smith S. Smith	scr. 8 516
Final J. Davis 1191, 1179, 1000, 997, 793, 592, 587, 580, 556, 550, 500	22 601 (146·0)	T. Newman 782, 774, 720, 671, 670, 603, 593, 588, 547	18 321 (118·0)
1938			
Semi-finals T. Newman 556, 771, 602, 599 J. Davis 1013, 840, 988, 666	8 959 15 238	S. Smith 740 S. Lee	7 227 6 048
Final J. Davis	20 933	T. Newman	19 542
1939-45 No contests			
1946			
J. Barrie	8 972	W. Leigh	6 782
1947			
S. Smith	7 002	J. Barrie	6 428
1948-49 No contests			
1950			
First round J. Barrie	7 645 (34·8)	S. Lee	5 593 (25·4)
Semi-finals J. Barrie K. Kennerley	7 009 (46·7) w.o.	W. Smith	5 941 (39·6)
Final J. Barrie	9 046 (48·9)	K. Kennerley	5 069 (27·4)
1951			
F. Davis	8 120	K. Kennerley	6 011

SNOOKER

ORIGINS

In 1875 Sir Neville Chamberlain was a young subaltern with the Devonshire Regiment stationed at Jubbulpore. During the rainy season the officers' long afternoons were spent at the mess billiards table where the parent game was less popular than various round games which were more suitable for more than two players and to which it was easier to add a modest gambling element.

Pyramids, perhaps snooker's most obvious forerunner, was a game played with 15 reds, initially placed in a triangle, with the apex red on what is now the pink spot but which was then known as the pyramid spot. Each time a player potted a red, all his opponents paid across the agreed stake money per ball.

In Life Pool, each player was given a cue-ball and an object-ball (eg white on red, red on yellow) so, for the second player, his object-ball was the first player's cue-ball and so on. The object was to pot one's specified object-ball three times. Each time a player's ball was potted, he lost a life and had to pay an agreed stake. When he had lost three 'lives' he paid an extra sum for a 'star' or extra life and when that was gone he was 'dead'. When only one player remained he scooped the kitty.

Black Pool was a development of Life Pool in that a black ball was added. When a player had potted his allocated ball, he could attempt the black. If he was successful, each of his opponents paid across an additional sum and he could then attempt the nearest ball. Joe Davis spent many of his youthful hours playing a similar game, Pink Pool.

Black Pool was the preferred game among the Devonshire officers but it was Chamberlain's inspiration to gradually add other coloured balls so that snooker came to be played with 15 reds, yellow, green, pink and black. Blue and brown were added some years later.

These new colours produced a game whose variety (and variety of monetary forfeits) immediately caught on. The concept of break building was much in the future and even the point values of the balls were not established until a little later; but it was in these casual and almost chance beginnings that the game undoubtedly had its origin.

When Compton Mackenzie, the novelist, interviewed him in 1938, Chamberlain recalled that the Devons one afternoon received a visit from a young subaltern who had been trained at the Royal Military Academy, Woolwich. In the course of conversation, the latter happened to remark that a first-year cadet at Woolwich was referred to as a 'snooker' with the implication that this was the status of the lowest of the low. The original word for a cadet had been the French 'neux' which had been corrupted to 'snooker'.

Chamberlain said: 'The term was a new one to me but I soon had the opportunity of exploiting it when one of our party failed to hole a coloured ball which was close to a corner pocket. I called out to him: "Why, you're a regular snooker"! I had to explain to the company the definition of the word and to soothe the feelings of the culprit I added that we were all, so to speak snookers at the game so it would be very appropriate to call the game snooker. The suggestion was adopted with enthusiasm and the game has been called snooker ever since.'

In 1876, when Chamberlain left the Devons to join the Central India Horse, he took the game with him. After being wounded in the Afghan War, he served with the Commander-in-Chief of the Madras Army and was with him every summer when he moved to the hill station at Ootacamund. Snooker came to be recognised as the speciality of the Ooty Club and the rules of the game were drawn up and posted in the billiards room.

During the 1880s rumours of this new game reached England and when John Roberts went out to India on one of his tours he had it in mind to find out the rules. One evening, in 1885, in Calcutta, Chamberlain was dining with the Maharajah of Cooch Behar when Roberts was introduced to him. Roberts duly brought the game back to England.

It was many a long day before snooker became

widely played. Not every hall nor every club could afford a snooker set of 22 balls though it was not long before the manufacturers appreciated snooker's superior commercial possibilities. Even so, billiards remained such a popular game to play that not until the Second World War could a billiard hall risk carrying fewer sets of billiard balls than they had tables.

By 1910 a measure of break building had come into the game as one F. H. Garside received a certificate for a break of 99 against Sir Charles Kirkpatrick at his home and Tom Aiken, the Scottish professional billiards champion, was reported to have made one of 102 at snooker and Cecil Harverson two. Phil Morris, a Tottenham marker, made a 103 at the Eagle Hotel, Tottenham.

In 1912 the official record, on tables with standard pockets, was 73, held jointly by John Roberts (1907) and James Harris (1908). In 1915 George Hargest, the manager of the Lucania Hall, made a break of 112, a total clearance with Durolite balls, at Blackwood, Monmouthshire. In the same year, William Murray made a 103 at the Collingwood Billiard Hall, Newcastle, of which he was manager. Tom Newman made an official break of 89 in 1919.

The rules of snooker, which had been subject to many local variations, were codified in when the Billiards Association and Billiards Control Club amalgamated in 1919. The drawn game was abolished when provision was made for the black to be respotted at the end of a frame if the scores were equal. The free ball was introduced to supersede the BCC rule that if a player was snookered after a foul he could have the snookering ball(s) taken up so that he could play onto the 'nearest ball playable', though, when in hand, a player was judged to be snookered or not from the brown spot only and not any part of the 'D'. The penalty for going in-off a red was still only one, the four point minimum penalty still being a few years away.

The touching ball rule was introduced in 1927.

In the earliest professional matches Fred Lawrence beat Albert Cope 31-27 for the Midland Professional Championship in 1921 and J. S. Nicholls beat W. Davies 1032-777 (the aggregate score of 18 frames) for the Welsh Professional Championship in 1922.

The first week's snooker match at a major London venue was staged as a season curtain-raiser at Burroughes and Watts, Soho Square in September 1922 when Arthur Peall beat Joe Brady 34-14.

George Nelson, a Leeds professional deeply involved in the promotion and trade aspects of the game, was publicly urging the BA & CC to wake up to snooker potentialities and the indefatigable Bill Camkin produced a book of rules. The Midland Counties Billiards Association with whom Camkin was closely associated imposed a minimum penalty of four points for a foul stroke, contrary to the then official rules.

From 1932-36, amateur snooker consolidated its popularity without its leading exponents noticeably improving their skill.

There was an important rule change in 1934 when the so-called crawl stroke, rolling the cue-ball up behind a nominated free ball, was outlawed, first as a six month's experiment but then permanently.

Snooker overtook billiards in popularity because it was a more sociable game to play and a more varied game to watch. Even at a friendly amateur level, one billiards player, noticeably superior to his opponent, could condemn him to an evening which consisted largely of fielding out, but at snooker breaks were of course much smaller, one player succeeded another at the table more speedily and the exchanges were more evenly balanced. With shrewd handicapping, games could be closer still.

As the top professional billiards players specialised more and more in nursery cannons and gained levels of expertise in break building sequences which, with small variations, were essentially repetitive, the game they played came to bear less and less resemblance to the one which amateurs themselves played or could identify with. As crowds for professional billiards dwindled away it was not long before professionals began to concentrate on snooker.

In 1936, the *Daily Mail* switched its annual sponsorship of a billiards tournament to snooker, the great feature of the event being a 133 break by Sidney Smith, the first ever official 'total clearance' and a new world record.

Tournaments sponsored by the *Daily Mail* and later the *Empire News*, *News of the World* and *Sporting Record* were to provide the staple fare at Thurston's and, after the war, at Leicester Square Hall: round robin events of three days or week's matches on handicap, involving seven or eight players and lasting at least half the season. It was a long drawn out procedure – in sharp contrast to the much shorter matches in today's major tournaments – and was eventually rejected by the public.

As the professional game contracted, fewer amateurs turned professional. The public tired of the same old players competing endlessly against each other and professional snooker, by the mid fifties, had virtually petered out. Nothing looked less likely for snooker's future than its affluent state today.

JOE DAVIS (1901-78)

If Joe Davis was a Master among Masters at Billiards, appreciably above Newman and McConachy, appreciably below Lindrum, he was indisputably King of Snooker, not only on the table but in all matters pertaining to the game.

In his days managing a billiard hall in Chesterfield, Davis realised at first hand that while billiards remained the championship game, snooker was increasingly becoming the people's game. It was more sociable in that breaks did not take as long and the inferior player did not therefore spend most of his time fielding out. With an appropriate handicap, a poor player could compete with an even chance with a good one. There was skill in the game but there was luck as well, more than there was at billiards, and this too enhanced its attractions as a gambling game.

As a young man, Davis also played a great deal of Pink Pool, a gambling game which employed 15 reds and the pink. Potting a red entitled the player to an agreed stake from all other players plus a chance, for a higher stake, to attempt the pink. He was so much too good for the local miners that he was made to play left-handed, thus acquiring the skill as a left-handed player which enabled him to deal with many positions

at billiards – and even more at snooker – for which he would otherwise require The Rest, an implement which he rarely employed with great confidence. (Joe's younger brother Fred later learnt to play left-handed for a similar reason and was also comparatively poor with The Rest.)

Another chance factor may well have contributed to Davis's extraordinary consistent and accurate potting. As his right eye was virtually useless, he automatically sighted with his left eye, almost like a marksman, his cue touching his chin beneath his good eye.

The Amateur Snooker Championship had started in 1916; there had been a Midland Professional Championship in 1921 and a Welsh Professional Championship in 1922; but snooker's role in the professional world was chiefly to fill out, with a couple of light-hearted frames, a billiards session which finished early. When it was suggested in 1924 that the BA & CC organise a professional championship their secretary, A. Stanley Thorn, replied: 'The suggestion will receive consideration at an early date but it seems

Fred Davis (*left*) and Joe Davis prepare to start a week's match at Leicester Square Hall in 1949.

a little doubtful whether snooker as a spectacular game is sufficiently popular to warrant the successful promotion of such a competition'.

Two billiard traders, George Nelson of Leeds and Bill Camkin of Birmingham, both friends of Davis, could see snooker's possibilities, even if the Establishment could not, and brought snooker to the fore whenever they could. Finally, Camkin and Davis drafted a letter to the BA & CC drawing up conditions for a professional championship and received this august body's blessings.

There was a five guinea entry fee and five guinea sidestake, half the money to be distributed in a 60–40 ratio between winner and runner-up, the other half to pass to the BA & CC. Gate receipts would be divided equally between the players. The entire organisation fell on Camkin who not only promoted the final but refereed it.

In those days, the prevailing idea was to pot a red or two, a couple of colours and play safe but in the time he could spare from billiards Davis devoted considerable thought and practice to evolving the positional and breakbuilding shots, sequences and techniques which are taken for granted today. In 1925, he made a break of 96 which superseded Tom Newman's official record of 89 which had stood since 1919.

Predictably, Davis won the inaugural 1926-27 championship with ease. His top break was 57 and he pocketed £6 10s 0d. The BA & CC used the players' half of the entry fees to buy a trophy. Few of the early championships were much more remunerative. Even by 1931, it was still held in such low esteem that the final was staged in the back room of a Nottingham pub owned by the other finalist, Tom Dennis.

In January 1928, Davis made his first public snooker century – he never counted anything he did in practice – against Fred Pugh at Manchester. He inched up the official record to 105 (1930), 109 (1933), 114 (1933), with a 132 on a non-standard table for good measure. His first championship century was 110 in 1935, the first year in which the event became a paying proposition.

Davis, according to his brother, 'a very good player before anyone else knew how to play the game', won the championship as regularly as clockwork each year. Though he never lost a frame on purpose, he was so far superior to his rivals that he could virtually pick his moment to tighten up if he needed to.

Even so, he trailed Dennis 10-14 and 16-19 before beating him 25-21 in the 1931 final. He cut it even finer against Horace Lindrum, the young Australian he had hammered 42-22 in a match for £100 plus all the gate money in Melbourne in 1933. Lindrum led 27-24 in the 1936 final before Davis won 34-27.

Lindrum, who had an exceptionally attractive style and personality was little if at all inferior to Davis in

technique but when the chips were really down the Englishman's infinitely superior temperament carried him through. Lindrum never beat Davis level but did so several times when receiving seven. Davis never lost on purpose but it no doubt crossed his mind that the audiences for week's matches between them might fall away if the same player always won.

In 1936, Lindrum equalled Davis's break record of 114 and later that year improved it to 131 though on the same evening as Sidney Smith made a 133. Davis improved his own best to 124, 128 and then regained the record with 135 in 1937 though Lindrum's break of 141 in January 1937 had been denied official status only on a technicality, the table not being tested *before* rather than *after* the match, a condition now abandoned.

On the first of many trips to South Africa, Davis made a 141 break that year which beat the all-comers record of 113 which had been set by Walter Lindrum, who did not take snooker seriously, in 1933. He increased the official record to 137 and three weeks later to 138 in the *Daily Mail* Gold Cup of 1938, the newspaper having switched its annual sponsorship from billiards to snooker in the 1936-37 season. It was also in 1938 that Davis first cleared the table from opening stroke with an effort of 134.

The championship record passed out of his hands but remained within the family as Fred made a 113 in their 1939 semi-final. Joe won narrowly 17-14 and even more narrowly in the 1940 final, clinching his 37-35 victory with a break of 100.

During the war, Davis raised over £125 000 for war charities and made a considerable name for himself on variety stages including the London Palladium, with a trick shot performance involving the use of a large tilted mirror. He married June Malo, the singer.

After the war, he was elected chairman of the resurrected Professional Billiards Players Association and formed a partnership with Sidney Smith and Bob Jelks, a billiard trader, to lease and promote at Leicester Square Hall (which opened on the old bombed Thurston's site in 1947).

His last title defence culminated in a fabulously successful fortnight's match against Horace Lindrum at the Royal Horticultural Hall, Westminster where crowds of 1200 a session poured £12 000 into the box office. Expenses were high and entertainment tax was reduced from 48 to 33$^1/_3$ per cent only the day before the match but each finalist pocketed a hitherto undreamt of £1500 for his efforts. Six century breaks (the two highest of the match, 133 and 136, being in turn championship records) helped Davis retain the title 78-67.

He retired from championship play, having held the world professional snooker title undefeated for 20 years, but like John Roberts before him continued to rule as king in exile. As the best player, the dominant personality, the chairman of the player's body, the man with the biggest say in who played at Leicester Square Hall, the game's showcase, he virtually ran professional snooker. When television came early in the 1950s, it was Joe with whom the BBC negotiated; when a player wished to turn professional he needed Davis's approval or he was frozen out. He had innumerable friends in show business, the professions, the city and the press. He was astute in business though, no matter what deal or conversation might have been occupying him only minutes before, his concentration was absolute when he reached the table. His instructional books, classics of their kind, sold hugely.

That Joe had the interests of the game at heart there is no doubt. With professional players squabbling and an ineffectual governing body there was a desperate need for a strong man to take charge as he did. Neither did anyone begrudge him his legitimate commercial pickings. But his retirement from championship play was soon to devalue the championship itself – just as Roberts's withdrawal had devalued it. In less than ten years, professional snooker was to decline from that peak of the 1946 final almost to the point of extinction.

Outside the world championship, professional tournaments were conducted on a handicap basis. Davis inevitably was the scratch man. Victory confirmed his supremacy, defeat did not threaten him because, of course, his opponent had received a certain number of points per frame. He played only the reigning official champion on level terms. He won the tournament twice in its ten-year history and was invariably near the top. Some players were so much in awe of his dominant personality that they were, literally, afraid to beat him.

It disappointed him that his brother allowed the title to pass outside the family in 1947 to Walter Donaldson, though there was some compensation in the crowds which flocked to Kelvin Hall, Glasgow, to see the king, a Scot himself, play the king in exile. During the week 10 000 spectators attended. Davis won 42-29 and made a new world record of 140.

Davis also made a break of 112 in which he took blacks with the first 14 reds. He could easily have left himself on the the blue from the last red and gone on to make 145 but elected to play the red very slowly to stay on the black. It failed to drop and he had to wait until 1955 to achieve snooker's first 147 maximum under standard conditions. (Murt O'Donoghue in 1934, Horace Lindrum in 1941, Leo Levitt in 1948, Clark McConachy in 1952 had previously made witnessed 147's on non-standard tables in practice frames.)

After his brother had beaten Donaldson in the 1948 final, Fred and Joe met in the *Empire News* tournament which ran throughout the 1948-49 season. The brothers played level but as Joe had never lost to anyone he was expected to be conceding two or three frames on the sealed handicap which was revealed at the end of the match.

Fred won a great victory, 36-35, having achieved a winning lead at 36-33, but when the sealed envelope was opened it was revealed that Fred was conceding two frames! The handicapper, Harold Mayes, sports editor of the *Empire News*, for whom Fred was writing a column in opposition to Joe's in the *News of the World*, had evidently thought it one-up to his paper to have 'their' man conceding start to Joe. As it was, this bizarre denouement, which enabled Joe to take the first prize of £450, obscured Fred's victory, which never achieved a sense of reality with the public.

In the 1949-50 season, Davis won the new £1500 *News of the World* tournament from the back mark, conceding 7 to Donaldson and at least 20 to every other competitor. George Chenier, a Canadian whom he had brought over after they had contested a week's match in Bermuda, snatched the world record with 144 but was Davis's opponent when the maestro wrested it back five weeks later with 146, taking a pink after his sixth red.

In 1951 in South Africa and twice in 1954, Davis made century breaks in three consecutive frames. On 22 January 1955, having just made his second 146 in the *News of the World* tournament, Davis achieved his dearly held ambition: against Willie Smith at Leicester Square Hall, only a few weeks before it closed due to the expiry of the lease, he made the first official 147 maximum.

Pettily and short-sightedly the BA & CC refused to recognise the break on the grounds that professionals were playing under their own 'play again' rule though this had not, of course, cropped up in this particular frame. Everyone knew what the break meant, however, and the BA & CC did in fact belatedly recognise it in April 1957, shortly before they themselves adopted the 'play again' rule for amateur play.

The break was the climax of Davis's career. He received the OBE in 1963 and continued to play until 1964. Whenever snooker was on television the formula was Joe *v.* A. N. Other.

In retrospect, the game suffered from revolving too closely round one man. By retiring from the championship (ie not risking his reputation) he devalued the game's premier event and, it followed, anyone who won it. No doubt he would have won many more world titles but the chances are that, at least once, he would have lost. His brother, after all, beat him four times on level terms in the fifties, admittedly far fewer times than Joe beat him but enough to constitute a real threat.

The future of professional snooker was not safeguarded in any way. He had had the vision to build up snooker as a public entertainment but always, quite understandably, in a context which allowed for his personal progress, standing and profit. His determination and that of his immediate colleagues to uplift the game's status had been wholly admirable but their lack of forethought in not only failing to encourage but actually discouraging leading amateurs of the day from turning professional was not in the best interests of the game.

Little was seen of Davis in the first few years of his retirement but as snooker gathered an unstoppable momentum in the late seventies he was regularly seen at big tournaments. Invariably, he received a mighty ovation.

It was tragic, if appropriate, that at the age of 77, he should be taken ill while watching his brother contest

THE WORLD PROFESSIONAL SNOOKER CHAMPIONSHIP

1927

First round: M. Inman beat T. Newman 8-5; T. Carpenter beat N. Butler 8-3.

Second round: T. A. Dennis beat F. Lawrence 8-7; A. Cope beat A. Mann 8-6; J. Davis beat J. Brady 10-5; Carpenter beat Inman 8-3.

Semi-finals: Davis beat Cope 16-7; Dennis beat Carpenter 12-10.

Final: Davis beat Dennis 20-11.

1928

First round: T. Newman beat F. Smith 12-6; A. Mann beat A. Cope 14-9.

Second round: Newman beat T. A. Dennis 12-5; F. Lawrence beat Mann 12-11.

Third round: Lawrence beat Newman 12-7.

Final: J. Davis beat Lawrence 16-13.

1929

First round: F. Lawrence beat A. Mann 13-12.

Semi-finals: J. Davis beat Lawrence 13-10; T. A. Dennis beat K. Prince 14-6.

Final: Davis beat Dennis 19-14.

1930

First round: F. Lawrence beat A. Mann 13-11; N. Butler beat T. Newman 13-11.

Semi finals: J. Davis beat Lawrence 13-2; T. A. Dennis beat Butler 13-11.

Final: Davis beat Dennis 25-12.

1931

Final: J. Davis beat T. A. Dennis 25-21.

1932

First round: C. McConachy beat T. A. Dennis 13-11.

Final: J. Davis beat McConachy 30-19.

1933

First round: W. Donaldson beat W. Leigh 13-11.

Semi finals: J. Davis beat Donaldson 13-1; W. Smith beat T. A. Dennis 16-9.

Final: Davis beat Smith 25-18.

1934

Final: J. Davis beat T. Newman 25-23.

1935

First round: W. Smith beat C. Stanbury 13-12.

Semi finals: Smith beat A. Mann 13-4; J. Davis beat T. Newman 15-10.

Final: Davis beat Smith 25-20.

1936

First round: C. O'Donnell beat S. Lee 16-15; H. Lindrum beat H. Terry 20-11; J. Davis beat T. Newman 29-2; W. Smith beat S. Smith 16-15; C. Stanbury beat A. Mann 22-9.

Second round: Alec Brown beat Stanbury 16-15; Lindrum beat O'Donnell 19-6 (retired); J. Davis beat W. Smith 22-9; S. Newman w.o.

Semi finals: Davis beat Brown 21-10; Lindrum beat S. Newman 29-2.

Final: Davis beat Lindrum 34-27.

1937

First round: W. A. Withers beat F. Davis 17-14.

Second round: J. Davis beat Withers 30-1; H. Lindrum beat S. Lee 20-11; W. Smith beat T. Newman 16-15; S. Smith beat Alec Brown 18-13.

Semi finals: Lindrum beat W. Smith 20-11; Davis beat S. Smith 18-13.

Final: Davis beat Lindrum 32-29.

1938

Qualifying
First round: H. Holt beat C. W. Read 21-10.

Second round: F. Davis beat Holt 23-8.

Competition proper
First round: F. Davis beat Alec Brown 14-6 (retired ill); S. Smith beat C. Stanbury 27-4; J. Davis beat S. Lee 24-7; W. Smith beat T. Newman 16-15.

Semi finals: Davis beat W. Smith (n.r.s.); S. Smith beat F. Davis (n.r.s.).

Final: J. Davis beat S. Smith 37-24.

1939

Qualifying
First round: W. Donaldson beat H. Holt 18-13; H. W. Laws beat S. Newman 19-12.

Second round: Donaldson beat Laws 18-13.

Competition proper
First round: S. Smith beat S. Lee 21-10; W. Donaldson beat C. Falkiner 21-10; T. Newman beat A. Mann 19-12; F. Davis beat C. Stanbury 19-12.

Second round: J. Davis beat W. Smith 19-12; F. Davis beat T. Newman 20-11; Alec Brown beat H. Lindrum 17-14; S. Smith beat Donaldson 16-15.

Semi finals: J. Davis beat F. Davis 17-14; S. Smith beat Alec Brown 20-11.

Final: J. Davis beat S. Smith 43-30.

1940

Qualifying
H. Holt beat C. Stanbury 18-13.

Competition proper
First round: W. Donaldson beat Holt 24-7; J. Davis beat Alec Brown 20-11; F. Davis beat S. Lee 20-11; S. Smith beat T. Newman 22-9.

Semi finals: J. Davis beat Donaldson 22-9; F. Davis beat S. Smith 17-14.

Final: J. Davis beat F. Davis 37-36.

1946

Qualifying
First round: K. Kennerley beat F. Lawrence 22-9; C. Stanbury beat J. Barrie 18-13; S. Newman beat W. Leight 16-15.

Second round: Kennerley beat T. Reece 8-2 (retired); S. Newman beat Stanbury 17-14.

Third round: S. Newman beat Kennerley 21-10.

Competition proper
First round: J. Davis beat W. Donaldson 21-10; S. Newman beat S. Lee 19-12; F. Davis beat Alec Brown 24-7; H. Lindrum beat H. Holt 17-14.

Semi finals: J. Davis beat S. Newman 21-10; Lindrum beat F. Davis 16-12.

Final: J. Davis beat Lindrum 78-67.

the 1978 semi-final against the South African Perrie Mans. He survived a 6½-hour operation but died a few months later from a chest infection while convalescing.

He died with the satisfaction of having seen, at Sheffield and on television, the game which he had pioneered at a peak of popularity and the championship he founded established, with events like Wimbledon and the Open Golf Championship, as one of Britain's great annual sporting spectacles.

FRED DAVIS (1913–)

With any other surname, Fred Davis would have made a very much more substantial impact on the general public than was the case as Joe's younger brother. Eight world titles in ten attempts would in ordinary circumstances have made him the dominant player of his generation but with Joe not playing in the championship, though otherwise pursuing a full playing career, Fred became immovably stuck in the public mind as the perennial number two. Four times (not of course counting short matches and exhibitions) Fred beat Joe on level terms but this affected their relative standings with the public not at all. It was even suggested that Joe had allowed Fred to beat him in order to give his brother a leg-up though anyone who was aware of Joe's intense pride of performance and his ambition to retire undefeated recognised the absurdity of this diagnosis.

Some twelve years the younger, Fred grew up so deeply in Joe's shadow that it was remarkable that he ever emerged from it. He began playing on a miniature table at his home on Wittingham Moor, near Chesterfield. No one as much as told him the rules but he picked up the basics very quickly and at the age of 12 was taken by his father to play at Burroughes Hall, London in the Boys (Under 16) Championship. A semi-final place in competition with older boys did not impress anyone in Chesterfield, least of all his family, who were now accustomed to Joe playing – and usually winning – at the very highest level and he was not even entered for the event for another three years, on which occasion he won it comfortably.

Easygoing, not a glutton for practice, Fred tended to be written off by Joe as not dedicated or ambitious enough. Apart from a forcible suggestion that he should wipe the grin off his face when he was practising, Fred received little advice and certainly no coaching from his elder brother. Through working in his family's billiard hall in Chesterfield he automatically became a professional on his sixteenth birthday but Joe held such a low opinion of his game that he was most reluctant that he should be allowed to enter the Junior Professional Billiards Championship. In fact, Fred won the event on each of the three occasions it was held.

Professional opportunities, though, were few and far between. There were a few club exhibitions – £1 was the fee for his first – but with professional billiards going out of existence at just the wrong time he did not surface again as a competitor until the 1937 World Professional Snooker Championship.

By this time he was self-consciously keeping to himself that he was suffering from myopia. He could tell the time from the large clock which stood in the family billiard hall only by standing right underneath it. When he played, the balls had a woolly edge. He lost 17-14 in the first round to Bill Withers, a Welshman of no previous or subsequent record.

Joe was furious at this affront to family honour. He berated Fred for losing . . . . . and beat Withers in the next round 30-1. Fred overcame his self-consciousness sufficiently to consult an optician and thus became the first professional to play with the special swivel joint spectacles which have since become the saviour of many an imperfectly sighted player.

His game improved rapidly. A semi-finalist in 1938, Fred lost only 17-14 to Joe in the 1939 semi-final and in 1940 reached the final, giving Joe his closest-ever championship battle before losing only 37-35. Fred, who had several times been told by Joe that he would never beat him, was thus very near to doing so before the Army spirited him away for almost the full duration of the war.

In the first post-war championship, Fred lost in the semi-final to Horace Lindrum but with Joe then retiring from championship play he was odds-on favourite to beat Walter Donaldson in the 1947 final. Their previous meetings had given Fred no great cause for anxiety but Donaldson, having locked himself away in the loft practising by himself for weeks on end, produced such a deadly mixture of brilliant single ball potting and, at the first semblance of risk, tight safety play that a name other than Davis was inscribed on the trophy for the first time.

This proved to be the first of eight consecutive world finals that Fred and Donaldson contested. Only once more was Donaldson successful, in 1950, but the matches were invariably hard work. The best tactics against Donaldson were to play him at his own patient, careful game, an approach which lent their contests an attritional aspect at times but which did not, strangely, deter spectators from attending in large numbers. Blackpool Tower Circus, which became established as the venue for the world final, was packed to near its considerable capacity every April.

Public interest would doubtless have been greater if Fred had been playing Joe with the title at stake. Even outside the championship they played some memorable matches. Joe preferred to concede a black start, a

59

handicap which hardly reduced his chances of winning but which safeguarded his reputation and record if he did lose. Nevertheless, on four occasions, Fred defeated Joe on level terms, the only player ever to do so.

Fred's first victory over Joe was in the *Empire News* tournament, a round robin event, with each match lasting a week, which ran through the 1948-49 season at Leicester Square Hall. Fred took a winning lead at 36-33 and won 36-35. However, the tournament was conducted on a sealed handicap basis with the handicapping entrusted to Harold Mayes, sports editor of the *Empire News*, for which Fred was writing a weekly column.

Several judges on the inside of snooker felt that around this time Fred was actually playing better than Joe but the fact remained that Joe had never lost level to anyone. Accordingly, when the sealed handicap

Snooker at Blackpool Tower Circus: Walter Donaldson and Fred Davis await the start of a session in one of their great finals.

revealed Fred to be conceding two frames start, Joe was presented with a 37-36 victory which not only obscured Fred's feat but gave Joe the £450 first prize.

The second victory, 37-34, occurred in a week's challenge match at Leicester Square Hall in 1949, the third, 20-17, in a three day match on level terms in the *News of the World* tournament in 1952 and the fourth, 21-16 in the *News of the World* tournament in 1954. In all fairness, these four close victories have to be set against a great many defeats, some by wide margins. Apart from his two championship defeats by Donaldson, though, Fred did not lose level to any other player before, on the grounds of dwindling financial return, he himself chose not to enter the 1957 championship.

Donaldson's retirement in 1954 had led to Fred meeting John Pulman in the 1955 and 1956 world finals, both of them close matches just as their 1954 semi-final had been. But the advent of television and the failure of professional snooker to provide new names was diminishing public support. Some leading

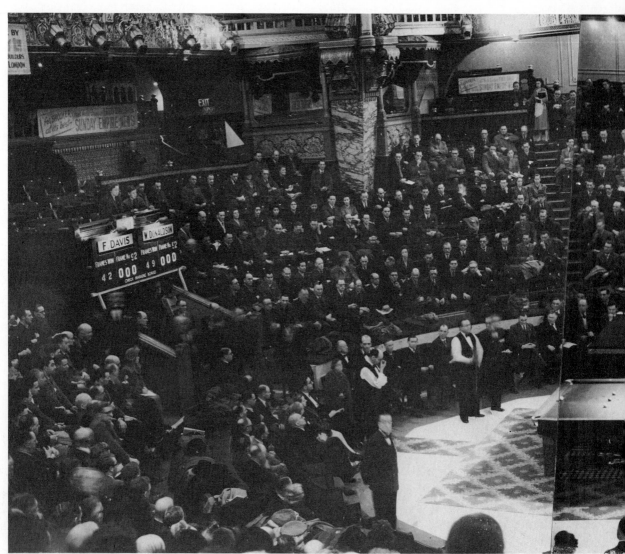

amateurs were vaguely thought to be 'not the right type' so the professional game grew ever more confined to a few familiar names. There was still a living to be earned from the club exhibition circuit but this had little to do with competitive sport. Fred, securely encamped at the Llandudno hotel which was run by his wife, felt less and less inclined to bestir himself.

This remained the position during Pulman's reign as champion from 1957-69. With the championship dormant from 1957-64 and only on a challenge basis from 1964-69, Fred challenged in 1964, in 1965 (when he was within one frame of victory) and in 1966 but, playing so infrequently, his standard inevitably suffered.

It became crystal clear, in 1968-69, when there was at last a new intake of professionals and the championship was restored to a knock-out basis, that the established players had gone soft through lack of exposure to competition.

Ten years in which Fred might otherwise have been in his prime had been frittered away when profes-

sional snooker once again began to gather momentum. Calling on his great experience, he beat Ray Reardon, then a new professional, 25-24 after winning five of the last seven frames in a 5 hour 33 minutes final session but lost easily to Gary Owen.

Though snooker's revival rekindled much of Fred's enthusiasm, this was inevitably negated by two heart attacks, in 1970 and 1974.

In the circumstances, it would clearly have been unrealistic to have expected him to recapture his former position in the game. Indeed, for someone born in 1913, it is amazing, so late in his career, that he should still compete so successfully at top level, winning the last three frames to beat Alex Higgins 15-14 in the 1974 world quarter-final, beating John Spencer in the 1975 Watney Open, losing only 11-10 to Ray Reardon in the 1976 Pontins Professional final, reaching the semi-final of the World Championship in 1978 and the quarter-final in 1979.

Though he has always been popular, Fred's efforts have been supported in the last few years by a special

THE WORLD PROFESSIONAL SNOOKER CHAMPIONSHIP

1947

Qualifying
First round: Albert Brown beat J. Pulman 21-14; W. Leigh beat H. F. Francis 19-16; S. Lee beat J. Lees 19-16; K. Kennerley beat C. Stanbury 23-12; E. Newman w.o. H. Holt.

Second round: J. Barrie beat F. Lawrence 25-10; Albert Brown beat Newman 28-7; Kennerley beat A. Mann 23-12; Leigh beat Lee 25-10.

Third round: Albert Brown beat Barrie 24-11; Kennerley beat Leigh 21-14.

Fourth round: Albert Brown beat Kennerley 21-14.

Competition proper
First round: H. Lindrum beat Albert Brown 39-34; S. Smith beat Alec Brown 43-28; W. Donaldson beat S. Newman 46-25; F. Davis beat C. McConachy 53-20.

Semi-finals: Donaldson beat Lindrum 39-32; Davis beat Smith 39-32.

Final: Donaldson beat Davis 82-63.

1948

Qualifying
First round: C. Stanbury beat E. Newman 26-9; W. Leigh beat H. Holt 18-17; J. Barrie beat H. F. Francis 19-16; J. Pulman w.o. S. Lee.

Second round: Leigh beat Barrie 21-14; Pulman beat Stanbury 19-16.

Third round: Pulman beat Leigh 18-17.

Competition proper
First round: F. Davis beat Alec Brown 43-28; C. McConachy beat J. Pulman 42-29; Albert Brown beat S. Smith 36-35; W. Donaldson beat K. Kennerley 46-25.

Semi-finals: Davis beat McConachy 43-28; Donaldson beat Alec Brown 40-31.

Final: Davis beat Donaldson 84-61.

1949

Qualifying
First round: C. Stanbury beat H. F. Francis 18-17.

Second round: Stanbury beat J. Rea 18-17.

Third round: Stanbury beat H. Holt 18-17.

Competition proper
First round: W. Donaldson beat Stanbury 58-13; J. Pulman beat Albert Brown 42-29; S. Smith beat Alec Brown 41-30; F. Davis beat K. Kennerley 50-21.

Semi-finals: Donaldson beat Pulman 49-22; Davis beat Smith 42-29.

Final: Davis beat Donaldson 80-65.

1950

Qualifying
First round: W. Smith beat W. A. Withers 28-7; H. Holt beat H. W. Laws 26-9; S. Lee beat C. Stanbury 20-15; K. Kennerley beat J. Barrie 21-14.

warmth. For all his steely determination and coolly analytical mind, his mild manner and ever-present sense of fun communicate an enjoyment of the game which, in an age of temperamental and overpaid superstars, the public find both endearing and refreshing.

Late in his career, Davis returned to billiards, his first love, which he had played only occasionally for more than 40 years as commercial reality had demanded that he concentrate on snooker. On one of his rare excursions into the three ball game he had won the 1951 United Kingdom Championship but declined to play Clark McConachy for the world title because he felt that the first week in September was too early in the season for a match of such importance.

Davis had long since abandoned all thoughts of playing for the Billiards Championship until Jim Williamson, proprietor of the Northern Snooker Centre, Leeds, persuaded Yorkshire Bank to sponsor a four day world title match with Rex Williams in May 1980.

A break of 583, the highest in the championship for 46 years, clinched Davis's convincing victory and enabled him to equal the record of his late brother Joe as the only player to have won the World Professional title both at snooker and billiards. He retained the Championship at Rugby later that year when the event was restored to a tournament basis.

Fred Davis, who adapted to contact lenses late in his career, in play in the Embassy World Professional Snooker Championship at the Crucible Theatre, Sheffield in 1980. Bill Girdwood is the referee.

WALTER DONALDSON (1907-73)

Walter Donaldson was the first winner of the British Boys Billiards Championship in 1922. He turned professional the following year and won the Scottish Professional Billiards Championship in 1928.

Combining hard practice with moves to Rotherham and Chesterfield to manage billiard halls, he began to concentrate on snooker and first entered the World Championship in 1932.

Heavily defeated by Joe Davis, he went away for no less than seven years to work on his game until he entered again in 1939, the year in which he established himself by finishing fourth in the *Daily Mail* Gold Cup.

After five years war service in the Eighth Army's desert and Italian campaigns he returned home in 1946 to undertake a relentless programme of solo practice to regain his form.

After Joe Davis's retirement had thrown the 1947 championship wide open, Donaldson shut himself away in a billiard room in a friend's loft for hours on end and to the surprise of the snooker world emerged to beat Fred Davis in the final.

These two were also to meet in the next four finals, Davis winning the first two and the last and Donaldson the other.

Donaldson's strong points were his imperturbability and the general consistency which arose from absolutely plain ball striking for he rarely used side in potting. This helped make his long potting the most consistently accurate the game had yet seen but it

---

Second round: Kennerley beat Smith 22-13; Lee beat Holt 16-8 (retired ill).

Third round: Kennerley beat Lee 21-14.

Competition proper
First round: Albert Brown beat J. Pulman 37-34; W. Donaldson beat K. Kennerley 42-29; G. Chenier beat P. Mans 37-34; F. Davis beat Alec Brown 44-27.

Semi-finals: Donaldson beat Albert Brown 37-34; Davis beat Chenier 43-28.

Final: Donaldson beat Davis 51-46.

1951

Qualifying
First round: J. Barrie beat S. Lee 23-12.

Second round: Barrie beat H. W. Laws 28-7.

Competition proper
First round: F. Davis beat Barrie 42-29; H. Lindrum beat Albert Brown 43-28; W. Donaldson beat K. Kennerley 41-30; J. Pulman beat S. Smith 38-33.

Semi-finals: Donaldson beat Lindrum 41-30; Davis beat Pulman 22-14 (retired ill).

Final: Davis beat Donaldson 58-39.

1952

First round: Alec Brown beat R. Williams 39-22; J. Rea beat J. Lees 38-32; Albert Brown beat J. Pulman 32-27 (records incomplete).

Semi-finals: W. Donaldson beat Albert Brown 31-30.

Final: F. Davis beat Donaldson 38-35.

1953

Qualifying
First round: W. Smith beat J. Lees 21-14; K. Kennerley beat R. Williams 25-12.

Second round: Kennerley beat Smith 42-29.

Competition proper
First round: Albert Brown beat Alec Brown 35-26; J. Pulman beat J. Rea 36-25; W. Donaldson beat Kennerley 42-19; F. Davis beat J. Barrie 32-29.

Semi-finals: Donaldson beat Brown n.r.s.; F. Davis beat Pulman 36-25.

Final: Davis beat Donaldson 37-34.

1954

First round: J. Pulman beat J. Rea 31-30.

Semi-finals: W. Donaldson beat Alec Brown 36-25; F. Davis beat Pulman 32-29.

Final: Davis beat Donaldson 39-21.

1955

First round: J. Pulman beat R. Williams 22-15; J. Rea beat H. Stokes n.r.s.

Semi-finals: F. Davis beat Rea 36-25; Pulman beat Alec Brown n.r.s.

Final: Davis beat Pulman 37-34.

1956

Semi-finals: J. Pulman beat J. Rea 36-25; F. Davis beat R. Williams 35-26.

Final: Davis beat Pulman 38-35.

Walter Donaldson

John Pulman in play during the 1980 Embassy World Professional Snooker Championship.

limited his positional play and restricted the number of centuries he made.

His dour approach and thrust out determined Scottish chin symbolised his approach to the game and indeed to life. He was a literal kind of man and he played a literal point-by-point type of game, making few concessions to the public. Though an excellent match player he was not in great demand for exhibitions and as professional snooker's appeal dwindled he acted out his disillusionment with the game by turning his billiard room at his Buckinghamshire home into a cowshed and breaking up the slates of his table to pave a path.

JOHN PULMAN (1926–)

John Pulman won the 1946 English Amateur snooker title as a 20-year-old unknown from Exeter and turned professional that year with the backing of a Bristol businessman, Bill Lampard, at whose house he stayed and in whose billiard room he practised intensively every day.

He won £400 in his first professional tournament, the *Empire News* event, but his progress to the championship was gradual. He gave Fred Davis a close match in the 1954 semi-final and another in the 1955 final. Leading 31-29 starting the last day he was on the brink of victory in the final the following year but Davis recovered to beat him and it was not until 1957, when Davis did not enter and when there were only four entries, that Pulman won the world title in Jersey.

He was unable to capitalise fully on his new status as champion as the game was entering an unprecedented depression and the championship became dormant until it was revived on a challenge basis in 1964. Public interest was limited but Pulman proved

his qualities as a competitor by defending the title against a variety of opponents in a variety of venues until the championship was restored to a knock-out basis in 1968-69.

When the established players were challenged by a wave of newcomers from the amateur ranks, Pulman stood up to the test better than any of his contemporaries, reaching the world final again in 1970. Thereafter, however, his standard gradually declined. There were, though, glimpses of his former quality and in 1978 he made a great personal effort to achieve his best form for some years in reaching the world semi-final. He has become chiefly known in recent years as a member of the BBC commentary team.

THE WORLD PROFESSIONAL SNOOKER CHAMPIONSHIP

1957

Semi-finals: J. Pulman beat R. Williams 21-16; J. Rea beat K. Kennerley 25-12.

Final: Pulman beat Rea 39-34.

Through lack of public support no championship was organised between 1957 and 1964. After a truce with the BA & CC a new system was adopted whereby the champion defended his title against a series of single challengers. These matches resulted:

1964

J. Pulman beat F. Davis 19-16.
J. Pulman beat R. Williams 40-33.

1965

J. Pulman beat F. Davis 37-36.
J. Pulman beat R. Williams 25-22 (matches).
J. Pulman beat F. van Rensburg 39-12.

1966

J. Pulman beat F. Davis 5-2 (matches).

1968

J. Pulman beat E. Charlton 39-34.

MODERN SNOOKER

A number of chance factors coincided to make professional snooker's revival possible. First, Gary Owen, John Spencer and Ray Reardon, three amateurs of high quality, decided to turn professional, thus giving the public new contests instead of the same tired old permutations; second, the developing sports sponsorship network led to the involvement of John Player in a British Amateur Team Championship, a series of exhibition tours by Pulman and, in 1968-69, to sponsorship of the World Championship which enabled it to revert to a knock-out tournament; third, *Pot Black*, the BBC-2 tournament series, was introduced when colour transmissions were in their infancy and it was modestly hoped that snooker, with its coloured balls of varying value, might stimulate sales of colour television sets. As it turned out, the programme offered snooker, more especially its top players, a priceless shop window, introducing the game to sections of the public who had known little or nothing of it, establishing the players as personalities and increasing the demand for their services for one-night club exhibitions. This coincided with a fourth factor, the legalisation of certain types of gaming machines, which transformed many a club's finances and thus made available more funds for professional exhibitions and re-conditioning of tables.

EDDIE CHARLTON (1930-)

Eddie Charlton has won the Australian Professional Championship every year, except 1968, since 1964 and has dominated the Australian scene not only on the table but through his chairmanship of the Australian Professional Association, his promotions company (who stage tournaments), through his connections in the billiard trade and through his contacts with sponsors and television companies. His status in Australia is akin to that which John Roberts and later Joe Davis achieved in Britain.

Charlton began playing when he was nine and at eleven played billiards exhibitions with Walter Lin-

Eddie Charlton

drum. He made his first billiards century at 15 and his first snooker century at 17 but spent much of his youth, with some success, playing more robust sports, including ten years First Grade soccer, the 1950 Australian surfing Championship with the Swansea Belmont crew, a string of victories in speed roller skating and competitive cricket, athletics, boxing, and tennis. He was one of the carriers of the Olympic torch for the 1956 Olympics in Melbourne and boxed an exhibition bout with Dave Sands, then world middleweight champion.

He turned professional in 1963 when he was still a miner and gradually began to concentrate on what was, after all, his number one game. He first visited England in 1968 to challenge John Pulman for the world title – this in the days when the champion defended against any challenger who could make a satisfactory commercial offer. He was beaten 39-34 and did not play in the Championship again until it was held in Australia in 1970 when he lost surprisingly to his fellow Australian Warren Simpson in the semi-final.

A man of immense physical reserves, he began his 1971-72 world quarter-final against David Taylor at Bolton the same day that he arrived. He won 31-25 and pushed John Spencer very hard to 37-32 in the semi but the highlight of his trip was winning the first of his two consecutive *Pot Black* titles, a success which may well have been material in the Australian Broadcasting Commission's decision to buy the series.

Though he has been very close many times, he has never won the world title or a major tournament in Britain. He led Ray Reardon 7-0 in the 1973 world final but was beaten 38-32; in the 1975 world final he recovered from 8-16 to lead Reardon 28-23 but was beaten 31-30; in 1976 he lost 20-18 to Alex Higgins in the semi-final; in 1979 he lost an epic semi-final to Terry Griffiths 19-17.

A cue action as straight as a gun barrel enables him to remain one of the game's cleanest and most consistent potters, though his unwillingness to use side for positional reasons for fear of endangering the certainty of the immediate pot symptomises the conservative side of his nature which has perhaps contributed to him losing a number of close matches which a more positive player might have won.

Some of his best qualities have been seen in adversity. In the first round of the 1978 World Professional Championship he beat Willie Thorne from three frames behind with four to play and in the following round beat Cliff Thorburn from four behind with five to play.

Outside the Professional Championship, Charlton's successes have included a 31-24 defeat of Reardon in the final of the controversial 'World' Matchplay Championship in Melbourne in 1976; a 23-19 defeat of John Spencer in the final of the biggest tournament South Africa has ever staged, the Limosin International, in Cape Town in 1979; and consecutive breaks of 135 and 137, neither opponent having a single shot, in an exhibition at the Kempsey Crescent Head Country Club, New South Wales in 1967. His break of 141 against Warren Simpson in the Australian Matchplay Championship, a challenge event which he has retained undefeated through numerous challenges, is the highest competitive break recorded in Australia.

Under the five pot rule he showed himself a useful billiards player in making a 488 break when he unsuccessfully challenged Rex Williams for the World Professional Billiards title in 1975.

STEVE DAVIS (1957-)

Steve Davis played like a living textbook long before he won any event of great importance. His model style, stance and cue delivery marked him as a player with a future even when he failed to win the British Junior Snooker Championship, a failure for which he compensated in part by winning the British Junior Billiards title in 1976.

His first notable success as an amateur, the Pontins Open, came in 1978, the year he also won the All England Club and Institute Union Snooker Championship from the club, Plumstead Common WMC, in which he had been taught to play by his father. The following year, having abandoned his A-level studies in order to play full time, he returned to Pontins as a professional, conceding 30 points per frame instead of receiving 30 as he had as an amateur the previous year. He won the tournament again.

The guiding hand in Davis's career has been that of Barry Hearn, chairman of Lucania Snooker Clubs, to whose Romford match room virtually every professional of note was invited to play in order to further Davis's match experience. He played every worthwhile tournament available to him and in only his

second year as a professional made a national reputation by beating Terry Griffiths, then the reigning world champion, in the 1980 Embassy World Championship before losing to Alex Higgins in the quarter-finals.

Encouraging as this was, it scarcely prepared the ground for Davis to dominate the 1980-81 British season with unparalleled severity. First prizes of £6000 from the Coral United Kingdom Championship, £5000 from the Wilson's Classic, £10 000 from the Yamaha Organs Trophy, £4000 from the John Courage English Professional Championship and, the jewel in the crown, £20 000 from the Embassy World Professional Championship, made a contribution of £45 000 to an annual income comfortably into six figures.

His draw for the 1981 World Championship could hardly have been more difficult but victories over Jimmy White, Alex Higgins, Terry Griffiths, Cliff Thorburn, and Doug Mountjoy proved that he is currently the toughest match player in a very hard school.

Flawless technique, mixed with the confidence engendered by success, is a deadly equation. Add to it the sober habits, single-mindedness and dedication of a Björn Borg and it is easy to visualise Davis as the leading player of the eighties.

Steve Davis: 1981 Embassy World Professional Snooker champion.

PATSY FAGAN (1951-)

A Republic of Ireland amateur international, Patsy Fagan reached the final of the English Amateur Championship at his first attempt in 1974 and turned professional two years later. He won the inaugural United Kingdom Professional Championship in 1977, the Dry Blackthorn Cup immediately afterwards and in the 1978 World Championship scored a memorable 13-12 win over Alex Higgins which took him to the quarter-final.

Patsy Fagan

TERRY GRIFFITHS (1947-)

Terry Griffiths began playing in his local snooker hall in Llanelli when he was 14 but by today's standards developed slowly. Although he won the West Wales Championship at 17, he was 24 before he made his first century break, the year in which he reached the final of the Welsh Amateur Championship at his first attempt.

After a few selections as reserve, Griffiths played 14 times for Wales in home amateur internationals, winning on 12 occasions, and also won the annual invitation tournament on HTV. The Welsh Amateur title in 1975 gave him a place in the World Amateur Championship in Johannesburg in 1976. He was beaten in the quarter-finals but returned home to win the English Amateur title in 1977 and 1978.

When a quarter-final defeat in the 1978 Welsh Amateur Championship ended his prospects of competing in the 1978 World Amateur, Griffiths turned professional but his professional tournament debut was a disaster. He led Rex Williams 8-2 in the qualifying section of the Coral United Kingdom Championship but was beaten 9-8.

Just before the 1979 World Professional Championship he was struggling to survive as a full time professional but in storybook fashion came through the qualifying competition and went on to win snooker's most prestigious title at his first attempt.

His 13-12 quarter-final win over Alex Higgins and his 19-17 semi-final victory over Eddie Charlton were among the most memorable matches the championship has seen. The contrasting styles of his opponents showed Griffiths's ability to play both types of game to the highest standards. Cool and positive under pressure, winning countless frames from losing positions with late clearances, Griffiths achieved a degree of concentration and inward harmony that he had never, by his own admission, achieved before.

The quarter-final, in which Higgins made centuries in consecutive frames and Griffiths a break of 107 in the decider, was superb attacking, break-building snooker, one mistake usually being sufficient to cost the frame. Charlton involved him in a gruelling battle of attrition including a 5 hours 25 minutes final session which did not finish until 1.40 a.m.

After defeating Dennis Taylor in the final – something of an anti-climax in view of the epic battles which had preceded it – Griffiths was inundated with demands for his services either for exhibitions or endorsements. He was voted 'Newcomer of the Year' by the Sports Writers Association, the first snooker player to be honoured in such a poll.

Although he could not maintain the fine edge of form which had enabled him to win the championship he was beaten only by a single frame in the final of the Canadian Open by Cliff Thorburn and by John Virgo in the final of the Coral United Kingdom later that year. He helped Wales to win the inaugural State Express World Cup and in early 1980 won the Benson and Hedges Masters and the Benson and Hedges Irish Masters.

He fell at the formidable first hurdle posed by Steve Davis in the 1980 World Championship and lost to Davis again in the semi-final of the Coral United Kingdom but helped Wales retain the World Cup and again reached the final of the Canadian Open.

Early in 1981, he retained the Benson and Hedges Irish Masters and won the Pontins professional title. He reached the final of the Benson and Hedges Masters but fell again to Davis, this time in the quarter-finals, in the Embassy World Championship.

ALEX HIGGINS (1949-)

Like George Best, Alex Higgins was born in Belfast, reached the top very quickly at a very early age and had problems coping with fame and fortune. Like Bobby Fischer, his instant grasp of situations, his unexpected moves and virtuoso shots brought gasps of admiration from the pundits. And it was his own

Terry Griffiths

instinctive genius that enabled him to play, usually in exhibitions but often in important matches when his confidence was high, with such speed and dash that crowds laughed at the ludicrous simplicity of it all.

He was only ten when he learned to play in a billiard hall called The Jampot which became his second home, living off Coke and Mars bars and learning in a tough school by playing for money. When he was 14 he was apprenticed to Eddie Reavey at Wantage but his career as a jockey foundered on a weight increase and after only one public ride he was back in Belfast where, at 19 he won the Northern Ireland Amateur Championship and almost single handed took Belfast YMCA to the British amateur team title.

He turned professional armed with a professional's ability but blithely ignorant of the political workings of the snooker scene or of how to organise himself as a true pro, giving exhibitions in clubs and playing public matches instead of playing impromptu money matches in dingy saloons.

The North of England soon began to hum with tales of four-minute centuries and high living and his career was re-launched under a Blackburn bingo tycoon, John McLoughlin. It was under Dennis Broderick, though, that Higgins, starting in the qualifying competition, came through to win the world professional title at his first attempt in 1972 at the age of 23.

Higgins progressed from folk hero to media personality, the first modern snooker had had. A Thames documentary *Hurricane Higgins* reached the top 20 in the week's ratings; he had a weekly column in *The Sun*; his exploits with wine, women and horses were well publicised; he earned an unenviable reputation for behaving badly under the influence of drink.

His form, though, began to desert him. An instinctive competitor, he compensated for a deterioration in his potting by improving the tactical side of his game. In time, his form returned, though rarely for the sustained periods of his crest of the wave days in 1971-72. He remained, through his boldness and flair and anti-hero status, the game's biggest box office attraction. He enjoyed a measure of success – one quarter-final, two semi-finals, and a final – in the world championship between 1973 and 1976 before losing twice in the first round and once in the quarter-final in 1977-79 though, ironically, on each of these three occasions, his skill and personality produced high adrenalin levels not only in the crowd but in his opponents, who each found inspiration from the atmosphere he had engendered.

Outside the World Championship, he beat Ray Reardon and Fred Davis to win the Watney Open in 1975 and Reardon to win the Canadian Club Masters in 1976. The Benson and Hedges Masters title came his way in 1978 and again in 1981 and he successfully defended the Irish Professional title, which he won from Jack Rea in 1972, twice against Dennis Taylor and twice against Patsy Fagan, before losing it to Taylor in 1980.

With Spencer, he is the only player to have compiled centuries in four consecutive frames and in February 1976 he became the first player to take 16 reds and all the colours in a total clearance, the 'extra' red of course, being from a free ball after his opponent had left him snookered after a foul with all 15 reds

Alex Higgins
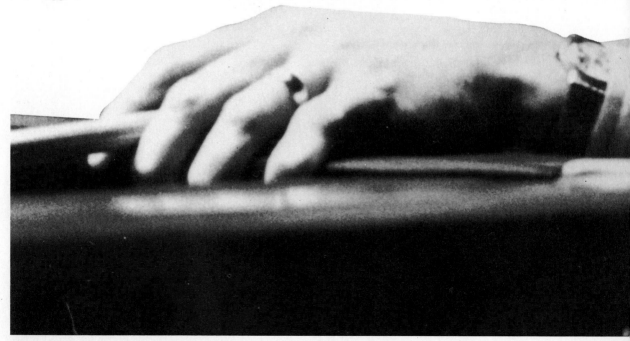

remaining. Sixteen reds, ten blacks, five pinks, one green and all the colours brought this break to 146. He has compiled six maximums.

PERRIE MANS (1940-)

Perrie Mans, whose father, Peter, was a World Professional Championship quarter-finalist in 1950, became in 1978 the first South African to reach the world final.

An outstanding single ball potter and a good competitor, with an unorthodox pattern of play which often disconcerted players technically more accomplished, Mans made good the comparative weakness of his positional play and breakbuilding in defeating John Spencer, Graham Miles and Fred Davis before losing to Ray Reardon in the final.

South African amateur champion in 1960, at his first and only attempt, Mans won the South African professional title from Freddie van Rensburg in 1965 and retained it until defeated by Derek Mienie in 1979. He regained the title the following year.

Mans, a left-hander, first competed in the World Professional Championship in 1970 but did not score a notable success until he sensationally defeated John Spencer 15-13 in a second round match in 1974. Two years later, he beat Graham Miles and Jim Meadowcroft to reach the semi-final.

Outside the Championship, Mans won the *Pot Black* tournament at his first attempt in 1977 and the Benson and Hedges Masters in 1979, beating Cliff Thorburn, Ray Reardon and Alex Higgins.

Perrie Mans

GRAHAM MILES (1941-)

Graham Miles first played snooker in a Birmingham Youth Club but he was 22 before he made his first century break. He won the Midland Amateur title twice but his record was still slim when he turned professional in 1969, in December of which year he made his first 147. As good a player as he was, he lacked the reputation readily to command tournament or exhibition invitations, but he made a breakthrough in the 1973 World Championship by beating former champion John Pulman.

Selected as reserve for *Pot Black*, he won the tournament when Fred Davis withdrew through illness, and retained the title the following year, two successes which enhanced his reputation and earning power dramatically.

His best championship was in 1974 when he took advantage of a number of upsets in his half of the draw to reach the final with wins over Paddy Morgan, John Dunning and Rex Williams, though he had little mental energy left for the final itself.

Miles reached the final of the Benson and Hedges

Graham Miles

Masters in 1976 by beating Higgins and Spencer but he was not engaged in another major final until the Holsten Lager International in 1979. He has never shown quite the flair or self belief to win a major title and his long potting has always been suspect but his close control round the black and pink spots is of the highest class and he is an able tactician. Distinctively, he sights his shots not with his cue on his chin but against his cheek-bone almost under his left ear.

DOUG MOUNTJOY (1942-)

Twice Welsh amateur champion, twice winner, as an amateur, of the Pontins Open, and world amateur champion in 1976, Doug Mountjoy's professional career began in a blaze of glory through winning the Benson and Hedges Masters in 1977, the UK Championship in 1978, the Pontins professional in 1979 and the Woodpecker Welsh Professional Championship in 1980 (beating both Terry Griffiths and Ray Reardon). Regarded by some as the best player currently on the circuit who has not won the world title, he is a fluent potter and breakbuilder seen at his best in a fast moving open type of game.

Winner of the first big event of the 1980-81 British season, the Champion of Champions, he suffered a worrying attack of Bell's Palsy, which paralysed one side of his face and affected the blinking function of one eyelid. This affected his performances for most of the season but he returned to form in time to make his best ever world championship showing, beating Willie Thorne, Eddie Charlton, Dennis Taylor and Ray Reardon to reach the final before losing 18-12 to Steve Davis. In his 16-10 semi-final defeat of Reardon, Mountjoy compiled a new world championship record break of 145.

Widely regarded as the best player currently on the circuit who has not won the world title, he was a member of the Welsh team which won the State Express World Cup both in 1979 and 1980.

GARY OWEN (1929-)

Gary Owen reached the final of the English Amateur Snooker Championship at his first attempt in 1950 but for a decade, until he entered again in 1963 and won the title easily, he was so preoccupied with family and working commitments that he played only as a hobby. With the professional game stagnant and the amateur game not yet offering a wide range of opportunity, there was not much apparent future in putting himself out.

He was still a Birmingham fireman when his success in the 1963 English Championship gave him the

Doug Mountjoy

right to represent England in the first ever World Amateur Snooker Championship in Calcutta. He did not win the English title again, but, as holder, he successfully defended the world amateur title in Karachi in 1966, when John Spencer, England's second player, finished runner-up. These events were the first which enabled amateur snooker players to hope that prowess with the cue might be a means of seeing the world.

For Owen his two world titles led to the award of the MBE and, in 1967, to being offered a £250 retainer to endorse a range of cues, the cue manufacturers by now being fairly desperate to carry a new line or at any rate a new name. He was the first new professional since 1951.

A fine potter and breakbuilder, as good a middle pocket potter as the game had ever seen, Owen achieved a hard competitive edge in the mid 1960s, when he could sense that his snooker was a passport to a more comfortable life, which arguably made him, for a couple of years, the best player in the world, amateur or professional. He reached the final of the World Professional Championship at his first attempt in 1969 but then lost to Spencer for the first time and never really looked a serious title contender again.

With a short backswing, which limited his cue power, there was always a suspicion of a jerk in his cue action and this gradually become more pronounced. A contract as the professional attached to the Western Suburbs Leagues Club, near Sydney, enabled him to emigrate to Australia but his tournament successes were surprisingly few, partly because he found it difficult to motivate himself as he had in the past.

RAY REARDON (1932-)

Ray Reardon was born into a snooker family in Tredegar, South Wales. His father and uncles all played local competitive snooker and he grew up in a snooker atmosphere, even to the extent of playing makeshift games on one of his aunt's kitchen tables with marbles for balls and books for cushions. He was barely tall

Gary Owen

enough to reach the table when he played his first full-size games in the Miners Institute but this acted to his later advantage in that he developed confidence in using the rest, an implement which even some professionals never manage to feel at home with, to such an extent that he is acknowledged as one of the finest rest players in the history of the game.

He went into the mines when he was 14 and competed in the British Boys and Junior Championship, but his first real success was the Welsh amateur when he was 17. This was the first of six consecutive wins, a sequence which was broken only when his family moved to Stoke.

This move also ended a period of intense rivalry with Cliff Wilson, another Tredegar boy, who won the British Junior Championship in 1952 and 1953 and who reached the final of the English Championship in 1954. The pattern of their matches was that Reardon tended to win in the Welsh Championship and Wilson in the English. There were also some raw battles in money matches with the town split into two camps, favouring either Reardon at the Miners Institute or Wilson who reigned at the Lucania billiard hall. Much later, in 1978, Tredegar was uniquely supplying both the world professional champion – Reardon – and the world amateur champion – Wilson.

At the Florence Colliery, Stoke, Reardon was buried in a roof fall, unable to move a muscle for three hours. He fought against the impulse to try to move by playing, in his mind, endless frames of snooker or games of marbles with his younger brother, a demonstration of his iron calmness and resolve which was to see him through many a crisis on the table.

Outstandingly talented as he was as an amateur, his besetting fault was a tendency to attempt too much. Partly because of this, he had to wait until 1964 to win his one and only English amateur title though he had been desperately unlucky in the 1956 final when he led Tommy Gordon 7-3 at the end of the first day only to lose his tip with his first shot on the second day and eventually lose 11-9.

It was at the expense of John Spencer, later a recurring professional adversary, that he won the English amateur title in 1964. This resulted in an amateur tour of South Africa which in turn led to an offer from Ken Shaw of Union Billiards to organise a professional tour for him. On the strength of this, Reardon resigned from the City of Stoke Constabulary in which he had served since shortly after his mine accident and in which he earned two commendations for bravery, one for disarming a man with a shotgun, the other for climbing across a frosty rooftop to drop through a skylight on to an unsuspecting burglar.

Having turned professional in 1967, Reardon won the world title at his second attempt in 1970 and in 1973 started a run of four consecutive wins. His other major tournament wins included the Benson and Hedges Masters once and the Pontins Professional twice though he did lose to Spencer in two excellent finals in the Norwich Union Open in 1974 and the inaugural Benson and Hedges Masters in 1975.

Ray Reardon

After a year's gap, he regained the world title in 1978 but apart from another success in the Pontins Professional in 1978 and the inaugural Welsh Professional title in 1977, he had no other major successes until he regained the Welsh title in 1981. However, the status which had accrued through his championship successes enabled him to establish himself more widely.

Through exposure as various as the subject of *This is your Life*, as a guest on *The Parkinson Show*, as a chooser of *Desert Island Discs*, as the centrepiece of a Tuborg television advertisement, as a *Sunday Mirror* columnist, his reputation did not rest on his playing success alone. He toured extensively in Australia, New Zealand, South Africa and India, crammed his diary full of exhibition engagements and negotiated many advantageous contracts with the snooker trade. His book, *Classic Snooker*, sold briskly and his instructional series, recorded by HTV, was well received. In summer, he fulfilled a demanding holiday camp exhibition contract with Pontins and even his favourite relaxation, golf, furthered his public image through Pro-Celebrity tournaments.

Highly organised, totally professional in presentation, Reardon was probably more successful financially than any player previously. Towards the end of the 70s his game fell away in consistency though never sufficiently for his opponents ever to forget his innate class. In contrast to the open – often wide open – style of his amateur days, he perfected a game more balanced between attack and defence, varying his tactics cleverly according to the opposition. He was particularly deadly when biding his time – and apparently conceding the initiative – only to pounce on a lapse and win the frame with a conclusive counter punch. His breakbuilding, clear and often subtle in design, was assisted by precise control of the cue-ball and, at his best, complete concentration.

WARREN SIMPSON (19??-80)

Warren Simpson, as cheerful and likeable a man as ever picked up a cue, won the Australian Amateur Snooker Championship in 1953 and 1957 and two Australian Open titles before he first won the Australian Professional Championship in 1963. He won the Australian title again in 1968, the only player to break Eddie Charlton's otherwise uninterrupted winning run from 1964 to the present day.

It was in 1970 that Simpson had his finest hour. Victories in the preliminary round robin over John Pulman, 21-16, and Gary Owen, 19-18, were enough, despite a 21-16 loss to Paddy Morgan, to put him through to the semi-final of the World Professional Championship.

Few fancied his chances against Charlton but Simpson played the game of his life to carry a 21-15

Warren Simpson

lead into the final day and hold on to win 27-22.

John Spencer, at the peak of his form, beat him 37-29 in the final and sadly Simpson never recaptured in matchplay the form which had so dramatically and so unexpectedly brought him within reach of the world title.

He was beaten 16-14 by Owen in the second round of the 1973 championship and in 1974 he lost 8-2 to Bernard Bennett, though it must be said of the latter match that he had spent the previous four days in hospital and discharged himself against medical advice. In 1975, he lost 15-11 in the second round to Ray Reardon.

As able a match player as he was, Simpson's scene was playing for money in clubs, particularly his beloved City Tatts in Sydney. With no head for or interest in business, Simpson was one of nature's punters for whom the thrill of picking or trying to be the winner was ultimately more important than the money of which he was perpetually in pursuit.

As quick around the table as Alex Higgins and almost as quick on the shot, Simpson was an easy, natural cueist with a deceptively loose style. He had less interest in century breaks than, for example, in taking bets all around the room, when there were seven or eight reds left, that he would clear the table. Talking and playing simultaneously, his standard was second to none.

He loved the game because he was fascinated by it. The most generous and correct of opponents, he was

John Spencer

also an avid watcher, quick to discern even a hint of quality – and start the applause.

He bore the diabetes with which he suffered without complaint and survived one heart attack before his death in 1980.

JOHN SPENCER (1935-)

John Spencer learnt to play on a makeshift home table with twelve nails knocked into a bagatelle board to form pockets and tape tied from one name to another to form cushions. His first snooker on a more traditional surface was played at the Radcliffe Sunday School Institute where, at the age of 15, less than a year after his first proper game, he made a break of 115, starting with a red and a yellow and followed by 14 reds and 14 blacks.

He played until he was 18 and then retired for 10 years until a friend of his recruited him for a local needle match. A succession of money matches, for sums between £10 and £20 followed. He won 14 in succession and was persuaded to enter the English Amateur Championship, the first tournament in which he had ever participated.

He reached the final, lost in the final again the following year but won it in 1966. He represented England in the 1966 World Championship in Karachi, finishing second to Gary Owen and, on his return, withdrew from all amateur events after a dispute with the governing body.

With no previous thought of turning professional,

he was contacted out of the blue by the National Spastics Society to play some exhibitions on their behalf. A summer engagement at Pontins holiday camp at Morecambe also came his way and when entries were invited for the 1968-69 World Professional Championship, a sympathetic bank manager advanced him the £100 entry fee.

Winning the title in an attractive style in which deadly long potting and prodigious screw shots were the more prominent elements, Spencer became almost overnight, snooker's biggest name. Even his defeat by Ray Reardon in the March 1970 semi-final did not much interrupt his reign for in November that year he regained the title in spectacular fashion when it was held in Australia for the first time.

When between January 1971 and February 1972, Park Drive sponsored four four-man tournaments, Spencer won three £750 first prizes and a £550 second prize. He won *Pot Black* in 1970 and 1971, he made, in Canada, his first 147 maximum and when, in February 1972, he was beaten by Alex Higgins in the world final, it was the greatest snooker upset for years.

There was another traumatic reverse in the 1973 world semi-final when he lost 23-22 to Reardon after leading 19-12. He won the Norwich Union Open both in 1973 and 1974 and the inaugural Benson and Hedges Masters in 1975 but his world championship performances gave him no cause for elation until, having sunk to number 8 in the world rankings, he won the 1977 title.

Some of his troubles stemmed from a car accident just before the 1974 Norwich Union in which the cue with which he had always played was broken into four pieces. Though it was expertly rebuilt, Spencer gradually lost confidence in it, until, only a few weeks before the 1977 World Championship, he changed to a Canadian two-piece. Shortly afterwards, he changed to the Japanese two-piece with which he compiled the first ever 147 maximum in tournament play in the Holsten Lager tournament at Slough in January 1979, his first major title win for eighteen months.

Even taking his cue difficulties into account, though, Spencer did not recapture, after 1972, except sporadically, the inspiration and sparkle of his early professional years. To some degree, he appeared to lose his love of the game and his style became much more carefully balanced between attack and defence. His best remained very good indeed but he did not consistently produce it.

KIRK STEVENS (1958-)
Canadian champion in 1978, Kirk Stevens became the youngest ever world championship semi-finalist in 1980 when he beat John Spencer and Eddie Charl-

David Taylor

Kirk Stevens

Dennis Taylor

Capped for England as an amateur on his residential qualification in 1971, he turned professional on a relatively slim amateur record making his first substantial impact in 1974 by reaching the final of the Canadian Open, in practice for which he scored 349 points in three frames without missing a shot – a 103 clearance, a total clearance of 134, and a break of 112.

He reached the semi-final of the World Professional Championship in 1975 and 1977 and in 1979 ousted the defending champion Ray Reardon in reaching the final.

Also the loser in two *Pot Black* finals, Taylor has often appeared to suffer from a certain tension creeping into his arm in the vital stages of important matches, particularly finals. Two unsuccessful challenges for the Irish Professional Championship, held by Alex Higgins, were followed, though, by a notable defeat of Higgins 21-15 in 1980 giving him his first major professional title. He retained the Irish title by winning seven of the last nine frames to beat Patsy Fagan 22-21 at Coleraine in 1981. With his ready wit and friendly personality, he also remains much in demand on snooker's exhibition circuit.

CLIFF THORBURN (1948-)

A beginner at 16 in his local pool hall in Victoria, British Columbia, Cliff Thorburn made his first century break when he was 19 and a break of 145 when he was 20. As Canadian snooker had no competitive structure, he acquired his experience playing cue games for money all over Canada and North America.

A job as a dishwasher on the Victoria to Seattle shuttle boat gave him a night in Seattle playing for money. Another job, cotton picking, led to him going into the nearby town with his earnings of $16.50 and converting it into $300 playing on a table which had a red cloth and, because of this, yellow balls instead of reds.

Hearing tales of George Chenier, the only Canadian to cut much ice in international competition before the present age, Thorburn hopped a freight train, hiding in the warm, dirty engine, to see him play in Toronto – though not before finding himself 400 miles off course in tee-shirt and raincoat with the temperature 30° below. On the road, he developed his unwavering concentration and determination in long sessions for money. Playing non-stop for 54 hours he once won $1000 – playing for no more than $40 a game – from one Canadian Dick in San Francisco. 'He came in with a jar of speed pills to stay awake', Thorburn recalls. 'But I really knew he had come to play when he laid out three pairs of socks.'

After Chenier died in 1970, Thorburn won the vacant North American and Canadian titles though he subsequently lost and regained the Canadian title and lost the North American title to Bill Werbeniuk. In

ton before losing to Alex Higgins. His break of 136 on the opening day of that championship would have superseded the then championship record of 142 but for a failure at the final black. Having made his first century break at the age of 12, there has never been any doubt of his exceptional ability. His attractive attacking style and happy personality have quickly made him very popular both with live and television audiences.

DAVID TAYLOR (1943-)

World amateur champion in 1968, David Taylor achieved little in his first ten years as a professional but in 1978 reached the final of the Coral United Kingdom Championship, beating Patsy Fagan, the holder, John Virgo and Alex Higgins before losing to Doug Mountjoy in the final.

In the 1980 Embassy World Professional Championship Taylor recorded victories over Ray Edmonds, Fred Davis and Ray Reardon before losing to the eventual winner, Cliff Thorburn, in the semi-finals. He took the £5000 second prize from the Yamaha Organs Trophy at Derby in 1981.

DENNIS TAYLOR (1949-)

Dennis Taylor, born in Coalisland, Co. Tyrone, moved to Lancashire when he was 17 and won the British Junior Billiards Championship in 1968, an event he had, ironically, entered only as an afterthought.

1970 too he saw British professionals for the first time, Fred Davis and Rex Williams. Discovering how authentic tournament professionals dressed and conducted themselves, he began to cherish an ambition to break into the authentic tournament circuit.

Late in 1971, Thorburn played John Spencer, then world champion, for three weeks, losing 56-49 in Calgary, 54-43 in Edmonton and 42-33 in Vancouver, narrow enough margins but wide enough to instil a special respect for Spencer's ability. Farcically, Thorburn possessed only one suit at the time and with morning, afternoon and evening sessions to be played could never get round to having it cleaned.

His conversations with Spencer, however, revealed the practical steps he had to take to become a tournament player and in 1973 he competed in the World Championship for the first time beating Dennis Taylor 9-8 before losing 16-15 to Rex Williams for a place in the quarter-final, a very creditable debut in view of the adjustment he had to make from the Vitalite balls used in Canada to the Super Crystalates used in other parts of the snooker world.

In 1974, he won the first Canadian Open in Toronto and the Victorian Masters, a television event, in Melbourne. He gradually enhanced his reputation until in 1977, he reached the world final for the first time.

He led Spencer by four frames but the feelings of awe and inferiority which belonged to their first encounters returned to undermine him as he went down 25-21. It did not help him either that his friends in Canada, oblivious to the five hours time difference, constantly disturbed his sleep to wish him well.

A marginal recession then set into his career. In Canada, he frequently compiled 147's – he had made 20 by 1 January 1981 – and beat back some notable challengers to win the Canadian Open in 1978, a success he repeated in 1979 and 1980. A leading light in the formation of the Canadian Professional Association, he won the inaugural championship the body organised in 1980. In Britain, he beat Spencer, thus overcoming a significant personal obstacle, to reach the 1978 final of the Benson and Hedges Masters.

Generally, though, he struggled and an old problem, clinching winning positions, tripped him up time and again, most notably when he lost to Eddie Charlton in the 1978 world quarter-final after leading by four frames with five to play. It seemed as if, for all his determination, dedication, and precise cue-ball control, Thorburn was not of the stuff of which world champions are made.

Triumphantly, he disproved this in the 1980 World Championship when after trailing 5-9 he beat Alex Higgins 18-16 in a memorable final. He was beaten in the semi-final by Steve Davis when he defended his title the following year.

John Virgo

Cliff Thorburn in play during the Benson and Hedges Masters tournament.

Bill Werbeniuk

JOHN VIRGO (1946-)

Having reached the semi-final of the World Championship for the first time in 1979, John Virgo captured his first major title, the Coral United Kingdom Championship at Preston in November that year. He also won the Bombay International tournament and, late in the season, the Pontins professional title at Prestatyn. As his bearded, glowering looks suggest, he has the artist's volatile temperament, full of flair and invention at his best but a little inconsistent.

BILL WERBENIUK (1947-)

Twice a world championship quarter-finalist and four times in the last 16, Bill Werbeniuk made a 142 break in the 1979 championship to equal the championship record set by Rex Williams in 1965. A Canadian World Cup player he holds the dubious distinction of being the first professional to split his trousers while playing on television, an incident which occurred during the State Express World Cup earlier this season.

Cliff Wilson *(left)* and Jimmy White *(right)*

JIMMY WHITE (1962-)

At 16, the youngest ever English amateur champion and at 18, the youngest ever world amateur champion, Jimmy White is the game's youngest professional. He made his first century break when he was only 13 and with his outstanding natural talent appears certain to make his mark very soon in the highest reaches of the professional game.

CLIFF WILSON (1934-)

Welsh amateur champion in 1956, and after a 15-year retirement from the game again in 1977 and 1979, Cliff Wilson won the World Amateur Snooker Championship in Malta in 1978 and turned professional the following year. Partly because of eye trouble he has not recaptured the consistency of his youth but at his best he remains an outstanding potter with a uniquely entertaining style.

JIM WYCH (1955-)

Canadian Amateur champion in 1979, Jim Wych gave up his chance to compete in the 1980 World Amateur in order to participate in the 1980 World Professional Championship in which he accomplished the outstanding feat of reaching the quarter-finals at his first attempt.

Jim Wych

All set for a season of the Embassy World Professional Championship at Crucible Theatre, Sheffield.

Bruce Donkin introduces a session in the 1980 Embassy World Championship at the Crucible Theatre, Sheffield. From left referee John William and players Denis Taylor, Jim Wych, Cliff Thorburn and Doug Mountjoy. A curtain descends between the two tables before play begins.

Above: Kirk Stevens

Right: Cliff Thorburn

Below: Doug Mountjoy

THE MODERN GAME: PROFESSIONAL TOURNAMENTS

1969
World Professional Snooker Championship

Sponsor: Players No 6	*Entries*: 8
Prize money: £3500	*First prize*: £1300

The eight man draw providentially brought the four established professionals against the four newcomers. The first match, at Wryton Stadium, Bolton, saw the end of Pulman's reign as champion at the hands of John Spencer. Pulman, at one time eleven frames behind, recovered to only three behind but was eventually beaten 25-18. Jack Rea was beaten 25-17 at Stratford Hippodrome by Gary Owen but Rex Williams scored a very comfortable victory over Bernard Bennett, a Southampton player who turned professional without any substantial amateur record, at Southampton. In the last first round match, Fred Davis just overcame Ray Reardon by the odd frame in 49 after several marathon sessions at Tunstall British Legion, Stoke.

There were thus two new and two established professionals remaining in the semi-finals though, at this stage, both newcomers were to record crushing victories, Spencer over Williams at the Co-op Hall, Bolton, and Owen over Davis at Wilstanton Miners Club, Stoke.

Owen, in view of the fact that he had always beaten Spencer in their previous important matches, started favourite for the final, a week's match at the Victoria Hall, London, but Spencer established a psychological ascendancy in the early stages and won very comfortably.

First round: J. Spencer beat J. Pulman 25-18; R. Williams beat B. Bennett 25-4; G. Owen beat J. Rea 25-17; F. Davis beat R. Reardon 25-24.
Semi-finals: Spencer beat Williams 37-12; Owen beat Davis 37-24.
Final: Spencer beat Owen 37-24.

1970 (April)
World Professional Snooker Championship

Sponsor: Players No 6	*Entries*: 9
Prize money: Not known	*First prize*: £1225

David Taylor, having turned professional after winning the 1968 World Amateur in Sydney, brought about an increase of one on the entry for the previous year. He held Pulman to 12-12 at Grimsby before going down 31-20. Pulman also crushed Owen in a semi-final at Middlesbrough and after trailing 14-27 to Reardon in the final at the Victoria Hall, London

recovered to 33-34 before losing 37-33. Controversy attended the other semi-final for which a diabolically difficult table was installed at Bolton. Spencer let the difficulties it presented get the better of him and Reardon, adapting himself better to the conditions, scored a narrow victory to reach the final.

First round: David Taylor beat B. Bennett 11-8.
Quarter-finals: J. Pulman beat David Taylor 31-20; G. Owen beat R. Williams 31-11; R. Reardon beat F. Davis 31-26; J. Spencer beat J. Rea 31-15.
Semi-finals: Pulman beat Owen 37-12; Reardon beat Spencer 37-33.
Final: Reardon beat Pulman 37-33.

1970 (November)
World Professional Snooker Championship

Sponsor: None	*Entries*: 9
Prize money: Not known	*First prize*: £2333

The championship was organised in Australia for the first time by Frank Holz on behalf of the Lewisham Hospital Sports Medicine Clinic. The four semi-finalists were obtained by means of an incomplete and thus unsatisfactory round robin. Matches were spread round Australia and thus involved competitors in a certain amount of air travel even, in some cases, on the day of a match.

Eddie Charlton, who had dominated the Australian scene since winning the Australian professional title in 1964, was expected to reach the final but lost to his compatriot Warren Simpson, a good potter with a deceptively casual and cheerful approach who spent most of his time playing for money in City Tattersall's Club, Sydney. Earlier, Simpson had beaten Pulman and, by a single frame, both Owen and the South African Perrie Mans.

With Spencer in his prime, however, he never looked like losing. The final saw him make three centuries in four frames, the first time this had been done in the championship.

Round robin: J. Spencer beat P. Mans 20-17; beat N. Squire 27-10; beat J. Pulman 23-14. R. Reardon beat Mans 22-15; beat E. Charlton 21-16; beat Spencer 21-16. W. Simpson beat G. Owen 19-18; beat Pulman 21-16; beat Mans 19-18. Charlton beat Squire 27-10; beat Mans 26-11; beat Owen 23-14. Owen beat P. Morgan 26-11; beat Squire 19-18. Pulman beat Morgan 25-12; beat Squire 26-11. Morgan beat Simpson 21-16.
Semi-finals: Spencer beat Reardon 34-15; Simpson beat Charlton 27-22.
Final: Spencer beat Simpson 37-29.

1971
Park Drive £2000

Gallahers first involvement with snooker, which was also that of their sports sponsorship consultants, West and Nally, was in the form of a triple round robin between four invited professionals with matches played over a single evening in 18 club venues. The top two in the final league table contested the final, which was televised by the BBC.

Final placings	P	W	L	Prize
John Spencer	9	8	1	£750
Rex Williams	9	5	4	£550
Gary Owen	9	5	4	£400
John Pulman	9	0	9	£300

Play off for first prize: Spencer beat Williams 4-1.

1971
Park Drive £2000

Park Drive repeated in October the tournament they had first staged in January. Reardon, who had been unable to take part in the first event because he was touring South Africa, finished second to Spencer in the round robin section but took the £750 first prize by winning the play-off 4-3 after needing a snooker with only pink and black remaining in the deciding frame.

Final placings	P	W	L	Prize
John Spencer	9	7	2	£550
Ray Reardon	9	4	5	£750
John Pulman	9	4	5	£400
Rex Williams	9	3	6	£300

Play off for first prize: Reardon beat Spencer 4-3.

1972
Park Drive £2000

The third Park Drive tournament was notable for a break of 146 by Reardon in the round robin section, the highest ever break in competitive play until Spencer's 147 in the 1979 Holsten Lager International. Spencer beat Higgins, playing in his first major professional tournament, 4-3 in the final which was played the day before they commenced their week long final of the 1972 World Professional Championship.

Final placings	P	W	L	Prize
John Spencer	9	6	3	£750
Alex Higgins	9	5	4	£550
John Pulman	9	4	5	£400
Ray Reardon	9	3	6	£300

Play off for first prize: Spencer beat Higgins 4-3.

1972
World Professional Snooker Championship

Sponsor: None   *Entries*: 16
Prize money: By arrangement with individual promoters.

Running from March 1971 to February 1972 this incredibly long drawn out event began with eight qualifiers being reduced to two to join the eight other entries in the competition proper. Those in the qualifying section included four former amateur champions, Ron Gross, Maurice Parkin, Pat Houlihan and Geoffrey Thompson, who all turned professional when well past their prime, but also Higgins, who was to make history as the first qualifier ever to go on to win the title.

He was not extended until the semi-final when Rex Williams led him by six frames before the Irishman got home in an exciting finish by the odd frame in 61.

The final proceeded on even lines until Higgins struck the front with a 6-0 victory in the Thursday evening session. This created a gap which Spencer was never able to close.

One of the surprises of the championship had come in the quarter-finals when Williams beat Reardon 25-23, the match being contested in five different club venues in Scotland.

Qualifying competition
First round: A. Higgins beat R. Gross 15-6; M. Parkin beat G. Thompson 11-10; J. Dunning beat P. Houlihan 11-10; G. Miles beat B. Bennett 15-6.
Second round: Higgins beat Parkin 11-3; Dunning beat Miles 11-5.
Competition proper
First round: J. Pulman beat Dunning 19-7; Higgins beat J. Rea 19-11.
Quarter-finals: J. Spencer beat F. Davis 31-21; E. Charlton beat David Taylor 31-25; Higgins beat Pulman 31-23; R. Williams beat R. Reardon 25-23.
Semi-finals: Higgins beat Williams 31-30; Spencer beat Charlton 37-32.
Final: Higgins beat Spencer 37-32.

1972
Park Drive £2000

Spencer finished second to Higgins in the round robin section but beat him 5-3 in the play-off in front of a crowd of 2000 at Belle Vue, Manchester, an attendance which sealed Park Drive's decision to enlarge their support from a four man tournament to the world championship itself.

Final placings	P	W	L	Prize
Alex Higgins	9	7	2	£550
John Spencer	9	6	3	£750
Ray Reardon	9	3	6	£400
John Pulman	9	2	7	£300

Play off for first prize: Spencer beat Higgins 5-3.

1973
Park Drive World Professional Snooker Championship

Sponsor: Gallaher	*Entries*: 23
Prize money: £8000	*First prize*: £1500

Snooker's box office potentialities, particularly when Higgins was playing, and the benefits it could offer a sponsor led to West and Nally devising the streamlined modern formula under which, with one or two alterations, the championship is still contested. Instead of dragging on interminably in diverse and often out of the way venues, with little sense of continuity and little or no publicity, the championship was telescoped into a fortnight at the City Exhibition Halls, Manchester with play taking place simultaneously, rather like Wimbledon, in eight different arenas. BBC Television covered the latter stages of the final, the first time it had done so. During the fortnight, there were 25 000 spectators. On site, betting was introduced through Ladbrokes, there were many successful trade stands and press coverage increased.

The championships provided one of the greatest recoveries in its history when Reardon, having trailed Spencer 12-19, won their semi-final 23-22. Reardon after losing the first session 0-7, went on to beat Charlton in the final. Higgins beat Davis in a memorable quarter-final but, burnt out by the accumulated pressures of the year following his 1972 title win, lost easily to Charlton in the semi-final.

First round: P. Houlihan beat J. Rea 9-2; D. Greaves beat B. Bennett 9-8; G. Miles beat G. Thompson 9-5; P. Mans beat R. Gross 9-2; W. Simpson beat M. Parkin 9-3; C. Thorburn beat Dennis Taylor 9-8; David Taylor beat J. Dunning 9-4.

Second round: F. Davis beat Greaves 16-1; Miles beat J. Pulman 16-10; E. Charlton beat Mans 16-8; G. Owen beat Simpson 16-14; R. Reardon beat J. Meadowcroft 16-10; R. Williams beat Thorburn 16-15; J. Spencer beat David Taylor 16-5; A. Higgins beat Houlihan 16-3.

Quarter-finals: Higgins beat Davis 16-14; Spencer beat Williams 16-7; Charlton beat Miles 16-6; Reardon beat Owen 16-6.

Semi-finals: Charlton beat Higgins 23-9; Reardon beat Spencer 23-22.

Final: Reardon beat Charlton 38-32.

1973
Norwich Union Open

Sponsor: Norwich Union	*Entries*: (invited) 24
Prize money: £3500	*First prize*: £1000

Norwich Union, another West and Nally sports sponsorship client, restored big time snooker to London with a tournament featuring both professionals and leading amateurs at the Piccadilly Hotel. This was the first notable Open since the removal of restrictions on amateurs accepting prize money but only one amateur, Sid Hood, with victories over Jack Rea, a professional, and Mannie Francisco, then an amateur, reached the quarter-finals. London Weekend Television covered an exciting final in which Pulman, having trailed 2-6, levelled at 7-7 before missing a vital green in the deciding frame which led to Spencer's 8-7 victory.

First round: *S. Hood beat J. Rea 4-0; *C. Ross beat *M. Owen 4-3; *A. Savur beat D. Greaves 4-1; David Taylor beat J. Karnehm 4-2; Dennis Taylor beat *A. Lloyd 4-1; *J. Barron beat R. Gross 4-2; J. Dunning beat J. Meadowcroft 4-2; P. Houlihan beat *J. Virgo 4-3.

Second round: G. Miles beat Savur 4-1; *R. Edmonds beat Barron 4-3; Hood beat *M. Francisco 4-3; E. Charlton beat Ross 4-0; C. Thorburn beat Houlihan 4-0; A. Higgins beat Dennis Taylor 4-3; J. Spencer beat Dunning 4-3; J. Pulman beat David Taylor 4-3.

Quarter-finals: Spencer beat Edmonds 4-0; Charlton beat Hood 4-0; Higgins beat Thorburn 4-2; Pulman beat Miles 4-3.

Semi-finals: Spencer beat Higgins 8-2; Pulman beat Charlton 8-3.

Final: Spencer beat Pulman 8-7.

(*amateur)

1974
Park Drive World Professional Snooker Championship

Sponsor: Gallaher	*Entries*: 31
Prize money: £10 000	*First prize*: £2000

Following the euphoria generated by the success of the 1973 championship, the 1974 event at Belle Vue, Manchester was a disappointment. The building was perhaps too reminiscent of a vast aircraft hangar and the pattern of results was a promoter's nightmare. Of the name players, Spencer lost his first match to Perrie Mans, the left-handed South African; Charlton went out to a lifetime best performance by John Dunning, a dour Yorkshireman; and Higgins lost the last three frames to Davis to lose their quarter-final by the odd frame. Reardon, a comfortable victor over Miles in the final, had his most difficult match in the quarter-final against Marcus Owen, who had turned professional after regaining in 1973 the English amateur title he had won three times between 1958 and 1967.

Qualifying round: J. Dunning beat D. Greaves 8-2; W. Simpson beat J. Rea 8-3; J. Meadowcroft beat P. Houlihan 8-5; C. Thorburn beat A. McDonald 8-3; J. Pulman beat J. Karnehm 8-0; David Taylor beat R.

Gross 8-7; M. Owen beat Dennis Taylor 8-1.

First round: B. Bennett beat Simpson 8-2; B. Werbeniuk beat G. Thompson 8-3; Meadowcroft beat K. Kennerley 8-5; M. Owen beat M. Parkin 8-5; P. Mans beat I. Anderson 8-1; Pulman beat S. Lee 8-0; Dunning beat David Taylor 8-6; P. Morgan beat Thorburn 8-4.

Second round: Mans beat J. Spencer 15-13; Dunning beat E. Charlton 15-13; M. Owen beat G. Owen 15-8; A. Higgins beat Bennett 15-4; G. Miles beat Morgan 15-7; R. Williams beat Pulman 15-12; F. Davis beat Werbeniuk 15-5; R. Reardon beat Meadowcroft 15-3.

Quarter-finals: Williams beat Mans 15-4; Miles beat Dunning 15-13; Davis beat Higgins 15-14; Reardon beat M. Owen 15-11.

Semi-finals: Miles beat Williams 15-7; Reardon beat Davis 15-3.

Final: Reardon beat Miles 22-12.

1974
Pontins Festival of Snooker

The new conception of having a large part of the snooker family under one roof at Pontins Holiday Camp, Prestatyn for a whole week's playing, talking and watching snooker created an event with a unique atmosphere and appeal.

The professional tournament, featuring the *Pot Black* cast, produced a great final before Reardon, having been 9-4 up, beat Spencer 10-9 to take the £1000 first prize but this event was overshadowed by the Open in which 398 amateurs were reduced to 24 to join the eight invited professionals in the last 32. With the amateurs each receiving 25 start and with a first prize of £1000 and subsidiary prizes going down to losers in the last 32, the format caught the snooker world's imagination and laid the foundations for what was to become one of its great annual jamborees. Doug Mountjoy, later a professional, became the first amateur ever to win a four-figure prize by beating Reardon and Spencer in the last two rounds.

Professional final: R. Reardon beat J. Spencer 10-9.

Open final: D. Mountjoy (receive 25) beat Spencer 7-4.

1974
Canadian Open

The Canadian National Exhibition Centre in Toronto, a large scale trade and entertainment complex, offered for the first time a snooker tournament among its many attractions promoted by Canadian snooker entrepreneur Terry Haddock. The Open tournament was joined in its late stages by a number of professionals with Canada's Cliff Thorburn securing the £1500 first prize, half the total prize money, in an event which was to develop over the next five years into a regular feature of the international circuit. Dennis Taylor, who reached the final, achieved an amazing sequence of 349 points, in pre-tournament practice, without missing a shot. This consisted of a 103 clearance, a 134 total clearance after fluking a red from the break off and 112 at his first visit in the following frame.

Semi-finals: C. Thorburn beat G. Miles 8-5; Dennis Taylor beat A. Higgins 8-6.

Final: Thorburn beat Taylor 8-6.

1974
Norwich Union Open

Sponsor: Norwich Union	*Entries*: (invited) 16
Prize money: £4750	*First prize*: £1500

Spencer, his cue broken into four pieces in a car accident just before the tournament, had it magically restored by Cliff Curtis of Riley Burwat with 13 plugs and a wood graft and won the tournament with it, both the semi-finals and the final providing first class matches.

First round: C. Thorburn beat F. Davis 5-4; B. Werbeniuk beat J. Dunning 5-1; J. Spencer beat *R. Edmonds 5-0; J. Pulman beat *G. Thomas 5-0; G. Miles beat *E. Sinclair 5-0; R. Williams beat M. Owen 5-3; A. Higgins beat Dennis Taylor 5-1; R. Reardon beat *P. Burke 5-2.

Quarter-finals: Higgins beat Werbeniuk 5-4; Thorburn beat Pulman 5-3; Spencer beat Miles 5-2; Reardon beat Williams 5-2.

Semi-finals: Reardon beat Higgins 9-8; Spencer beat Thorburn 9-7.

Final: Spencer beat Reardon 10-9.

(*amateur)

1975
Benson and Hedges Masters

Sponsor: Gallaher	*Entries*: (invited) 10
Prize money: £5000	*First prize*: £2000

Another West and Nally sponsor achieved at the first attempt only a partial success at the West Centre Hotel, Fulham, too far out of town, it seemed, to attract big crowds. Spencer and Reardon contested a final which could not have been closer – though the overall standard, partly because of the ultra-fast table, was disappointing.

First round: J. Pulman beat C. Thorburn 5-3; A. Higgins beat B. Werbeniuk 5-0.

Quarter-finals: E. Charlton beat F. Davis 5-3; J. Spencer beat Pulman 5-3; R. Reardon beat G. Miles 5-3; R. Williams beat Higgins 5-3.

Semi-finals: Spencer beat Charlton 5-2; Reardon beat Williams 5-4.

Final: Spencer beat Reardon 9-8.

1975
World Professional Snooker Championship

Sponsor: None	*Entries*: 27
Prize money: £18 900	*First prize*: Not known

With Park Drive somehow having slipped away as a sponsor the world championship was awarded to Eddie Charlton Promotions to stage in Australia. The WPBSA's seeding system, which was based only on previous world championships, or rather the promoter's failure to carry it out in full, led to Reardon (no 1) and Spencer (No 8) clashing in the quarter-final, a match which many saw as the real final. Dennis Taylor achieved his best championship showing so far to reach the semi-final in the other half before a choppy Sydney to Brisbane plane journey on the morning of his semi-final against Charlton contributed to him making a poor start from which he never recovered.

The final fluctuated amazingly. Reardon led 16-8; Charlton led 29-23; Reardon led 30-29 and after Charlton had levelled took the decider for his 31-30 victory.

Qualifying round: P. Tarrant beat B. Bennett 15-8; L. Condo beat M. Parkin 15-8; D. Greaves beat J. Charlton 15-14.

First round: W. Simpson beat R. Mares 15-5; J. Pulman beat Tarrant 15-5; David Taylor beat R. King 15-8; I. Anderson beat Condo 15-8; Dennis Taylor beat P. Mans 15-12; G. Owen beat Greaves 15-3; B. Werbeniuk beat J. Meadowcroft 15-9; C. Thorburn beat P. Morgan 15-6.

Second round: R. Reardon beat Simpson 15-11; J. Spencer beat Pulman 15-10; A. Higgins beat David Taylor 15-2; R. Williams beat Anderson 15-4; Dennis Taylor beat F. Davis 15-14; Owen beat J. Dunning 15-8; E. Charlton beat Werbeniuk 15-11; Thorburn beat G. Miles 15-2.

Quarter-finals: Reardon beat Spencer 19-17; Higgins beat Williams 19-12; Dennis Taylor beat Owen 19-9; Charlton beat Thorburn 19-12.

Semi-finals: Charlton beat Dennis Taylor 19-12; Reardon beat Higgins 19-14.

Final: Reardon beat Charlton 31-30.

1975
Pontins Festival of Snooker

Reardon, jet-lagged from his Australian trip, scored a great double by beating Spencer to win the professional tournament and, conceding 25, John Virgo, later a professional, to win the Open also. There were 657 amateur entries and vast crowds, including one of 1500 at 10.30 a.m. which saw Reardon recover from the loss of the first three frames to beat Patsy Fagan 4-3 in the Open semi-final.

Professional final: R. Reardon beat J. Spencer 10-4.
Open final: Reardon beat J. Virgo (receive 25) 7-1.

1975
Canadian Open

With prize money increased to $10 000 in all with $5000 for the winner there was a cascade of big breaks, albeit on sympathetic tables, in which a break of 142 by Cliff Thorburn was the highest of 23 centuries. The big surprise was a 9-7 quarter-final win for Willie Thorne, then an amateur, over Spencer.

Semi-finals: J. Pulman beat W. Thorne 9-6; A. Higgins beat G. Miles 9-5.
Final: Higgins beat Pulman 15-7.

1976
Benson and Hedges Masters

Sponsor: Gallaher	*Entries*: (invited) 10
Prize money: £5200	*First prize*: £2000

A new central London venue, the New London Theatre, attracted capacity crowds to its 1500 seat arena and gave the event its distinctive character. Reardon took the £2000 first prize with a comfortable victory over Miles, a surprise semi-final winner over Spencer, though the match of the tournament was Reardon's 5-4 semi-final victory over Charlton.

First round: F. Davis beat C. Thorburn 4-2; J. Pulman beat Dennis Taylor 4-2.

Quarter-finals: G. Miles beat A. Higgins 4-1; R. Reardon beat J. Pulman 4-1; J. Spencer beat Davis 4-0; E. Charlton beat R. Williams 4-1.

Semi-finals: Miles beat Spencer 5-4; Reardon beat Charlton 5-4.

Final: Reardon beat Miles 7-3.

1976
Embassy World Professional Snooker Championship

Sponsor: W. D. and H. O. Wills	*Entries*: 27
Prize money: £15 300	*First prize*: £6000

Embassy's first sponsorship of the championship was attended by all sorts of organisational difficulties. 'Q' Promotions, who became defunct shortly afterwards, overstretched their resources and the decision to play the top half of the draw at Middlesbrough Town Hall with the bottom half and the final at Wythenshawe Forum created all sorts of problems. There was trouble over the pockets on one table not conforming to official standards and in the final the table, the television lighting and the refereeing all attracted initial criticism.

Reardon comfortably retained the title; Perrie Mans reached the semi-final for the first time; and Higgins, as usual, kept the crowd alight by winning three desperately close matches to reach the final. Charlton made a break of 137 against Pulman and Spencer one of 138 against David Taylor.

Qualifying competition

First round: J. Rea beat I. Anderson 8-5; D. Greaves beat J. Charlton 8-5; J. Meadowcroft beat D. Wheelwright 8-1; R. Gross beat M. Parkin 8-5; L. Condo beat M. Owen 8-6.

Second round: Rea beat B. Bennett 8-5; David Taylor beat Greaves 8-1; Meadowcroft beat Gross 8-4; W. Thorne beat Condo 8-3.

Third round: David Taylor beat Rea 8-7; Meadowcroft beat Thorne 8-5.

Competition proper

First round: R. Reardon beat J. Dunning 15-7; Dennis Taylor beat G. Owen 15-9; P. Mans beat G. Miles 15-10; Meadowcroft beat R. Williams 15-7; E. Charlton beat J. Pulman 15-9; F. Davis beat B. Werbeniuk 15-12; A. Higgins beat C. Thorburn 15-14; J. Spencer beat David Taylor 15-5.

Quarter-finals: Reardon beat Dennis Taylor 15-2; Mans beat Meadowcroft 15-8; Charlton beat Davis 15-13; Higgins beat Spencer 15-14.

Semi-finals: Reardon beat Mans 20-10; Higgins beat Charlton 20-18.

Final: Reardon beat Higgins 27-16.

1976
Pontins Festival of Snooker

The match of the season provided a 10-9 victory for Reardon over Fred Davis to give him the £1000 professional first prize after the veteran former champion had failed to pot a brown in the final which would have left him needing only the blue to win.

Mountjoy won the Pontins Open for the second time in three years from an entry of 693 amateurs and eight professionals. Receiving 25, Mountjoy beat Reardon 4-3 in the last 32.

Professional final: R. Reardon beat F. Davis 10-9.

Open final: D. Mountjoy (receive 25) beat L. Pibworth (receive 25) 7-1.

1976
Canadian Open

Spencer took the $5000 first prize by beating Higgins 17-9 in the final. The match of the tournament was the victory of Bernie Mikkelsen, a 6 ft 5 in Canadian amateur over John Pulman in the quarter-finals, Mikkelsen making a break of 141 in the deciding frame.

Semi-finals: J. Spencer beat J. Virgo 9-4; A. Higgins beat B. Mikkelsen 9-1.

Final: Spencer beat Higgins 17-9.

1976
World Professional Matchplay Championship

A 16 man international tournament promoted by Eddie Charlton in Melbourne was confusingly given world title recognition by the WPBSA. When Charlton won the event, beating Reardon 31-24 in the final, sections of the uninformed media and public believed that he had won the World Professional Championship. Despite strong criticism of the title of the tournament, the WPBSA sanctioned it twice more, but on both occasions organisational difficulties prevented it from taking place.

1977
Benson and Hedges Masters

Sponsor: Gallaher   *Entries*: (invited) 10
Prize money: £5200   *First prize*: £2000

Doug Mountjoy, brought into his first major professional tournament only as a late replacement, duly won it as the 33/1 outsider.

Having turned professional only a couple of months previously after winning the world amateur title in Johannesburg, Mountjoy confirmed how narrow was the gap between professionals and top amateurs by beating three former world professional champions before defeating the current title holder Ray Reardon in a thrilling finish 7-6 on the final pink.

First round: D. Mountjoy beat J. Pulman 4-2; J. Spencer beat Dennis Taylor 4-2.

Quarter-finals: R. Reardon beat R. Williams 4-1; G. Miles beat Spencer 4-1; A. Higgins beat P. Mans 4-2; Mountjoy beat F. Davis 4-2.

Semi-finals: Mountjoy beat Higgins 5-3; Reardon beat Miles 5-2.

Final: Mountjoy beat Reardon 7-6.

1977
Embassy World Professional Snooker Championship

Sponsor: W. D. and H. O. Wills   *Entries*: 24
Prize money: £17 000   *First prize*: £6000

A new promoter, Mike Watterson, a plush but intimate theatre in the round venue, the Crucible Theatre, Sheffield, and increased television coverage enabled snooker's premier event to take a massive step forward. Record crowds of over 20 000 for the championship fortnight saw some memorable finishes – Mountjoy sinking a daring black down the side cushion to beat Higgins 13-12, Thorburn beating Charlton 13-12 after a 62-minute final frame – and the end of Reardon's reign as champion as he went out tamely to Spencer in the quarter-finals. Spencer did not show the flair and brilliance of his vintage years but grit, determination and a high level of confidence carried him to the title by defeating Thorburn, the first ever Canadian finalist. Spencer was the first player to win the title with a two-piece cue.

Qualifying competition
First round: J. Virgo beat R. Andrewartha 11-1.
Second round: P. Fagan beat J. Meadowcroft 11-9; Virgo beat J. Dunning 11-6; W. Thorne beat B. Bennett 11-4; J. Pulman w.o.; David Taylor beat D. Greaves 11-0; C. Thorburn beat C. Ross 11-0; Dennis Taylor beat J. Karnehm 11-0; D. Mountjoy beat J. Rea 11-9.

Competition proper
First round: R. Reardon beat Fagan 13-7; J. Spencer beat Virgo 13-9; G. Miles beat Thorne 13-4; Pulman beat F. Davis 13-12; E. Charlton beat David Taylor 13-5; Thorburn beat R. Williams 13-6; Dennis Taylor beat P. Mans 13-11; Mountjoy beat A. Higgins 13-12.
Quarter-finals: Spencer beat Reardon 13-6; Pulman beat Miles 13-10; Thorburn beat Charlton 13-12; Dennis Taylor beat Mountjoy 13-11.
Semi-finals: Spencer beat Pulman 18-16; Thorburn beat Dennis Taylor 18-16.
Final: Spencer beat Thorburn 25-21.

1977
Pontins Festival of Snooker

Higgins, omitted from *Pot Black* and thus from the professional invitation list for Pontins, took advantage of a new dispensation whereby uninvited professionals could, by giving 21 points start per frame, play through the qualifying rounds of the Open event. With enormous popular support, Higgins went through the tournament on a crest of a wave and won the £1500 first prize by defeating Terry Griffiths, to whom he was conceding three blacks per frame, 7-4.
Professional final: J. Spencer beat J. Pulman 7-5.
Open final: A. Higgins beat T. Griffiths (receive 21) 7-4.

1977
Warners Open

A second holiday camp chain joined the snooker circuit with a modest 27 entry tournament at Sinah Warren. Tony Meo, then 17, receiving 21 start, took the £250 first prize with a 5-4 final victory over Doug Mountjoy.

1977
Canadian Open

With the usual permanent building unavailable, the tournament went on in heat wave conditions in a circus tent. Kirk Stevens, subsequently a professional, surfaced for the first time in a major event at the age of eighteen to lead Reardon 5-3 in the last 16 before losing 9-6. Spencer made a break of 146, taking a pink after the eleventh red, in beating Kevin Robitaille 9-3 in the quarter-finals after this young Canadian had eliminated Mountjoy 9-8. Higgins won the $6000 first prize with Spencer taking $2000 as runner-up.
Semi-finals: A. Higgins beat R. Reardon 9-7; J. Spencer beat Dennis Taylor 9-6.
Final: Higgins beat Spencer 17-14.

1977
Super Crystalate United Kingdom Professional Snooker Championship

Sponsor: Super Crystalate   *Entries*: 22
Prize money: £7000   *First prize*: £2000

Fired by his promotional success with the Embassy World Professional Championship, Mike Watterson instituted this new championship with sponsorship from manufacturers of Super Crystalate balls. The venue, Blackpool Tower Circus, had a strong snooker tradition from the April world finals of the 1950s but Blackpool in December proved a different proposition and crowds were poor. Partly because matches were short, there were a number of upsets, Reardon going out 5-4 to Jim Meadowcroft in his first match. Only one established player, Higgins, reached the semi-finals and the £2000 first prize went to Patsy Fagan, a London-based Dubliner, a professional for less than a year.
First round: C. Ross beat J. Karnehm 5-4; P. Fagan beat J. Rea 5-1; J. Meadowcroft beat P. Houlihan 5-1; D. Mountjoy beat R. Andrewartha 5-2; W. Thorne beat B. Bennett 5-1; J. Dunning beat M. Parkin 5-4; David Taylor beat D. Greaves 5-4.
Second round: J. Virgo beat Dennis Taylor 5-2; G. Miles beat Ross 5-1; Fagan beat F. Davis 5-0; Meadowcroft beat R. Reardon 5-4; Mountjoy beat J. Spencer 5-3; Thorne beat R. Williams 5-4; Dunning w.o.; A. Higgins beat David Taylor 5-4.
Quarter-finals: Virgo beat Miles 5-2; Fagan beat Meadowcroft 5-4; Mountjoy beat Thorne 5-4; Higgins beat Dunning 5-0.
Semi-finals: Fagan beat Virgo 9-8; Mountjoy beat Higgins 9-2.
Final: Fagan beat Mountjoy 12-9.

1977
Dry Blackthorn Cup

Wembley Conference Centre was used for snooker for the first time as Mike Barrett, best known for his boxing promotions, ventured into snooker for the first time with a one-day event covered by London Weekend Television which offered a £2000 first prize. Fagan beat Spencer 4-2 and Higgins 4-2 to double the money he had won a couple of weeks previously at the UK Championship.

1978
Benson and Hedges Masters

Sponsor: Gallaher	Entries: (invited) 10
Prize money: £8000	First prize: £3000

Higgins, straight from a successful defence of his Irish professional title against Dennis Taylor, won the title for the first time with a 5-1 semi-final win over Reardon as the highlight of the week.
First round: J. Pulman beat P. Fagan 4-2; G. Miles beat F. Davis 4-3.
Quarter-finals: J. Spencer beat Pulman 4-2; A. Higgins beat Dennis Taylor 4-3; C. Thorburn beat D. Mountjoy 4-2; R. Reardon beat Miles 4-1.
Semi-finals: Higgins beat Reardon 5-1; Thorburn beat Spencer 5-3.
Final: Higgins beat Thorburn 7-5.

1978
Benson and Hedges Irish Masters

The beautifully appointed sales ring at Goffs, Kill provided an unusual setting for the inaugural Benson and Hedges Irish Masters, John Spencer taking the £1000 first prize with a 5-3 final victory over Doug Mountjoy.

1978
Embassy World Professional Snooker Championship

Sponsor: W. D. and H. O. Wills	Entries: 28
Prize money: £24 000	First prize: £7500

Through the championship's daily coverage snooker became a front rank television sport. A five million audience on the first day built to seven million by the end of the fortnight. Reardon won the championship for the fifth time in six years; Mans became the first ever South African finalist by defeating Fred Davis in a semi-final so gripping that the nervous tension precipitated the collapse of Joe Davis, a highly involved spectator, and in turn led to his fatal illness. Reardon's hardest match was in his 18-14 semi-final defeat of Charlton after the Australian had led 12-9. Charlton had earlier won the last four frames to beat Willie Thorne 13-12 and the last five to beat Thorburn 13-12.
Qualifying competition
First round: M. Parkin beat B. Bennett 9-4; R. Andrewartha beat J. Karnehm 9-0; J. Barrie beat D. Greaves 9-3; P. Houlihan beat C. Ross 9-1.

Second round: D. Mountjoy beat Andrewartha 9-3; P. Fagan beat J. Dunning 9-5; W. Thorne beat R. Williams 9-3; B. Werbeniuk beat Parkin 9-2; P. Mans beat Barrie 9-6; David Taylor beat P. Morgan 9-7; Houlihan beat J. Meadowcroft 9-6; F. Davis beat J. Virgo 9-8.
Competition proper
First round: Mans beat J. Spencer 13-8; G. Miles beat David Taylor 13-10; Fagan beat A. Higgins 13-12; Davis beat Dennis Taylor 13-9; E. Charlton beat Thorne 13-12; C. Thorburn beat Houlihan 13-8; Werbeniuk beat J. Pulman 13-4; R. Reardon beat Mountjoy 13-9.
Quarter-finals: Mans beat Miles 13-7; Davis beat Fagan 13-10; Charlton beat Thorburn 13-12; Reardon beat Werbeniuk 13-6.
Semi-finals: Mans beat Davis 18-16; Reardon beat Charlton 18-14.
Final: Reardon beat Mans 25-18.

1978
Pontins Festival of Snooker

Two players shortly to enter the professional ranks, Steve Davis, 20, and Tony Meo, 18, contested an exciting Open final with Davis taking the £1500 first prize by the odd frame in 13.
Professional final: R. Reardon beat J. Spencer 7-2.
Open final: S. Davis (receive 30) beat T. Meo (receive 30) 7-6.

1978
Warners Open

Entries rose to 64 and Spencer, conceding 21, beat Tony Knowles 7-4 for the £250 first prize.

1978
Canadian Open

Cliff Thorburn recovered from 6-10 overnight arrears to beat Tony Meo 17-15 for the $6000 first prize. Meo was the outstanding personality of the tournament, achieving a 9-7 semi-final win over Higgins as he took $2000 as runner-up.
Semi-finals: C. Thorburn beat K. Robitaille 9-5; T. Meo beat A. Higgins 9-7.
Final: Thorburn beat Meo 17-15.

1978
Coral United Kingdom Professional Snooker Championship

Sponsor: Coral Racing	Entries: 24
Prize money: £12 500	First prize: £3500

An impressive new venue, Preston Guildhall, and a

new sponsor, Coral Racing, transformed the status of this championship in its second year and ensured its continuance.

The most dramatic match came in the qualifying section when Terry Griffiths, only a few months later to win the world professional title, was beaten 9-8 by Rex Williams after leading 8-2.

The championship proper also provided plenty of surprises. Fagan, the holder, went out 9-7 in the first round to David Taylor who, after a decade in the professional ranks, reached his first major final by beating Higgins 9-5 in the semi. In the other half, Roy Andrewartha beat Spencer 9-8 and Willie Thorne beat Reardon 9-6 only to collapse 9-1 against Miles, whose 139 break set a tournament record. In the semi-finals it was Miles's turn to collapse 9-1 to Mountjoy who, keeping his best till last, clinched his final victory over Taylor with a break of 120.

Qualifying competition
W. Thorne beat B. Bennett 9-4; R. Andrewartha beat P. Houlihan 9-3; D. Mountjoy beat J. Barrie 9-5; R. Williams beat T. Griffiths 9-8; J. Dunning beat D. Greaves 9-3; J. Virgo beat R. Edmonds 9-4; David Taylor beat M. Parkin 9-2; J. Meadowcroft beat J. Rea 9-5.

Competition proper
First round: David Taylor beat Fagan 9-7; Virgo beat J. Pulman 9-3; F. Davis beat Dunning 9-2; A. Higgins beat Meadowcroft 9-6; Thorne beat R. Reardon 9-6; G. Miles beat Williams 9-8; Mountjoy beat Dennis Taylor 9-4; Andrewartha beat J. Spencer 9-8.
Quarter-finals: David Taylor beat Virgo 9-2; Higgins beat Davis 9-4; Miles beat Thorne 9-1; Mountjoy beat Andrewartha 9-4.
Semi-finals: David Taylor beat Higgins 9-5; Mountjoy beat Miles 9-1.
Final: Mountjoy beat David Taylor 15-9.

1979
Forward Chemicals £10 000 Tournament

The Park Drive 2000 format which had launched snooker's modern era was resurrected with Reardon, Spencer, Mountjoy and Higgins each playing each other three times with the top two from the round robin contesting the final. Reardon won six matches, Spencer five, Mountjoy four and Higgins three with Reardon going on to beat Spencer 9-6 in the final at the Royal Exchange Theatre, Manchester. Reardon took £3000 and Spencer £2300.

1979
Holsten Lager International

Spencer made history at the Fulcrum Centre, Slough by compiling the first ever 147 maximum in tourna-

ment play, albeit on a table whose pockets were more generous than standard and which thus prevented the break being recognised as an official record. Ironically, the cameras of Thames Television, who covered the last three days of the four day tournament, were idle when the break was made. Union agreements within the television industry over hours and meal breaks were such that without two complete production crews not every frame of the day's play could be recorded.

Spencer and Thorburn arrived late for their quarter-final and the decision was taken to rest the crew then rather than later. The public, believing the match had been deferred, drifted out so only a handful of spectators saw Spencer win the first three frames 106-1, 147-0, 119-0.

The tournament departed from normal practice in that all matches except the semi-final were decided on aggregate score. Under this system, there were some amazing recoveries. Spencer, in the first round, trailed Fagan by 91 with only one frame remaining but took victory with a break of 109; Williams, in the second round, was 97 behind early in the last frame against Reardon before, with the aid of 72 break, he won on the final black. The semi-finals and final were comparatively straightforward though Spencer did raise hopes of a second maximum when he reached 96 by dint of 12 reds and 12 blacks in the penultimate frame of his 11-7 final victory over Miles. The tournament contained one final irony: at a time when many events were starting to offer a jackpot prize of £5000 or more for a 147 this one did not do so.

Semi-finals: J. Spencer beat R. Williams 6-2; G. Miles beat A. Higgins 6-3.
Final: Spencer beat Miles 11-7.

1979
Benson and Hedges Masters

Sponsor: Gallaher	*Entries*: (invited) 10
Prize money: £8000	*First prize*: £3000

Perrie Mans, having survived a five hour 5-4 struggle with Thorburn, went on to beat Reardon and Higgins to win the first Masters to be staged at Wembley Conference Centre. Curiously, he failed to make a 50 break in any match but he once again proved, with his awkward style, a difficult man to beat. Higgins's break of 132 against Charlton was a tournament record.

First round: D. Mountjoy beat F. Davis 5-2; David Taylor beat P. Fagan 5-4.
Quarter-finals: A. Higgins beat E. Charlton 5-2; P. Mans beat C. Thorburn 5-4; Mountjoy beat J. Spencer 5-0; R. Reardon beat Taylor 5-2.
Semi-finals: Higgins beat Mountjoy 5-1; Mans beat Reardon 5-3.
Final: Mans beat Higgins 8-4.

1979
Benson and Hedges Irish Masters

Doug Mountjoy recovered from 0-3 and 3-5 to beat Ray Reardon 6-5 for the £2000 first prize, Reardon missing an easy brown which would have given him a 6-4 victory.

1979
Bombay International

The easing of foreign exchange regulations gave India a chance to stage its most ambitious ever professional tournament, a six man round robin in which Spencer won four of his five matches to take the £2000 first prize. Dennis Taylor, second with three wins, took £1200.

1979
Tolly Cobbold Classic

After the initial four man round robin had put Higgins and Reardon through to the final, Higgins snatched the £600 first prize with a 63 clearance which gave him his 5-4 victory on the final black. The event was covered in its entirety from the Corn Exchange, Ipswich by Anglia Television.

1979
Embassy World Professional Snooker Championship

Sponsor: W. D. and H. O. Wills   *Entries:* 35
Prize money: £35 000   *First prize:* £10 000

That Terry Griffiths won the title at his first attempt (as only Joe Davis, John Spencer and Alex Higgins had done before him) was not only an amazing personal success story but confirmation that the old order was changing. Two memorable if radically different matches were the key to his success, his 13-12 quarter-final win over Higgins and his 19-17 semi-final victory over Charlton.

The first four frames of the Higgins match took only 46 minutes, Griffiths winning the first and fourth on the black with 61 and 63 clearances, Higgins the second and third with consecutive centuries of 105 and 112. When Higgins went on to lead 6-2 at the first interval he hardly looked beatable but Griffiths levelled at 8-8 at close of play and after a gripping final session won the deciding frame with a break of 107.

Griffiths led Charlton 10-4 but lost the first six frames of the third session and led only 11-10 overnight. A gruelling fourth session with Charlton slowing the tempo with long bouts of safety and taking no risks ended with Griffiths leading 15-13 but Charlton led for the first time at 16-15 and again at 17-16.

The Welshman led 18-17 but the match seemed certain to go the full distance when Charlton led 48-0 in what was scheduled to be the penultimate frame. One mistake, though, was all the encouragement Griffiths needed to steady himself to compile a winning 97 clearance. The final session, which ended at 1.40 a.m., occupied 5 hours 25 minutes.

The final, against Dennis Taylor, was something of an anti-climax. Level at 15-15 starting the final day, Griffiths raised his game when the winning post came in sight to clinch the title by taking nine of the next ten frames.

Taylor had earlier distinguished himself by ousting Reardon, the holder, 13-8 in the quarter-final and John Virgo, appearing in his first semi-final, 19-12. The bulky Canadian, Bill Werbeniuk, eliminated Spencer in the first round and in the quarter-final equalled the 142 championship record set by Rex Williams in 1965 before losing 13-9 to Virgo.

Qualifying competition
First round: D. Mountjoy beat D. Mienie 9-1; T. Griffiths beat B. Bennett 9-2; P. Houlihan beat J. Barrie 9-5; W. Thorne beat J. Charlton 9-3; J. Virgo beat M. Parkin 9-0; J. Dunning beat J. Rea 9-5; R. Williams beat D. Greaves 9-2; J. Meadowcroft beat J. van Rensburg 9-7; R. Andrewartha beat R. Edmonds 9-8; S. Davis beat I. Anderson 9-1; K. Stevens beat R. Amdor 9-1.

Second round: Virgo beat Thorne 9-8; B. Werbeniuk beat Andrewartha 9-2; David Taylor beat Dunning 9-8; Mountjoy beat Houlihan 9-6; S. Davis beat P. Fagan 9-2; Griffiths beat Meadowcroft 9-6; Stevens beat J. Pulman 9-0; G. Miles beat Williams 9-5.

Competition proper
First round: E. Charlton beat Mountjoy 13-6; Werbeniuk beat J. Spencer 13-11; Virgo beat C. Thorburn 13-10; F. Davis beat Stevens 13-8; Dennis Taylor beat S. Davis 13-11; A. Higgins beat David Taylor 13-5; Griffiths beat P. Mans 13-8; R. Reardon beat Miles 13-8.

Quarter-finals: Charlton beat F. Davis 13-4; Dennis Taylor beat Reardon 13-8; Virgo beat Werbeniuk 13-9; Griffiths beat Higgins 13-12.

Semi-finals: Griffiths beat Charlton 19-17; Dennis Taylor beat Virgo 19-12.

Final: Griffiths beat Dennis Taylor 24-16.

1979
Pontins Festival of Snooker

Steve Davis, winner of the Pontins Open in 1978 when receiving the 30 points amateur allowance, won it again as a professional, giving 30 and a 7-3 beating in the final to Jimmy White, who just short of his seventeenth birthday had a few weeks earlier become the youngest ever English amateur champion. The event was, in one immediate sense, too successful: 1034 competitors, their families and supporters produced a chronic overcrowding at the camp, a problem resolved in 1980 by Pontins organising a second week's tournament at Camber Sands, Rye to split the numbers.

Professional final: D. Mountjoy beat G. Miles 8-4.
Open final: S. Davis beat J. White (receive 30) 7-3.

1979
Warners Open

Tony Meo won the Warners title for the second time in three years by beating Jimmy White 5-2 in the final. All four invited professionals, who conceded 21 start, fell before the semi-finals. There were 67 entries, a record.

1979
Limosin International

South Africa's most valuable ever professional tournament, staged at the Good Hope Centre, Capetown, saw Charlton carry off the R5000 (£2747) first prize by beating Spencer 23-19, his first victory over Spencer in a long distance match. Charlton went on to beat Reardon 7-4 to win the R2500 first prize in the Kronenbrau 1308 Classic in Johannesburg the following week.

1979
Canadian Open

Thorburn won the event for the third time by beating Griffiths 17-16 in a desperate finish after leading 10-3. In the semi-finals Thorburn had made consecutive centuries, 108 and 116, in beating Higgins 9-6 but Griffiths scraped home only 9-8 over Kirk Stevens after the young Canadian had failed to clinch several good chances for victory.

The pick of the remaining matches was a 9-8 win for Jim Wych, another talented young Canadian, over Meo. Wych led 6-2 but Meo with a 142 total clearance levelled at 8-8 before refereeing blunders in the decider effectively cost him the match.

Semi-finals: C. Thorburn beat A. Higgins 9-6; T. Griffiths beat K. Stevens 9-8.
Final: Thorburn beat Griffiths 17-16.

1979
State Express World Cup

Sponsor: British American Tobacco	*Entries*: six teams
Prize money: £27 500	*First prize*: £7500

Any doubts that a world team championship might not command the interest of snooker followers or television audiences were triumphantly set at rest at Haden Hill Leisure Centre, near Birmingham. Mike Watterson, promoter of the Embassy World Professional Championship and the Coral United Kingdom Championship, thus completed a notable hat-trick.

Six three-man teams were drawn into two groups of three with the winners contesting the final. Professionals, some of whom had never played team matches even as amateurs, found themselves coping with new pressures and many of the matches were close and tense. The final, however, provided an overwhelming 14-3 victory for Wales (Terry Griffiths, Ray Reardon and Doug Mountjoy) over England (Fred Davis, John Spencer, Graham Miles).

Group 'A': England beat Rest of the World 8-7; England beat Northern Ireland 8-7; Northern Ireland beat Rest of the World 8-7.
Group 'B': Wales beat Canada 9-6; Wales beat Australia 9-6; Australia beat Canada 8-7.
Final: Wales beat England 14-3.

1979
Coral United Kingdom Professional Snooker Championship

Sponsor: Coral Racing	*Entries*: 27
Prize money: £15 000	*First prize*: £4500

John Virgo, 33, confounded those who doubted his ability to win on the big occasion by defeating Griffiths, the reigning world champion, by the odd frame of a final chiefly notable for the award of two frames to Griffiths to penalise Virgo's late arrival for the deciding session.

The general pattern of results indicated a new generation about to emerge to take over from most of the players who had dominated the seventies. Of the quarter-finalists, only Ray Edmonds, himself a relatively new professional, was over 35.

First round: J. Rea beat B. Bennett 9-8; M. Hallett beat M. Parkin 9-1; J. Dunning beat D. Greaves 9-8.
Second round: W. Thorne beat R. Andrewartha 9-4; P. Houlihan beat Rea 9-3; S. Davis beat Dunning 9-3; P. Fagan beat Hallett 9-4; B. Werbeniuk beat J. Johnson 9-3; R. Edmonds beat J. Meadowcroft 9-3; T. Meo beat David Taylor 9-7; C. Wilson beat J. Pulman 9-7.
Third round: S. Davis beat D. Mountjoy 9-5; T. Griffiths beat Wilson 9-4; A. Higgins beat Houlihan 9-3; Fagan beat G. Miles 9-5; Werbeniuk beat J. Spencer 9-8; Dennis Taylor beat Thorne 9-8; J. Virgo beat Meo 9-6; Edmonds beat F. Davis 9-6.
Quarter-finals: Werbeniuk beat Edmonds 9-8; Dennis Taylor beat Fagan 9-6; Virgo beat S. Davis 9-7; Griffiths beat Higgins 9-7.
Semi-finals: Virgo beat Dennis Taylor 9-4; Griffiths beat Werbeniuk 9-3.
Final: Virgo beat Griffiths 14-13.

1980
Bombay International

John Virgo beat Cliff Thorburn 13-7 to take the £3000 first prize. Thorburn, who had beaten Virgo 6-1 in the qualifying round robin took £2200 as runner-up and £500 for the highest break, 123. The tournament could not be repeated in 1981 because of currency difficulties.

1980
Padmore/Super Crystalate International

The original promoters, though armed with the promise of seven ATV slots, failed to produce a sponsor to guarantee the £15 000 prize money the players were expecting. The tournament was rescued from cancellation at the eleventh hour by world championship promoter Mike Watterson and two trade interests, Padmore's and Super Crystalate, who between them guaranteed £5000 prize money and £3000 towards the costs of staging the event at the Gala Baths, West Bromwich.

Higgins despite being rushed to hospital with a painful ear infection on the first night of the tournament survived a deciding frame with Willie Thorne in the semi-final before taking the £2000 first prize with a 4-2 victory over Perrie Mans in the final.

1980
Wilsons Classic

John Spencer took the £3000 first prize, a record for a two day tournament, by beating Alex Higgins 4-3 in the final of an eight man event recorded at the New Century Hall, Manchester by Granada Television and shown in the North West in seven Wednesday night programmes. Higgins took £1500 as runner-up.

1980
Benson and Hedges Masters

Sponsor: Gallaher	*Entries*: (invited) 10
Prize money: £14 000	*First prize*: £4500

A crowd of 2323, a record for Britain, saw Terry Griffiths clinch his 9-5 final victory over Higgins with a superb total clearance of 131.
First round: C. Thorburn beat J. Virgo 5-3; A. Higgins beat F. Davis 5-1.
Quarter-finals: R. Reardon beat Dennis Taylor 5-3; T. Griffiths beat Thorburn 5-3; J. Spencer beat E. Charlton 5-2; Higgins beat P. Mans 5-1.
Semi-finals: Griffiths beat Spencer 5-0; Higgins beat Reardon 5-2.
Final: Griffiths beat Higgins 9-5.

1980
Woodpecker Welsh Professional Championship

With the media expecting a confrontation in the final between Terry Griffiths, reigning world champion, and Ray Reardon six times world champion, Doug Mountjoy scored victories over both at Ebbw Vale Leisure Centre to take the £2250 first prize. Reardon had held the Welsh professional title since beating Mountjoy, then the only other Welsh professional, 12-8 at Caerphilly under the sponsorship of William Hill in 1977.
Semi-finals: D. Mountjoy beat T. Griffiths 9-6; R. Reardon beat C. Wilson 9-3.
Final: Mountjoy beat Reardon 9-6.

1980
Benson and Hedges Irish Masters

Terry Griffiths, having led 6-3, 7-4 and 8-5, beat Doug Mountjoy 9-8 for the £2500 first prize.

1980
British Gold Cup

A new event at Derby Assembly Rooms, jointly sponsored by three companies in the billiard trade, E. J. Riley, Composition Billiard Ball Supply and Strachan's, was conducted initially through four round robin groups with a knock-out semi-final and final.

Higgins provided a memorable conclusion to his group when, needing to beat Griffiths 3-0 to qualify, he achieved his target with consecutive breaks of 135 and 134.

He also played brilliantly to beat Tony Meo 4-0 in the semi-final and Ray Reardon, with a break of 132, 5-1 in the final to take the £4000 first prize. Reardon, who beat Dennis Taylor 4-3 in the other semi-final, took £3000 as runner-up.

1980
Tolly Cobbold Classic

Between his group matches in the British Gold Cup and the semi-finals and final, Higgins won another first prize, this time of £1500, by beating Dennis Taylor 5-4 at the Corn Exchange, Ipswich. An incident in the final, added to others in which he had been involved in other tournaments, led to Higgins subsequently being fined £200 for 'foul and abusive language to referees and bringing the game into disrepute'.

1980
Embassy World Professional Snooker Championship

Sponsors: W. D. and H. O. Wills *Entries:* 49
Prize money: £60 000   *First prize:* £15 000

The title left Britain for the first time when Thorburn scored a dramatic 18-16 victory over Higgins in the final after the Irishman, leading 9-5, had lost the last four frames of the first day.

Higgins, who had had to win the last two frames to beat Tony Meo 10-9 in the first round, came within the last five colours of a 147 maximum in beating Steve Davis 13-9 in the quarter finals before loss of position on the green ended his hopes of a £10 000 jackpot.

Kirk Stevens gave the tournament a dramatic start with a break of 136 in his 10-3 first round win over Graham Miles, failing at the final black which would have given him a new championship record.

Stevens, with some fearless potting, then eliminated two seasoned campaigners, John Spencer and Eddie Charlton, before losing to Higgins 16-13 in an exciting semi-final.

Jim Wych, at his first attempt, gave Canada a third representative in the last eight and Steve Davis made his name by beating the defending champion Terry Griffiths 13-10 in their second round match before losing to Higgins.

The climax of the final attracted 14·5 million viewers. There was 70 hours of television coverage.

Qualifying competition
Group 1: J. Rea beat B. Bennett 9-1; W. Thorne beat K. Robitaille 9-4; Thorne beat Rea 9-1.
Group 2: S. Davis beat C. Ross 9-3; P. Morgan beat P. Thornley 9-4; S. Davis beat Morgan 9-0.
Group 3: M. Hallett beat K. Kennerley 9-2; K. Stevens beat D. Greaves 9-3; Stevens beat Hallett 9-3.
Group 4: J. Johnson beat R. Andrewartha 9-5; P. Houlihan beat Johnson 9-6; T. Meo beat J. van Rensburg 9-1; Meo beat Houlihan 9-1.
Group 5: R. Amdor beat B. Mikkelsen 9-7; R. Williams beat Amdor 9-4; J. Wych beat J. Bear 9-5; Wych beat Williams 9-7.
Group 6: F. Jonik beat M. Wildman 9-7; C. Wilson beat Jonik 9-6.
Group 7: R. Edmonds beat M. Parkin 9-2; S. Hood beat J. Dunning 9-7; Edmonds beat Hood 9-6.
Group 8: E. Sinclair beat M. Morra 9-5; Sinclair beat D. Mienie 9-7; J. Meadowcroft beat Sinclair 9-1.
Competition proper
First round: S. Davis beat P. Fagan 10-6; A. Higgins beat Meo 10-9; D. Mountjoy beat Wilson 10-6; Wych beat J. Pulman 10-5; J. Virgo beat Meadowcroft 10-2; Stevens beat G. Miles 10-3; David Taylor beat Edmonds 10-3; B. Werbeniuk beat Thorne 10-9.

Second round: S. Davis beat T. Griffiths 13-10; Higgins beat P. Mans 13-6; Stevens beat J. Spencer 13-8; E. Charlton beat Virgo 13-12; C. Thorburn beat Mountjoy 13-10; Wych beat Dennis Taylor 13-10; R. Reardon beat Werbeniuk 13-6; David Taylor beat F. Davis 13-5.
Quarter-finals: David Taylor beat Reardon 13-11; Thorburn beat Wych 13-6; Stevens beat Charlton 13-7; Higgins beat S. Davis 13-9.
Semi-finals: Thorburn beat David Taylor 16-7; Higgins beat Stevens 16-13.
Final: Thorburn beat Higgins 18-16.

1980
Pontins Festival of Snooker

Willie Thorne scored the most significant success of his professional career by beating another professional, Cliff Wilson, 7-3 for the £1500 first prize in the Open section at Prestatyn while John Virgo earned the £2000 winners cheque in the professional section by beating Ray Reardon 9-6.

Pontins promoted a second festival week at Camber Sands with Alex Higgins beating Dennis Taylor 9-7 for the professional title and Taylor beating the London amateur Geoff Foulds 7-5 in the final of the Open.
Prestatyn
Professional final: J. Virgo beat R. Reardon 9-6.
Open final: W. Thorne beat C. Wilson 7-3.
Camber Sands
Professional final: A. Higgins beat Dennis Taylor 9-7.
Open final: Dennis Taylor beat G. Foulds (receive 30) 7-5.

1980
Warners Open

Steve Davis, conceding 21, beat Portsmouth amateur Brian Watson 5-1 for the £2000 first prize.

1980
Canadian National Exhibition Open

Television, new to Canadian tournaments, made a fiasco of the first day of the final by installing lighting so glaring and dazzling that the players could not give of their best.

Cliff Thorburn, who had been less impressive than Terry Griffiths (winner over both Steve Davis and Alex Higgins) in the earlier rounds, maintained his concentration and will to win more single-mindedly in taking a commanding 13-3 lead by the end of the first day's play.
Semi-finals: C. Thorburn beat K. Stevens 9-5; T. Griffiths beat A. Higgins 9-6.
Final: Thorburn beat Griffiths 17-10.

1980
Champion of Champions

Snooker returned to the New London Theatre (home of the Benson and Hedges Masters until 1978) with an ambitious 10-man event, split initially into two round robin sections, but without television coverage or sponsorship the event was financially disastrous. Doug Mountjoy beat John Virgo 10-8 in the final to take the £5000 first prize but the tournament itself made an estimated loss of £30 000.

1980
State Express World Cup

Sponsor: British American Tobacco   *Entries*: 6 teams
Prize money: £31 555   *First prize*: £9000

Wales, again represented by Ray Reardon, Terry Griffiths and Doug Mountjoy, retained the title though Reardon needed a 50 break, in which he displayed all his old icy calm, to take his last frame against Alex Higgins to give his team an 8-7 semi-final win over Ireland, this year represented by Higgins and Dennis Taylor from the North and the Dubliner Patsy Fagan. Wales also trailed Canada 4-5 in the final before taking the next four frames for victory.
Group 'A': Wales beat Canada 10-5; Canada beat Rest of World 9-6; Wales beat Rest of World 13-2.
Group 'B': England beat Ireland 11-4; Australia beat England 8-7; Ireland beat Australia 10-5.
Semi-finals: Wales beat Ireland 8-7; Canada beat England 8-5.
Final: Wales beat Canada 8-5.

1980
Coral United Kingdom Professional Championship

Sponsor: Coral Racing   *Entries*: 32
Prize money: £22 500   *First prize*: £6000

With television coverage increased to eight days the championship was the most successful in its four year history. Steve Davis took his first major professional title in the most convincing style imaginable, annihilating Terry Griffiths in the semi-final and disposing of Alex Higgins in the final with almost equal comfort.
Preliminary round: M. Hallett beat B. Bennett 9-4; S. Hood beat C. Ross 9-3.
Qualifying round: Hallett beat R. Edmonds 9-8; E. Sinclair beat K. Kennerley 9-1; M. Wildman beat C. Wilson 9-8; J. Meadowcroft beat D. Greaves 9-1; R. Andrewartha beat A. Knowles 9-8; R. Williams beat J. Barrie 9-1; J. Johnson beat J. Dunning 9-6; T. Meo beat Hood 9-5.

Competition proper
First round: Meo beat P. Houlihan 9-1; S. Davis beat Hallett 9-1; P. Fagan beat Johnson 9-4; Sinclair beat G. Miles 9-5; W. Thorne beat Meadowcroft 9-1; Wildman beat J. Spencer 9-7; Williams beat D. Mountjoy 9-8; Andrewartha beat Pulman 9-6.
Second round: Meo beat J. Virgo 9-1; S. Davis beat B. Werbeniuk 9-3; Dennis Taylor beat Sinclair 9-6; T. Griffiths beat Fagan 9-8; A. Higgins beat Thorne 9-7; F. Davis beat Wildman 9-6; Reardon beat Andrewartha 9-3; Williams beat David Taylor 9-7.
Quarter-finals: S. Davis beat Meo 9-5; Griffiths beat Dennis Taylor 9-2; Higgins beat F. Davis 9-6; Reardon beat Williams 9-4.
Semi-finals: S. Davis beat Griffiths 9-0; Higgins beat Reardon 9-7.
Final: S. Davis beat Higgins 16-6.

1980
Wilsons Classic

Steve Davis took his second first prize within a week, this time of £5000, by beating Dennis Taylor 4-1 in the final at Blighty's, Farnworth.

1981
Benson and Hedges Masters

Sponsor: Gallahers   *Entries*: (invited) 12
Prize money: £20 500   *First prize*: £6000

Alex Higgins, having trailed 1-5, extraordinarily beat Cliff Thorburn 6-5 to reach his fourth consecutive Masters final and reversed the result of the 1980 final against Terry Griffiths, who had himself made a dramatic recovery to beat John Spencer 6-5 in the semi-finals after trailing 2-5 and needing two snookers in the eighth frame. Griffiths set a new tournament record break of 136 in the final. The tournament attracted 18 742 spectators in its six days including a new British tournament record of 2422 for the final session.
First round: P. Mans beat S. Davis 5-2; D. Mountjoy beat E. Charlton 5-0; F. Davis beat K. Stevens 5-4; J. Spencer beat Dennis Taylor 5-2.
Quarter-finals: A. Higgins beat Mountjoy 5-1; C. Thorburn beat Mans 5-4; Spencer beat R. Reardon 5-1; T. Griffiths beat F. Davis 5-2.
Semi-finals: Higgins beat Thorburn 6-5; Griffiths beat Spencer 6-5.
Final: Higgins beat Griffiths 9-6.

1981
Woodpecker Welsh Professional Championship

Ray Reardon, two and a half years after winning his last major event, regained his national title by beating

Cliff Wilson, with whom he grew up in Tredegar, for the £3000 first prize.
Semi-finals: R. Reardon beat T. Griffiths 9-6; C. Wilson beat D. Mountjoy 9-6.
Final: Reardon beat Wilson 9-6.

1981
Benson and Hedges Irish Masters

The round robin system which had previously been favoured for the early stages was abandoned in favour of a straight knock-out. Terry Griffiths retained the title and took the £5000 for so doing by beating Cliff Thorburn 6-5 in the semi-finals, winning the last two frames with breaks of 93 and 91, and Ray Reardon 9-7 in the final. Reardon, who took £2500 as runner-up, beat Alex Higgins 6-5 in the other semi-final.

1981
Tolly Cobbold Classic

Graham Miles took the £2000 first prize by beating Cliff Thorburn 5-1 in the final.

1981
Yamaha Organs Trophy

Sponsor: Yamaha Organs	*Entries*: 28
Prize money: £30 000	*First prize*: £10 000

Taking over the date, venue and playing format of 1980's British Gold Cup, this became the first major tournament to be extensively covered on the ITV network with each day's action shown later that night. Its four days coverage produced viewing figures so impressive that they seemed likely to mark a turning point in ITV's attitude to snooker.

Three of the four groups ended in exciting finishes but Steve Davis won his group with comfort and went on to score decisive victories in both semi-final and final to take his third major first prize of the season.
Semi-finals: David Taylor beat K. Stevens 5-3; S. Davis beat Dennis Taylor 5-2.
Final: S. Davis beat David Taylor 9-6.

1981
John Courage English Professional Championship

Steve Davis enriched himself by a further £4000 in becoming the inaugural title holder. The event was staged at Haden Hill Leisure Centre, Sandwell.
Semi-finals: S. Davis beat R. Edmonds 9-0; T. Meo beat W. Thorne 9-8.
Final: S. Davis beat Meo 9-3.

1981
Embassy World Professional Snooker Championship

Sponsor: W.D. and H.O. Wills	*Entries*: 46
Prize money: £75 000	*First prize*: £20 000

Steve Davis, winner of four major first prizes earlier in the season, triumphantly justified his status as favourite by beating five tough opponents to take the title.

After leading 8-4, he was only one frame in front of Jimmy White at 9-8 before winning 10-8 and after leading Alex Higgins 6-2 he was pulled back to 9-7 before going away to win 13-8. Both matches revealed the young Londoner's ability to respond with his best when he came under the most severe pressure.

From 4-4 against Terry Griffiths in the quarter-final, Davis led 9-5 after so protracted a second session that it had to be curtailed two frames early and went on to clinch victory at 13-9.

Davis's semi-final against Cliff Thorburn was even more arduous. A three hours, 34 minutes first session saw Davis 4-3 ahead but Thorburn appeared to be right on top when, with his opponent's concentration apparently broken, he led 8-6 at the end of the session. That evening, though, Davis's concentration was amazingly restored and when the session ended at 12.58 a.m. he led 12-10. The first four frames the following morning gave him his place in the final.

Although he won the first six frames against Doug Mountjoy, Davis had to withstand a determined recovery which four times brought the Welshman to within two frames. From 14-12 at the start of the final session, however, Davis won four frames in succession to assure himself of snooker's record cheque of £20 000.

Mountjoy added to his £10 000 runner's-up prize one of £5000 for his new world championship record break of 145 in beating Ray Reardon 16-10 in the semi-final. This break also earned him the tournament break of £1200.

Qualifying
Group A: W. Thorne beat M. Morra 9-5; D. Greaves beat M. Parkin 9-5; Thorne beat Greaves 9-3.
Group B: J. White beat B. Mikkelsen 9-4; White beat J. Meadowcroft 9-8.
Group C: R. Edmonds beat M. Wildman 9-3; R. Williams beat S. Hood 9-4; Edmonds beat Williams 9-7.
Group D: T. Meo beat J. Johnson 9-8; M. Hallett beat F. Jonik 9-1; Meo beat Hallett 9-4.
Group E: J. Dunning beat B. Bennett 9-6; Dunning beat P. Fagan 9-7.
Group F: D. Martin beat I. Anderson 9-3; Martin beat J. Pulman 9-2.

Group G: C. Wilson beat R. Andrewartha 9-4; E. Sinclair beat P. Morgan 9-8; Wilson beat Sinclair 9-4.
Group H: T. Knowles beat C. Ross 7-0 (retired); Knowles beat J. Wych 9-3.
First round: G. Miles beat Knowles 10-8; David Taylor beat Wilson 10-6; D. Mountjoy beat Thorne 10-6; K. Stevens beat Dunning 10-4; Meo beat J. Virgo 10-6; S. Davis beat White 10-8; B. Werbeniuk beat Martin 10-4; J. Spencer beat Edmonds 10-9.
Second round: C. Thorburn beat Miles 13-2; David Taylor beat F. Davis 13-3; T. Griffiths beat Meo 13-6; S. Davis beat A. Higgins 13-8; Mountjoy beat E. Charlton 13-7; Dennis Taylor beat Stevens 13-11; Werbeniuk beat P. Mans 13-5; R. Reardon beat Spencer 13-11.
Quarter-finals: Thorburn beat David Taylor 13-6; S. Davis beat Griffiths 13-9; Mountjoy beat Dennis Taylor 13-8; Reardon beat Werbeniuk 13-10.
Semi-finals: S. Davis beat Thorburn 16-10; Mountjoy beat Reardon 16-10.
Final: S. Davis beat Mountjoy 18-12.

1981
Guinness World of Snooker

With Warners moving their annual May tournament to October, Top Spot Promotions added to the list of holiday camp events by organising an ambitious festival, sponsored by Guinness, at Thorness Bay, Isle of Wight.

Steve Davis, conceding 25, beat Mike Darrington, the Home Counties amateur champion, 6-4 to win the £2000 first prize in the Open Snooker and Ray Edmonds beat Eddie Charlton 1202-598 to take the £1000 winners cheque in the Open Billiards but in many ways the most interesting event was the first World Mixed Pairs Championship. This, played over the aggregate score of four frames, was won by the Canadian partnership, Cliff Thorburn and Natalie Stelmach, who beat John Virgo and Vera Selby 262-239 in the final. Mrs Selby won the Women's World Championship which was also staged as part of the festival.

1981
Pontins Festival of Snooker

Terry Griffiths, after trailing 1-5, beat Willie Thorne, 9-8 on the final black to win the £3500 first prize in the professional tournament. English amateur international John Hargreaves beat Cliff Wilson, conceding 30, 7-2, to win the Open first prize of £1500. There were 796 entries.
Professional final: T. Griffiths beat W. Thorne 9-8.

MODERN
BILLIARDS

From 1951, when Clark McConachy won the World Professional Billiards Championship and returned to New Zealand with the trophy, until 1968, when Rex Williams travelled to Auckland to challenge him for the title, professional billiards was dormant. Williams's capture of the title and four successful defences in his 12 year reign as champion revived it fitfully but it was not until the late seventies, notably with the revival of the United Kingdom Championship in 1979, that the professional game could look beyond mere survival. To some extent, though, the explosion of interest in snooker carried the fall-out effect of stimulating new interest in the parent game. Sponsors began to be attracted to it and real hopes are in the air of television bringing the game to a new public.

Rex Williams

REX WILLIAMS (1933-)
It was ironic that Rex Williams should become world professional champion at billiards, his 'second' game, which he did not play seriously for some 15 years while failing to fulfil the expectations of those who saw in him, as English amateur snooker champion at the age of 17, a future world professional snooker champion.

He was an outstanding junior at both games, winning the Boys (under 16) Billiards and Snooker Championships twice each and the Junior (under 19) Championships twice each before turning professional when he was 17. At this point, he virtually abandoned billiards – apart from 20 minutes or so as a curtain raiser to an evening of exhibition snooker it had no place in the professional scene – in favour of working on his snooker.

In 1965, in Capetown, Williams equalled Joe Davis's official break record of 147 but it was his misfortune, at an important stage of his development, to have few tournaments to get his teeth into. Sound as his technique was, he did not develop into a great winner of matches.

Away from the table, it was entirely through his efforts that the World Professional Snooker Championship which fell into abeyance from 1957-64 through want of public support, was revived on a challenge basis and the Professional Billiards Players Association was resurrected. Williams himself twice challenged the title holder, John Pulman, unsuccessfully.

He did though, on a predominantly snooker trip to Australia, decide, in 1968, to call at Auckland to play Clark McConachy, the 73-year-old New Zealander who had held the world professional billiards title unopposed since 1951. With McConachy suffering from Parkinson's disease in his cue arm and Williams having played little recent billiards, the standard of play was a travesty of what it had been in the heyday of the championship but it did at least bring the event back to life.

Unfortunately, it was also to prove the straw which broke the always fragile bridge between the PBPA and the BA & CC. Williams, not unreasonably, said that he would require a £250 guarantee to defend the title. The BA & CC characteristically hardly appearing to appreciate the financial aspect which loomed so large for professionals, ordered him to defend within six months. No proposal was placed before him by the expiry of this period but he then accepted an offer to defend against Albert Johnson, an Australian. The

Fred Davis receives the World Professional Billiards Championship trophy in May 1980 from 95-year-old Willie Smith, champion in 1920 and 1923.

BA & CC then insisted that he should defend against Leslie Driffield, newly-turned professional who still sat on the BA & CC council. Williams declined and was stripped of the title.

The PBPA feeling that there was a hidden intention for Driffield to play Jack Karnehm, the BA & CC's chairman for the title, dissociated themselves from the BA & CC renaming themselves the World Professional Billiards and Snooker Association and claimed autonomy for the professional game in December 1970. Driffield and Karnehm, the only professionals not to challenge the authority of the BA & CC did subsequently meet for the BA & CC's version of the title and Driffield defended it against Johnson.

Williams, meanwhile, continued to be recognised by everyone except the BA & CC (who no longer had any authority in professional matters) as champion though it hardly enhanced the status of the event that his first challenger was Bernard Bennett, who provided the venue and the required financial guarantee but hardly the appropriate quality of opposition in 1971 at his own Castle Club in Southampton.

Karnehm, by now accepted as a WPBSA member, was beaten by almost half the game when he challenged Williams at the Marconi Athletic Club, Chelmsford in September 1973. Two defences in Australia against Eddie Charlton, in 1974 and 1976, yielded two more comfortable wins.

Williams took the leading role in persuading the WPBSA to revert from 'five' to 'two' pots in late 1978. This ruled out the British Open Championship which Jim Williamson intended to run at the Northern Snooker Centre, Leeds. With amateurs now committed to 'three' pots the B & SCC withdrew its support and sanction on behalf of the amateur world.

Williamson then decided to revive the United Kingdom Professional Championship which had lain dormant since 1951. Williams won this event but sustained a surprise defeat at the hands of Karnehm in the 1980 final. His reign as world champion was ended by Fred Davis in a Williamson promotion, sponsored by Yorkshire Bank, in May 1980.

Even during his reign, Williams's energies were generally devoted to snooker, his chairmanship of the WPBSA and his trade interests, notably Power Glide cues, which he founded. His best snooker championship performance was in 1972 when he beat Ray Reardon 25-23 in the quarter-final before losing only by the odd frame, 31-30 to Alex Higgins in the semi-final, though in 1974 he again reached the semi-final with wins over John Pulman and Perrie Mans. He slipped down the snooker rankings thereafter but had one notable success in the qualifying section of the 1978 Coral UK Championship when he beat Terry Griffiths, a few months later to become world champion, 9-8 after trailing 8-2.

WORLD PROFESSIONAL BILLIARDS CHAMPIONSHIPS (1968-80)

Winner (breaks)	Score (average)	Loser (breaks)	Score (average)
1968			
R. Williams 293	5499 (n.r.)	C. McConachy 236, 200	5234 (n.r.)
1971			
R. Williams 480, 372, 353, 325, 302	9250 (n.r.)	B. Bennett 132	4058 (n.r.)
1973			
R. Williams 528, 363, 309	8360 (50·7)	J. Karnehm 215	4336 (26·1)
1974			
R. Williams 506, 365, 308, 307	7017 (43·6)	E. Charlton 488, 401	4916 (30·4)
1976			
R. Williams 532, 349, 382, 306	9105 (42·1)	E. Charlton 333	5149 (23·9)
1980 (May)			
Challenge: F. Davis 403, 225, 234, 239, 275, 583	5978 (39·9)	R. Williams 226, 202, 439, 229	4452 (29·9)
1980 (Nov)			
Qualifying P. Morgan	1655 (21·5)	J. Dunning	1107 (12·9)
M. Wildman	1968 (26·2)	B. Bennett	678 (9·0)
S. Davis	1809 (16·9)	K. Kennerley	965 (9·1)
Quarter-finals J. Barrie 335	2186 (53·3)	S. Davis	870 (21·8)
F. Davis 309	1907 (43·3)	Morgan	978 (22·2)
R. Edmonds	1513 (19·4)	J. Karnehm	1306 (17·0)
Wildman	1476 (25·9)	R. Williams	1415 (24·8)
Semi-finals F. Davis 501	1253 (34·8)	Barrie	1153 (32·0)
Wildman 204	1629 (21·4)	Edmonds	955 (12·6)
Final F. Davis 200, 361	3037 (30·4)	Wildman	2064 (20·6)

SUPER CRYSTALATE UK PROFESSIONAL BILLIARDS CHAMPIONSHIPS (1979-81)

Winner (breaks)	Score (average)	Loser (breaks)	Score (average)
1979			
Quarter-finals			
J. Karnehm 281, 286	2041 (35·8)	J. Dunning	760 (13·1)
R. Williams 259, 309	1557 (31·8)	R. Edmonds	1350 (27·0)
J. Barrie 238, 404, 206 (unf.)	2292 (46·8)	S. Davis	629 (12·6)
F. Davis	1953 (34·9)	B. Bennett	679 (12·1)
Semi-finals			
Williams 224, 372	1539 (32·7)	Karnehm	1182 (24·6)
Barrie 227, 444	1548 (43·0)	F. Davis 245	1031 (28·6)
Final			
Williams 228, 388, 253	2952 (44·4)	Barrie 379	2116 (32·0)
1980			
First round			
S. Davis	1670 (21·7)	S. Hood	1029 (13·4)
B. Bennett	1093 (12·0)	C. Ross	933 (10·1)
Quarter-finals			
J. Barrie	2001 (32·8)	M. Wildman	815 (13·1)
J. Karnehm 322	1990 (28·0)	K. Kennerley	842 (11·9)
R. Edmonds	1380 (17·7)	Bennett	914 (11·6)
R. Williams 205	1871 (33·4)	S. Davis	862 (15·4)
Semi-finals			
Karnehm 225, 230	1755 (35·1)	Barrie 229	1085 (21·3)
Williams 230, 234 (unf.)	2159 (41·5)	Edmonds	789 (15·2)
Final			
Karnehm 205, 208	2518 (28·0)	Williams 256, 423	2423 (26·6)
1981			
Qualifying			
S. Davis	980	B. Bennett	770
R. Edmonds 206	1881	G. Miles	473
J. Pulman	1078	K. Kennerley	879
Quarter-finals			
J. Karnehm 207	1307 (22·2)	Edmonds	935 (15·8)
J. Barrie 381	1743 (41·5)	Pulman	509 (12·1)
R. Williams 265, 385, 290	1575 (50·8)	S. Davis	579 (18·1)
F. Davis 217	1304 (29·0)	M. Wildman	805 (17·9)
Semi-finals			
Karnehm 390	1338 (23·1)	Barrie	1074 (18·5)
Williams 217, 505, 231	2003 (74·2)	F. Davis	999 (37·0)
Final			
Williams 393, 385	1592 (45·5)	Karnehm	1112 (31·8)

ROUND THE WORLD

ENGLAND

Late in the nineteenth century – indeed for at least the first 30 years of the twentieth – it was assumed by all loyal Englishmen that England was the centre of the universe. Britain had an Empire which was sustained by acceptance of the class divisions within it and an understanding not only that England knew best but that its governing class knew best of all. It seemed entirely natural that the sports world should be run by paternalistic amateurs rather than professionals.

Against this trend, the Billiards Association was founded in 1885 by professional and trade figures but before long amateur enthusiasts were in control. Amateur and professional interests coexisted uneasily and there were several partial and temporary ruptures until the final split between the amateur and professional sides of the game in 1971 when the professionals dissociated themselves from the Billiards and Snooker Control Council (then the Billiards Association and Control Council) and reconstituted the Professional Billiard Players Association as the World Professional Billiards and Snooker Association, thus declaring its autonomy.

Also in 1971, representatives of overseas national associations, increasingly conscious of the anomaly of the same body governing both the English domestic and international amateur games and dissatisfied, moreover, at the BA & CC's conduct of international amateur issues brought into being the World Billiards and Snooker Council.

To placate England's wrath this name was changed to the International Billiards and Snooker Federation in 1973. The IBSF, a one nation, one vote body, took over the conduct of World Amateur Championships and effectively became the rule amending body. The IBSF did not challenge the copyright on the rules which the B & SCC claimed (together with the income therefrom) but persuaded the B & SCC to make no alteration without consulting them.

In 1980, the B & SCC still described itself as the world governing body but its functions in reality were largely those of an English national amateur association with a senior standing among equals in the international amateur sphere.

The word 'English' was superfluous to the amateur billiards championship, founded in 1888. If the event took place in England it followed that it was the leading event of its kind just as the World Professional Billiards Championship was known simply as 'The Championship' until 1933.

It was in 1920 that Arthur Walker, a South African millionaire, first suggested a British Empire Amateur Billiards Championship but the BA & CC resisted this on the grounds that the amateur championship was sufficient. The Australian champion J. R. Hooper, visited London for the Amateur Championship of 1921 and was beaten by Sidney Fry in the semi-final.

In 1922 an Empire championship was approved in principle but there were various delays before the inaugural event was held at Thurston's, Leicester Square in 1926. At this point, Scotland opted out of the Amateur Championship in order to run its own national championship while the BA & CC decided that it could no longer accept entries from Scottish, Irish or colonial players, though it continued to do so from Wales. The present position is that entries are accepted from Scottish, Welsh and Irish players (though not if they are resident in Ireland) so the event retains some of its original open character. This is also true of the English Amateur Snooker Championship, founded·in 1916.

A rigid definition of amateurism survived until the 1960s when, in common with other sports, under the table payments for amateurs became so widespread that after a period of turning a blind eye it was tacitly agreed that the time had come for a new formula. An international agreement in 1972 provided that an amateur would be defined as a player who was not a member of the WPBSA, had not declared himself a professional or who did not lend his name to advertising or endorsing goods in connection with the playing of the game. In effect, this made the distinction between amateurs and professionals not one of cash but of which governing body a player chose to acknowledge.

The first championship was a fiasco. S. S. Christey beat W. D. Courtney to win the Southern division (the 44 competitors from England, Scotland and Ireland being divided into four areas) but was then objected to on the grounds that he was a professional. Christey had played against professionals in a tournament the previous year which had been advertised as 'open to amateurs and markers' but nevertheless the objection was upheld. All the players whom Christey had beaten claimed the right to play again and H. A. O. Lonsdale eventually emerged as the first champion.

Christey, who was subsequently reinstated, won the title three times though this total was exceeded in the early days of the championship by A. P. Gaskell (six) and A. R. Wisdom (four). Many of the early championships were conducted on a challenge basis with the winner of a challengers tournament earning the right to play the holder for the title. In 1893, indeed, S. H. Fry had to play Wisdom, the holder, two games of 1000 up. Having won both, Fry then had to play a further 1500 up for the first of the eight titles he won before his last success in 1925. The championship was not played on what is now recognised as an orthodox knock-out basis until 1913.

The standard of play now seems modest. Christey made a break of 146 in the first championship but it was not until the sixth that there was another century,

114 by Gaskell, a useful spot stroke exponent. A. W. T. Good, a red ball player, who won the title four times between 1902 and 1915, made a championship record of 155 (153 off the red) in 1902. This was broken in 1905 by G. Heginbottom (174), in 1913 by J. G. Taylor (210) and in the same year by Fry (236).

H. C. Virr, a very consistent red ball player, won the title six times between 1907 and 1914 and the immediate post-war years were dominated by Fry, also a championship class golfer, and J. Graham-Symes, three times champion, both of whom were products of London's gentlemen's clubs and thus exuded either privilege or the Corinthian spirit depending on your point of view.

In 1926, composition balls, which were not only cheaper but more consistent, replaced ivories as the approved championship ball. This, together with a

Sydney Lee: a 16-year-old billiards prodigy.

Sydney Lee, who specialised in coaching and club exhibitions before he became referee of BBC-2's *Pot Black*.

reduction in the entry fee from two guineas to half a guinea made the championship socially less exclusive. The beginnings of this trend had already been apparent when W. P. McLeod, a Middlesbrough man with a small plumbing business, had won both in 1923 and 1924, following which he had to fight off a challenge to his amateur status after touring more widely than was felt appropriate to his supposed income.

With composition balls and a wider spectrum of entries, the standard rose spectacularly. Joe Earlam, 20, made a new championship record of 278 (165 off the red) in the Liverpool area; Laurie Steeples made a 377 in the Sheffield area, albeit on a table which did not pass championship specifications.

Earlam, so good a red ball player that the 25 hazard limit was imposed after he won the title, also ran away with the inaugural Empire Championship but did not make the grade as a professional. Steeples, whose game was more polished, more balanced, more professional in approach, won two English and two Empire titles before ill-health forced him into premature retirement.

Maurice Boggin increased the championship record to 349 in 1929, Steeples to 354 in 1930 and Horace Coles to 363 in 1933 but it was Sydney Lee, who in 1931 won the first of his four consecutive titles, supplemented by the Empire title in 1933, who dominated the early thirties. In 1931, acknowledging rising amateur standards, the hazard limit was reduced to fifteen and matches were played on a time limit basis rather than to a points target.

It was Lee's misfortune that he turned professional just as billiards was fading fast as a public entertainment. His long, flowing, in some respects rather flowery cue action was not suited to snooker but with a great deal of hard work he carved a comfortable niche in the game with club exhibitions, coaching and, with the advent of *Pot Black*, refereeing.

Kingsley Kennerley, who won four consecutive titles from 1937-40, was also a victim of the same syndrome although his snooker, which had been good enough to win two English amateur titles – only Wisdom, Fry and Steeples in times when snooker standards were much lower having previously performed the double – stood up better than Lee's did to the demands of the professional game.

Kennerley was a fine top of the table player, a fast, consistent scorer who set championship records which survived 40 years and several changes to easier rules. His break of 549 in 1937 stood as a championship record until 1938. He made five centuries in a session in 1938; 4234 points in four sessions in 1939; 1218 in a session in the same year though this was just exceeded by Arthur Spencer, his opponent in the final that year, with 1266.

In statistical terms, Kennerley was the finest Eng-

lish amateur champion there had yet been but he was well beaten by the Australian, Bob Marshall, in the 1938 Empire Championship in Melbourne, an event which confirmed that it could no longer be assumed that whoever led English billiards led the world.

After the war, Frank Edwards, (five wins), Leslie Driffield (eight), Herbert Beetham (three) and pre-eminently Norman Dagley (twelve) dominated English billiards. They were players of contrasting styles.

Edwards, a first time striker who played at headlong pace, had a flair for recovery shots and improvisation. He was very entertaining to watch, but with rare exceptions his statistics were much less impressive than those of the two great Australians, Marshall and Tom Cleary. After his English championship hat

Two great English amateurs, Joe Thompson (*left*) and Kingsley Kennerley, leave Burroughes Hall, Soho Square after one of the afternoon sessions in the 1938 final of the English Amateur Championship.

The High Commissioner for Australia, T. W. White,
performs the opening ceremony in the 1951 World
Amateur Billiards Championship in Burroughes
Hall, Soho Square, watched by the seven
competitors, Edmund Haslem (Northern Ireland),
(*left*), Wilson Jones (India), Frank Edwards
(England), Willie Pierce (Wales), Tom Cleary
(Australia), Walter Ramage (Scotland) and Bob
Marshall (Australia).

trick in 1949-51, Edwards also found Driffield, whom
he beat only once in championship play, too consistent. In 1949, though, he did exceed Spencer's 1266
session aggregate record by two in equalling Kennerley's record of five centuries in a session. He broke the
latter with six in 1953 and in 1956 set a new four hour
aggregate record of 2339. He finished behind Marshall and Cleary in his two world amateur championship appearances in 1951 and 1954.

Driffield's game was greatly influenced by Willie
Smith, with whom he played a great deal in his home
town of Leeds. He rarely lingered long at the top of
the table but his all-round game, based largely on
in-offs, was played with relentless efficiency and concentration. His finest hour was his defeat of Marshall
in the key match of the 1952 World Championship,
his most disappointing defeat to the Indian Wilson
Jones in the 1958 championship after leading by 660
with 90 minutes to play.

Resembling his fellow Yorkshireman, Geoffrey
Boycott, the England batsman, in the personal importance he attached to averages and statistics, Driffield
had an insatiable appetite for points whatever the
state of the game. He was a great accumulator of

Leslie Driffield

breaks and of high averages and he fought grittily in adversity. His highest championship break was 499 and his best session average one of 102·1, both during the 1958 World Amateur, but his career was studded with averages and breaks not far short of these figures.

Beetham backed an outstanding in-off game with sound all round play and a fine temperament. Beaten four times in the final, once by a mere 30, Beetham won the English title three times in four years in 1960-63 with the 1960 World Amateur title for good measure. All his championship wins came within the period in which the hazard limit was increased from 15 to 25.

Dagley, like Driffield, won two world amateur titles and reached in addition one final and one semi-final. No one ever dominated the English Championship so thoroughly. After his only losing appearance in the final in 1963 he won 12 titles in 18 attempts, securing in the process every break and average record. In the 1978 semi-final, he compiled a new World and English championship record break of 862 in a session which led to an English record session average of 116·6. In the final, he set further records of 98·9 (highest 2¹/₂ hour session average), highest final average (67·8), highest 5 hour aggregate (2381) and highest 10 hour aggregate (4611).

A top of the table artist of the first order, a well nigh faultless in-off player, a master in fact of all phases of

Norman Dagley

the game except nursery cannons – which no amateur has ever mastered – Dagley's greatest strength is a temperament which enables him to respond to pressure or impose it at the crucial moment.

The Amateur Snooker Championship was founded in 1916 as a charity effort for the British Sportsmen's Motor Ambulance Fund. An American, H. H. Lukens, with only a few weeks' practice at the Palmerston Restaurant, won the 1918 event under the pseudonym T. N. Palmer and the standard remained low until players from London's gentlemen's clubs were overtaken by provincials with an upbringing in money games.

The final was decided on an aggregate score of seven frames until F. T. W. Morley won four of the seven against W. Nash in the 1926 final only to lose the match 383-356. Since 1927, in this as in every championship of stature, matches have been decided on frames.

Cagey, tactical players like Jack McGlynn (two wins), Walter Coupe (two), Pat Matthews (four) and Charles Beavis (two), or billiards players who turned to snooker like Laurie Steeples (two wins) and Kingsley Kennerley (two) dominated the inter-war period. Kennerley, who reached four consecutive finals, displayed the most professional breakbuilding technique and in 1939 set a new amateur championship record with 69, W. L. Crompton's 62 having stood since 1925.

Kennerley was the first amateur champion to make even a marginal impact on professional snooker but several subsequent winners and not a few who failed to become champion did so afterwards. John Pulman (1946), Ray Reardon (1964), John Spencer (1966) and Terry Griffiths (1977, 1978) went on to win the world professional title. Gary Owen (1963), David Taylor (1968), Ray Edmonds (1969, 1974) and Jonathan Barron, who in 1970, 1971 and 1972 recorded the only

BILLIARDS CHAMPIONSHIP

Year	Result	Score	Year	Result	Score
1888	H. A. O. Lonsdale–J. Tither	500- 356	1930	L. Steeples–H. F. E. Coles	3000-2462
	A. P. Gaskell–H. A. O. Lonsdale	1500-1349	*1931	S. Lee–M. A. Boggin	3793-3134
1889	A. P. Gaskell declared champion		1932	S. Lee–F. Edwards	4674-3508
	A. P. Gaskell–E. W. Alabone	1500-1278	1933	S. Lee–H. F. E. Coles	4458-3237
1890	A. P. Gaskell–S. H. Fry	1500-1395	1934	S. Lee–F. Edwards	3929-3509
	A. P. Gaskell–N. Defries	1500-1395	1935	H. F. E. Coles–M. A. Boggin	3707-3272
	W. D. Courtney–A. P. Gaskell	1500-1141	1936	J. Thompson–J. H. Beetham	3179-3149
1891	W. D. Courtney–A. P. Gaskell	1500- 971	1937	K. Kennerley–J. Thompson	4703-3633
	A. P. Gaskell–W. D. Courtney	1500-1188	1938	K. Kennerley–J. Thompson	4714-3925
1892	A. R. Wisdom–'Osbourne'	1500-1094	1939	K. Kennerley–A. Spencer	4423-3264
	S. S. Christey–S. H. Fry	1500- 928	1940	K. Kennerley–A. Spencer	3931-3749
1893	A. R. Wisdom–Mr Buxton	1500- 852	1941-45	No contests	
	S. H. Fry–A. R. Wisdom	1500-1239	1946	M. Showman–J. H. Beetham	3077-2539
	A. H. Vahid–S. S. Christey	1500-1395	1947	J. Thompson–A. Hibbert	4104-3185
1894	H. Mitchell–A. Vinson	1500-1464	1948	J. Thompson–H. G. Terry	5202-2816
	W. T. Maughan–H. Mitchell	1500-1202	1949	F. Edwards–J. Tregoning	4813-3297
1896	S. H. Fry–W. T. Maughan	1500-1439	1950	F. Edwards–J. Tregoning	4968-3385
1899	A. R. Wisdom–S. H. Fry	1500-1297	1951	F. Edwards–J. Tregoning	5015-3791
1900	S. H. Fry–A. R. Wisdom	1500-1428	1952	A. L. Driffield–J. H. Beetham	2894-2793
1901	S. S. Christey–W. S. Jones	1500-1305	1953	A. L. Driffield–F. Edwards	4136-3016
1902	A. W. T. Good–S. S. Christey	2000-1669	1954	A. L. Driffield–F. Edwards	4165-3030
	A. W. T. Good–A. J. Browne	2000-1669	1955	F. Edwards–A. Nolan	4194-3206
1903	A. R. Wisdom–A. W. T. Good	2000-1783	1956	F. Edwards–A. L. Driffield	3395-3327
	S. S. Christey–C. V. Diehl	2000-1314	1957	A. L. Driffield–F. Edwards	4464-2894
1904	W. A. Lovejoy–A. W. T. Good	2000-1733	1958	A. L. Driffield–J. T. Wright	4483-2587
1905	A. W. T. Good–G. A. Heginbottom	2000-1739	1959	A. L. Driffield–J. H. Beetham	4968-3385
1906	E. C. Breed–A. W. T. Good	2000-1620	1960	J. H. Beetham–R. C. Wright	3426-2289
1907	H. C. Virr–J. Nugent	2000-1896	1961	J. H. Beetham–R. C. Wright	4060-2043
1908	H. C. Virr–G. A. Heginbottom	2000-1841	1962	A. L. Driffield–J. H. Beetham	4312-2993
1909	Major Fleming–H. C. Virr	2000-1501	1963	J. H. Beetham–N. Dagley	4052-2759
1910	H. A. O. Lonsdale–Major Fleming	2000-1882	1964	A. Nolan–A. L. Driffield	3455-2188
1911	H. C. Virr–Major Fleming	3000-2716	1965	N. Dagley–A. Nolan	2983-2757
1912	H. C. Virr–Major Fleming	3000-2993	1966	N. Dagley–A. Nolan	3018-2555
1913	H. C. Virr–J. Nugent	3000-1956	1967	A. L. Driffield–C. Everton	3395-2328
1914	H. C. Virr–J. Nugent	3000-1962	1968	M. Wildman–C. Everton	2652-2540
1915	A. W. T. Good–G. A. Heginbottom	2000-1444	1969	J. Karnehm–M. Wildman	3722-2881
1916	S. H. Fry–G. A. Heginbottom	2000-1417	1970	N. Dagley–A. Nolan	4467-2372
1917	J. Graham-Symes–S. H. Fry	2000-1540	†1971	N. Dagley–W. J. Dennison	3672-2019
1918	J. Graham-Symes–'Osbourne'	2000-1121	1972	N. Dagley–A. Nolan	3115-2469
1919	S. H. Fry–J. Graham-Symes	2000-1729	1973	N. Dagley–C. Everton	2804-1976
1920	S. H. Fry–W. B. Marshall	3000-2488	1974	N. Dagley–A. Nolan	2961-2677
1921	S. H. Fry–J. Graham-Symes	3000-2591	1975	N. Dagley–R. Close	2917-2693
1922	J. Graham-Symes–W. P. McLeod	3000-2661	1976	R. Close–C. Everton	2413-2194
1923	W. P. McLeod–J. Graham-Symes	3000-2867	1977	R. Close–J. H. Beetham	2951-2031
1924	W. P. McLeod–J. Graham-Symes	3000-2862	1978	N. Dagley–R. Close	4611-2309
1925	S. H. Fry–W. B. Marshall	3000-2778	1979	N. Dagley–K. Shirley	3311-1549
1926	J. Earlam–C. M. Helyer	3000-1751	1980	N. Dagley–C.Everton	2825-2172
1927	L. Steeples–H. F. E. Coles	3000-2449	1981	N. Dagley–R. Close	3805-2190
1928	A. Wardle–A. W. T. Good	3000-2189	*	twelve hour finals	
1929	H. F. E. Coles–S. Lee	3000-2215	†	ten hour finals	

Jonathan Barron

Ray Edmonds

hat-trick of championship wins, went on to win the World Amateur Championship which was instituted in 1963.

Rex Williams, later world professional billiards champion, was an outstanding winner in 1951, making a break of 74 and demonstrating a technique which was professional in all departments of the game in taking the title, at the age of 17 for the loss of only five frames in the whole event. Geoffrey Thompson, who dramatically made the championship's first century, 115, in 1962, won the first two day final in 1954.

Consistency, steadiness and competitiveness were the hallmarks of the success of Tommy Gordon and Ron Gross, both of whom won the title three times. Marcus Owen, younger brother of Gary, who won four titles, had all these qualities and flair besides. Had he been able to organise his life more clearly he might well have become world professional champion.

Barron, a quiet, competitive Cornishman, who visibly expressed, while his opponent was at the table, the intense nervous strain of championship play, retired when he felt the pressure of travelling and competing was getting too much for him. He was the first champion since 1961 who did not turn professional and indeed never considered doing so.

The 1979 champion, Jimmy White, was at 16 years 11 months the youngest ever. His 130 break in beating Dave Martin, in the final at the Godolphin Club, Helston, was disallowed for record purposes since the pockets were found to be considerably oversize.

Through its senior status and because it is the only

national association large enough to maintain a permanent paid staff, the B & SCC also organises a number of British championships. These include the British Snooker Pairs Championship, sponsored from 1975-80 by Joe Coral and thereafter by Guinness, the State Express British Team Snooker Championship and the British Junior (Under 16 and Under 19) Billiards and Snooker Championships.

Although four-handed snooker has always been popular in clubs, there was no national championship until Watneys sponsored one in 1969. This was won by Stan Haslam and Stan Holden (Horwich British Legion) but the sponsorship was then discontinued. Corals came forward in 1974-75 and the event is now firmly established. The following pairs have won the championship:

1975 M. Berni and J. Selby beat G. Wood and F. McCourt
1976 P. Medati and J. Virgo beat D. Hughes and W. Kelly
1977 R. Bales and C. Everton beat H. Laws and J. Pike
1978 D. Martin and D. Reed beat H. Laws and J. Pike
1979 C. Wilson and S. Newbury beat J. Fitzmaurice and M. Suckling
1980 H. Burns and D. French beat T. Green and D. Grimmer
1981 R. Cole and W. Oliver beat H. Burns and D. French.

When Leicester Square Hall closed in 1956, its historic match table was offered as first prize in a national five-a-side championship sponsored by the *News Chronicle*. This was won by Abertillery Central.

An unsponsored event the following year was won by Barnstaple Liberal but there were no further team championships until Players No 6 sponsored a three-a-side championship in 1968, won by Abertysswg, and in 1969, won by Belfast YMCA with Alex

SNOOKER CHAMPIONSHIP						
1916	C. N. Jacques–n.r.		1951	R. Williams–P. Bendon	6-1
1917	C. N. Jacques–n.r.		1952	C. Downey–J. Allen	6-1
1918	T. N. Palmer–n.r.		1953	T. C. Gordon–G. Humphries	6-5
1919	S. H. Fry–n.r.		1954	G. Thompson–C. Wilson	11-9
1920	A. R. Wisdom–n.r.		1955	M. Parkin–A. Nolan	11-7
1921	M. J. Vaughan–S. H. Fry	384-378	1956	T. C. Gordon–R. Reardon	11-9
1922	J. McGlynn–C. Cox Jnr	423-301	1957	R. Gross–S. Haslam	11-6
1923	W. Coupe–E. Forshall	432-337	1958	M. Owen–J. T. Fitzmaurice	11-8
1924	W. Coupe–H. G. Olden	413-333	1959	M. Owen–A. Barnett	11-5
1925	J. McGlynn–W. L. Crompton	392-308	1960	R. Gross–J. Price	11-4
1926	W. Nash–F. T. W. Leaphard	383-356	1961	A. Barnett–R. Edmonds	11-9
1927	O. T. Jackson–A. W. Casey	4-2	1962	R. Gross–J. Barron	11-9
1928	P. H. Matthews–F. Whittall	5-4	1963	G. Owen–R. Gross	11-3
1929	L. Steeples–F. Whittall	5-4	1964	R. Reardon–J. Spencer	11-8
1930	L. Steeples–F. Whittall	5-1	1965	P. Houlihan–J. Spencer	11-3
1931	P. H. Matthews–H. Kingsley	5-4	1966	J. Spencer–M. Owen	11-5
1932	W. E. Bach–O. T. Jackson	5-3	1967	M. Owen–S. Hood	11-5
1933	E. Bedford–A. Kershaw	5-1	1968	D. Taylor–C. Ross	11-6
1934	C. H. Beavis–P. H. Matthews	5-2	1969	R. Edmonds–J. Barron	11-9
1935	C. H. Beavis–D. Hindmarch	5-3	1970	J. Barron–S. Hood	11-10
1936	P. H. Matthews–C. H. Beavis	5-3	1971	J. Barron–D. French	11-9
1937	K. Kennerley–W. H. Dennis	6-3	1972	J. Barron–R. Edmonds	11-9
1938	P. H. Matthews–K. Kennerley	6-5	1973	M. Owen–R. Edmonds	11-6
1939	P. Bendon–K. Kennerley	6-4	1974	R. Edmonds–P. Fagan	11-7
1940	K. Kennerley–A. Brown	8-7	1975	S. Hood–W. Thorne	11-6
1941-45	No contests		1976	C. Ross–R. Andrewartha	11-7
1946	H. J. Pulman–A. Brown	5-3	1977	T. Griffiths–S. Hood	13-3
1947	H. Morris–C. A. Kent	5-1	1978	T. Griffiths–J. Johnson	13-5
1948	S. Battye–T. Postlethwaite	6-3	1979	J. White–D. Martin	13-10
1949	T. C. Gordon–S. Kilbank	6-4	1980	J. O'Boye–D. Martin	13-9
1950	A. Nolan–G. Owen	6-5	1981	V. Harris–G. Wood	13-9

Higgins playing a starring role. Langs Whisky sponsored in 1974, when Abertysswg won again, but their withdrawal after only one year was followed by Double Diamond sponsoring a championship for teams of two – each player playing three frames rather than two players playing several frames as a pair. Des May and John Prosser won the title for Merthyr Ex-Servicemen's in 1975 and John Virgo and Paul Medati for Potters, Salford in 1976.

An unsponsored three-a-side championship, won by Romford Lucania, was organised in 1978. There was full sponsorship by State Express in 1979, when the event was won by Western Social, Middlesbrough, in 1980 when the winners were the North Midlands Snooker Centre, Worksop and, in 1981 when the Ron Grass Snooker Centre, Neasden provided the winning trio.

The Boys (Under 16) Billiards Championship, the inspiration of a journalist, Harry Young, was staged at and organised by Burroughes and Watts, London. A group of enthusiasts at Scunthorpe initiated a Boys Snooker Championship in 1944 though this too transferred to Burroughes and Watts five years later.

The BA & CC initiated Youths (Under 19) Championships at both games in 1949. With the closure of Burroughes Hall in 1966, the snooker championships lapsed, the Boys Billiards having already done so in 1962 and the Youths Billiards in 1964.

They were revived by Clive Everton, a journalist, in 1968 and were staged in the social club of Accles and Pollock, Birmingham, manufacturers of metal cues, who sponsored the event until 1974 when the B & SCC took over full responsibility for the events. The Youths Championships were renamed Junior

BRITISH BOYS (UNDER 16) BILLIARDS CHAMPIONSHIP

Year	Winners
1922	W. Donaldson–H. Renaut
1923	W. Leigh–F. Edwards
1924	L. Steeples–G. Cooper
1925	S. Lee–G. Cooper
1926	R. Gartland–S. Lee
1927	R. Gartland–R. L. Bennett
1928	R. L. Bennett–J. Forrester
1929	F. Davis–H. J. Bennett
1930	H. J. Bennett–W. H. Dennis
1931	C. Desbottes–T. Steeples
1932	D. Hawkes–W. Swinhoe
1933	n.r.
1934	W. Swinhoe–n.r.
1935	D. Cruikshank–R. Ballard
1936	D. Cruikshank–H. Stokes
1937	D. Curson–W. Milburn
1938	J. Hamilton–n.r.
1939	R. Smith–n.r.
1940	B. Smith–n.r.
1941-47	No contests
1948	R. Williams–J. Carney
1949	R. Williams–M. Leyden
1950	M. Owen–M. Leyden
1951	E. Parry–M. Owen
1952	M. Wildman–J. Burgess
1953	C. Everton–J. Lambert
1954	H. Burns–D. Deakes
1955	D. Deakes–G. Waite
1956	C. Dean–A. Gadsden
1957	P. Shelley–D. Roots
1958	P. Morgan–D. Bend
1959	n.r.
1960	A. Matthews–R. Tumman
1961	B. Whitehead–K. Richardson
1962-67	No contests
1968	C. Williamson–D. Ross
1969	P. Bardsley–C. Bowden
1970	W. Thorne–P. Bardsley
1971	P. Bardsley–N. Fairall
1972	P. Bardsley–T. Wells
1973	T. Wells–D. Rothwell
1974	P. Allan–C. Houlihan
1975	S. McNamara–J. Barnes
1976	D. Bonney–K. Martin
1977	D. Bonney–J. Calvey
1978	K. Walsh–D. Adds
1979	A. Pyle–K. Walsh
1980	K. Walsh–P. Jones
1981	D. Presgrave–I. Marks

BRITISH JUNIOR (UNDER 19) BILLIARDS CHAMPIONSHIP

Year	Winners
1949	G. Toner–R. G. Gross

Year	Winners
1950	R. Williams–J. Carney
1951	R. Williams–J. Carney
1952	J. Sinclair–B. Simpson
1953	M. Wildman–E. Parry
1954	M. Wildman–D. Scott
1955	D. Scott–C. Everton
1956	C. Everton–G. Hampson
1957	C. Myers–C. Dean
1958	C. Marks–C. Dean
1959	P. Morgan–P. Shelley
1960	D. Bend–C. Davies
1961	P. Morgan–A. Matthews
1962	A. Matthews–D. Rhodes
1963	A. Matthews–M. McCann
1964–67	No contests
1968	D. Taylor–D. Burgess
1969	D. Burgess–J. Terry
1970	J. Terry–W. Blake
1971	W. Thorne–R. Toombes
1972	W. Thorne–C. Palmer
1973	W. Thorne–P. Edworthy
1974	T. Wells–D. Rothwell
1975	E. Hughes–I. Williamson
1976	S. Davis–I. Williamson
1977	I. Williamson–J. Barnes
1978	I. Williamson–J. Barnes
1979	M. Garvey–P. McGowan
1980	G. Charville–M. Goodwill
1981	S. Hawkins–M. Heller

BRITISH BOYS (UNDER 16) SNOOKER CHAMPIONSHIP

Year	Winners
1944	G. Owen–n.r.
1945	R. Baker–n.r.
1946	D. Thomas–n.r.
1947	M. Knapp–n.r.
1948	R. Williams–G. Hobbs
1949	R. Williams–n.r.
	D. Lewis–I. Cheetham
1950	M. Owen–D. Williams
1951	M. Owen–E. Parry
1952	M. Wildman–D. Breese
1953	J. Board–K. Preston
1954	D. Bond–B. Allen
1955	P. Shelley–P. Ferrari
1956	A. Hart–D. Bond
1957	P. Shelley–A. Orchard
1958	D. Bond–D. Trevelyan
1959	J. Doyle–P. Cox
1960	N. Cripps–A. Matthews
1961	No contest
1962	J. Virgo–A. Grant
1963	J. Hollis–T. McCarver
1964	D. Clinton–J. Hollis
1965	No contest

Year	Winners
1966	J. Terry–R. Reardon
1967	No contest
1968	E. Stone–A. Vincent
1969	P. Hughes–W. Thorne
1970	W. Thorne–S. Mays
1971	J. Mills–R. Dean
1972	J. Mills–T. Wells
1973	P. Bardsley–K. Jones
1974	S. Holroyd–D. Battye
1975	M. Hallett–P. Hargreaves
1976	W. Jones–D. Bonney
1977	J. White–D. Bonney
1978	D. Adds–M. Jackson
1979	A. Pyle–J. Parrott
1980	T. Whitthread–J. Parrott
1981	C. Hamson–S. Ventham

BRITISH JUNIOR (UNDER 19) SNOOKER CHAMPIONSHIP

Year	Winners
1949	A. Kemp–L. R. Watts
1950	J. Carney–R. Reardon
1951	R. Williams–C. Wilson
1952	C. Wilson–M. Owen
1953	C. Wilson–M. Owen
1954	M. Wildman–E. Parry
1955	W. McGivern–M. Wildman
1956	E. Sinclair–A. Hope
1957	H. Burns–G. Wright
1958	W. West–D. Bond
1959	D. Root–D. Bend
1960	D. Bend–I. Rees
1961	I. Rees–T. Clarke
1962	A. Matthews–T. Collison
1963	A. Matthews–A. Stringer
1964	J. Fisher–R. Dolbea
1965	J. Virgo–J. Hollis
1966	J. Hollis–M. Colleran
1967	No contest
1968	J. Maughan–D. Clinton
1969	J. Terry–J. Peacock
1970	J. Terry–W. Blake
1971	J. Johnson–G. Crimes
1972	A. Knowles–M. Gibson
1973	W. Thorne–P. Edworthy
1974	A. Knowles–P. Smith
1975	E. Hughes–P. Bain
1976	I. Williamson–P. Death
1977	I. Williamson–W. Jones
1978	T. Meo–I. Williamson
1979	J. O'Boye–D. Gilbert
1980	T. Murphy–K. Hayward
1981	D. Reynolds–T. Murphy

Championships in 1968.

Wales instigated the first official amateur international match to mark the investiture of Prince Charles as Prince of Wales. The success of the first venture, when Wales received England at Port Talbot in June 1969, led to a triangular series with Scotland the following year with the Republic of Ireland making it a four-cornered contest a year later.

Matches (six players each playing three frames) were arranged for various weekends throughout the season but in view of heavy travelling expenses and the limited public appeal of some of the contests, the series was an uncertain financial proposition.

In September 1978 the championship was brought under one roof when Pontins provided sponsorship which enabled the event to be completed within a week at their Prestatyn camp. Isle of Man joined the competition in 1978 and Northern Ireland in 1979. Des May (Wal) holds the break record for the event with 111 in 1980.

NORTHERN IRELAND

The Northern Ireland BA & CC was founded in May 1924 and first ran a billiards championship the following year. Her first international competitor was Tom McCluney, their amateur billiards champion of 1925 and 1926, who finished last in the inaugural Empire Championship in London in the latter year. Domestic standards were modest and their next representative, Joe Blackburn, was also last in 1933, as was Edmund Haslem in 1951 though, ironically, Jack Bates, whom Haslem beat for the national title that year, was a player of considerable quality who was qualified at various times to represent both the Republic of Ireland and Scotland. Bobby Taylor's 278 in 1952 is the championship break record.

Bates won four consecutive Northern Ireland billiards titles from 1947 to 1950 (with snooker titles also in the last three years), the Scottish Billiards Championship in 1953 and 1954 and the Eire billiards title in 1963 and 1964. After illness and when past his best, he regained the Northern Ireland billiards title in 1971 and won again in 1979. He also acquitted himself creditably in an unofficial World Open billiards in Christchurch in 1977.

Bates, who set an all-Ireland break record of 307 in

HOME INTERNATIONAL SNOOKER CHAMPIONSHIP

1969

| England beat Wales | Port Talbot | 10-8 |

1970-71

England beat Wales	Harringay	14-4
England beat Ireland	Dublin	14-4
Wales beat Ireland	Port Talbot	17-1

	W	D	L	For	Agst	Pts
England	2	0	0	28	8	4
Wales	1	0	1	21	15	2
Ireland	0	0	2	5	31	0

1971-72

England beat Scotland	Newcastle	10-8
England beat Ireland	Harringay	14-4
England drew with Wales	Neath	9-9
Scotland drew with Wales	Edinburgh	9-9
Scotland beat Ireland	Dublin	12-6
Wales beat Ireland	Dublin	13-5

	W	D	L	For	Agst	Pts
England	2	1	0	33	21	5
Wales	1	2	0	31	23	4
Scotland	1	1	1	29	25	3
Ireland	0	0	3	15	39	0

1972-73

England beat Scotland	Edinburgh	16-2
England beat Ireland	Dublin	13-5
England drew with Wales	Hull	9-9
Wales beat Ireland	Pontygwaith	15-3
Wales beat Scotland	Llay	10-8
Scotland beat Ireland	Dublin	13-5

	W	D	L	For	Agst	Pts
England	2	1	0	38	16	5
Wales	2	1	0	32	22	5
Scotland	1	0	2	23	31	2
Ireland	0	0	3	15	41	0

1973-74

England beat Wales	Garnant	14-4
England beat Scotland	Carlisle	11-7
England drew with Ireland	Bolton	9-9
Wales beat Ireland	Dublin	11-7

| Wales beat Scotland | Edinburgh | 14-4 |
| Ireland drew with Scotland | Dublin | 9-9 |

	W	D	L	For	Agst	Pts
England	2	1	0	34	20	5
Wales	2	0	1	29	25	4
Ireland	0	2	1	25	29	2
Scotland	0	1	2	20	34	1

1974-75

Wales beat Ireland	Neath	12-6
Wales beat Scotland	Maerdy	14-4
Wales beat England	Exeter	10-8
England beat Scotland	Edinburgh	12-6
England beat Ireland	Glasnevin	11-7
Scotland beat Ireland	Dundee	12-6

	W	D	L	For	Agst	Pts
Wales	3	0	0	36	18	6
England	2	0	1	31	23	4
Scotland	1	0	2	22	32	2
Ireland	0	0	3	19	35	0

1975-76

Wales beat Ireland	Dublin	13-5
Wales beat Scotland	Edinburgh	11-7
Wales beat England	Merthyr	11-7
England beat Ireland	Grimsby	13-5
England beat Scotland	Southport	12-6
Scotland beat Ireland	Dun Laoghaire	12-6

	W	D	L	For	Agst	Pts
Wales	3	0	0	35	19	6
England	2	0	1	32	22	4
Scotland	1	0	2	25	29	2
Ireland	0	0	3	16	38	0

1976-77

England beat Ireland	Dublin	13-5
England beat Wales	Doncaster	12-6
England beat Scotland	Glasgow	11-7
Wales beat Scotland	Trealaw	14-4
Wales beat Ireland	Cardiff	13-5
Scotland beat Ireland	Edinburgh	12-6

1949 which he increased to 370 in 1963, turned professional in 1951 to claim the Irish Professional title. He lost it to Jack Rea the following year who in turn held it until deposed by Alex Higgins in 1972.

Higgins, who had won the Northern Ireland Amateur Championship at his first attempt in 1968, defended his title successfully both against Patsy Fagan and Dennis Taylor before losing it to Taylor in April 1980. Taylor retained the title by beating Fagan in March 1981.

Severely restricted by lack of funds and even more seriously in recent years by the country's troubled domestic situation, Northern Ireland has played a comparatively small part in the international game except for its nationals who have chosen to live elsewhere.

A remarkable if isolated success was that of Belfast YMCA, with Higgins playing the starring role, in capturing the British Team Championship in 1968. Dennis Taylor, born in Coalisland, County Tyrone but resident in Lancashire from the age of 17, won the British Junior Billiards title in 1968 but Northern Ireland has not been represented in the World Amateur Billiards Championship since 1960 when Bill Dennison gave the ultimate winner, Herbert Beetham, one of his hardest matches. Dennison later emigrated to Preston, Lancashire and reached the English Amateur final of 1971.

Northern Ireland has competed in each World Amateur Snooker Championship since 1974 and the Home International Championships since 1979 but so far without conspicuous success.

Northern Ireland captured the British Junior Snooker Championship for the first time in 1980 through Tommy Murphy.

The Northern Ireland amateur break record of 87, set by Maurice Gill in 1957, was broken by Sam Pavis with 90 in 1980.

REPUBLIC OF IRELAND

In 1905, when the Amateur Championship, hitherto confined to Londoners and wealthy provincials, was thrown open to the whole of the UK, qualifying rounds were staged in London, Manchester and Dublin. In 1911, Dublin staged the final and in the early years of the century, the Irishman, Joe Nugent, was

	W	D	L	For	Agst	Pts
England	3	0	0	36	18	6
Wales	2	0	1	33	21	4
Scotland	1	0	2	23	31	2
Ireland	0	0	3	16	38	0

1977-78

Wales beat England	Caerphilly	10-8
Wales beat Scotland	Dublin	12-6
Wales beat Ireland	Dublin	15-3
England beat Scotland	Doncaster	10-8
England beat Ireland	Portsmouth	11-7
Scotland beat Ireland	Dublin	12-6

	W	D	L	For	Agst	Pts
Wales	3	0	0	37	17	6
England	2	0	1	29	25	4
Scotland	1	0	2	26	28	2
Ireland	0	0	3	16	38	0

1978-79

England beat Isle of Man	Prestatyn	15-3
England beat Ireland		14-4
England beat Scotland		16-2
England beat Wales		10-7
Wales beat Isle of Man		16-2
Wales beat Ireland		11-7
Wales drew with Scotland		9-9
Scotland beat Isle of Man		15-3
Scotland drew with Ireland		9-9
Ireland beat Isle of Man		15-3

	W	D	L	For	Agst	Pts
England	4	0	0	55	16	8
Wales	2	1	1	43	28	5
Scotland	1	2	1	35	37	4
Rep. of Ireland	1	1	2	34	38	3
Isle of Man	0	0	4	11	61	0

1979-80

England beat Northern Ireland	Prestatyn	16-2
England beat Isle of Man		16-2
England beat Republic of Ireland		11-7
England beat Scotland		10-8
England beat Wales		10-7
Wales beat Northern Ireland		12-6
Wales beat Isle of Man		16-2
Wales beat Scotland		11-7
Wales drew with Republic of Ireland		9-9
Republic of Ireland beat Scotland		10-8
Republic of Ireland drew with Northern Ireland		9-9
Republic of Ireland beat Isle of Man		12-6
Scotland beat Isle of Man		13-5
Scotland beat Northern Ireland		10-8
Northern Ireland beat Isle of Man		14-4

	W	D	L	For	Agst	Pts
England	5	0	0	63	26	10
Wales	3	1	1	55	34	7
Republic of Ireland	2	2	1	47	43	6
Scotland	2	0	3	46	44	4
Northern Ireland	1	1	3	39	51	3
Isle of Man	0	0	5	19	71	0

1980-81

England beat Northern Ireland	Prestatyn	15-3
Scotland beat Isle of Man		14-4
Wales beat Northern Ireland		10-8
England beat Isle of Man		15-3
Wales beat Scotland		12-6
Republic of Ireland beat Northern Ireland		11-7
Northern Ireland beat Isle of Man		12-6
Wales beat Republic of Ireland		14-4
Republic of Ireland drew with Scotland		9-9
Wales beat Isle of Man		15-3
England beat Republic of Ireland		12-6
Scotland drew with Northern Ireland		9-9
Republic of Ireland beat Isle of Man		13-5
England beat Scotland		14-4
Wales beat England		10-7

	W	D	L	For	Agst	Pts
Wales	5	0	0	61	28	10
England	4	0	1	63	26	8
Republic of Ireland	2	1	2	43	47	5
Scotland	1	2	2	42	48	4
Northern Ireland	1	1	3	39	51	3
Isle of Man	0	0	5	21	69	0

NORTHERN IRELAND

BILLIARDS CHAMPIONSHIP

1925	T. McCluney–B. Craig	1963	W. Hanna–W. Ashe	1945	J. McNally–C. Downey
1926	T. McCluney–J. Sloan	1964	D. Anderson ⎱	1946	J. McNally–J. Rea
1927	J. Sloan–R. Mulholland		D. Turley ⎰	1947	J. Rea–J. Bates
1928	A. Davison–S. Stranaghen	1965	W. Ashe–E. Loughran	1948	J. Bates–E. Haslem
1929	J. Blackburn–W. Morrison	1966	D. Anderson–P. Morgan	1949	J. Bates–J. Stevenson
1930	J. Blackburn–n.r.	1967	W. Loughran–D. Anderson	1950	J. Bates–J. Dickson
1931	J. Blackburn–W. Mills	1968	D. Anderson–W. Loughran	1951	J. Stevenson–E. Haslem
1932	W. Lowe–R. Mulholland	1969	W. Loughran–D. Anderson	1952	J. Stevenson–D. Turley
1933	W. Mills–J. Dubois	1970	S. Crothers–P. Donnelly	1953	J. Stevenson–J. Thompson
1934	W. Lowe–J. Presley	1971	J. Bates–n.r.	1954	W. Seeds–J. Stevenson
1935	W. Morrison–W. Lowe	1972-73	No contests	1955	J. Stevenson–M. Gill
1936	J. Blackburn–G. Hutton	1974	P. Donnelly–M. Osborne	1956	S. Brooks–G. Lyttle
1937	J. Blackburn–E. Haslem	1975	P. Donnelly–D. Anderson	1957	M. Gill–D. Anderson
1938	W. Lowe–W. Mills	1976	P. Donnelly–J. Bates	1958	W. Agnew–W. Hanna
1939	W. Lowe–E. Haslem	1977	T. Taylor–G. Connell	1959	W. Hanna–W. Seeds
1940	No contest	1978	W. Loughan–P. Donnelly	1960	M. Gill–D. Anderson
1941	E. Haslem–R. Scleater	1979	J. Bates–E. Sharkey	1961	D. Anderson–M. Gill
1942-44	No contests	1980	S. Clarke–W. Loughan	1962	S. McMahon–D. Anderson
1945	E. Haslem–W. Webb	1981	W. Loughan–S. Clarke	1963	D. Anderson–J. Clint
1946	J. Holness–C. McErlean			1964	P. Morgan–M. Gill
1947	J. Bates–J. Sloan			1965	M. Gill–S. Crothers
1948	J. Bates–E. Haslem	**SNOOKER CHAMPIONSHIP**		1966	S. Crothers–W. Caughey
1949	J. Bates–E. Haslem	1927	G. Barron–G. R. Duff	1967	D. Anderson–S. Crothers
1950	J. Bates–E. Haslem	1928	J. Perry–n.r.	1968	A. Higgins–M. Gill
1951	E. Haslem–J. Bates	1929	W. Lyttle–Capt. J. Ross	1969	D. Anderson–A. Higgins
1952	R. Taylor–D. Turley	1930	J. Luney–n.r.	1970	J. Clint–N. McCann
1953	W. Scanlon–C. McErlean	1931	J. McNally–W. R. Mills	1971	S. Crothers–n.r.
1954	W. Scanlon–W. Dennison	1932	Capt. J. Ross–W. R. Mills	1972	P. Donnelly–S. Pavis
1955	D. Turley–J. Stevenson	1933	J. French–J. Chambers	1973	J. Clint–S. McMahon
1956	J. Stevenson–R. Lough	1934	Capt. J. Ross–W. Price	1974	P. Donnelly–S. Pavis
1957	W. Scanlon–R. Taylor	1935	W. Agnew–Capt. J. Ross	1975	J. Clint–S. McMahon
1958	W. Hanna–R. Hanna	1936	W. Lowe–S. Brooks	1976	E. Swaffield–D. McVeigh
1959	W. Hanna–W. Dennison	1937	J. Chambers–J. Blackburn	1977	D. McVeigh–G. Maxwell
1960	W. Dennison–R. Taylor	1938	J. McNally–W. Sankon	1978	D. McVeigh–L. McCann
1961	R. Hanna–D. Anderson	1939	J. McNally–S. Brooks	1979	R. Burke–J. Begley
1962	N. McQuay–D. Turley	1941	J. McNally–A. Heron	1980	S. Clarke–D. McVeigh
				1981	T. Murphy–W. Mills

ALL-IRELAND BILLIARDS CHAMPIONSHIP

1935	S. Fenning (E)–W. Lowe (NI) joint holders
1936	S. Fenning (E)–n.r.
1937	J. Blackburn (NI)–n.r.
1938	S. Fenning (E)–n.r.
1939	W. Lowe (NI)–n.r.
1940	T. O'Brien (E)–n.r.
1941	T. O'Brien (E)–n.r.
1942-44	No contests
1945	E. Haslem (NI)–n.r.
1946	P. Merrigan (E)–n.r.
1947	J. Bates (NI)–n.r.
1948	J. Bates (NI)–n.r.
1949	J. Bates (NI)–n.r.
1950	S. Fenning (E)–J. Bates (NI)
1951	E. Haslem (NI)–C. McErlean (E)
1952	M. Nolan (E)–R. Taylor (NI)
1953	D. Turley (E)–W. Sanlon (NI)
1954	W. Sanlon (NI)–M. Nolan (E)
1955	D. Turley (NI)–M. Nolan (E)
1956	M. Nolan (E)–J. Stevenson (NI)
1957	W. Sanlon (NI)–M. Nolan (E)
1958	W. Dennison (E)–W. Hanna (NI)
1959-61	No contests
1962	J. N. McQuay (NI)–K. Smith (E)
1963	J. Bates (E)–W. Hanna (NI)
1964	J. Bates (E)–D. Anderson (NI)
1965	W. Ashe (NI)–L. Codd (E)
1966	D. Anderson (NI)–L. Codd (E)
1967	P. Morgan (E)–W. Loughan (NI)
1968	P. Morgan (E)–D. Anderson (NI)
1969	W. Loughan (NI)–J. Rogers (E)
1970	S. Crothers (NI)–L. Drennan (E)
1971	J. Bates (NI)–L. Codd (E)
1972-73	No contests
1974	P. Donnelly (NI)–T. Moore (E)
1975-78	No contests
1979	J. Bates (NI)–L. Codd (E)
1980	S. Clarke (NI)–P. Burke (E)

ALL-IRELAND SNOOKER CHAMPIONSHIP

1935	S. Fenning (E)–W. Agnew (NI)
1936	S. Fenning (E)–W. Lowe (NI)
1937	P. O'Connor (E)–J. Chambers (NI)
1938	J. McNally (NI)–n.r.
1939	S. Fenning (E)–J. McNally (NI)
1940	P. Merrigan (E)–J. McNally (NI)
1941	P. Merrigan (E)–J. McNally (NI)
1942-44	No contests
1945	J. McNally (NI)–n.r.
1946	J. McNally (NI)–n.r.
1947	J. J. Rea (NI)–C. Downey (E)
1948	J. Bates (NI)–n.r.
1949	J. Bates (NI)–W. Brown (E)
1950	J. Bates (NI)–J. Redmond (E)
1951	J. Stevenson (NI)–P. O'Connor (E)
1952	J. Stevenson (NI)–W. Brown (E)
1953	J. Stevenson (NI)–n.r.
1954	S. Fenning (E)–W. Seeds (NI)
1955	J. Stevenson (NI)–S. Fenning (E)
1956	W. Brown (E)–S. Brooke (NI)
1957	M. Gill (NI)–J. Connolly (E)
1958	J. Gibson (E)–W. Agnew (NI)
1959-61	No contests
1962	J. Weber (E)–S. McMahon (NI)
1963	D. Anderson (NI)–J. Rogers (E)
1964	P. Morgan (NI)–J. Rogers (E)
1965	M. Gill (NI)–n.r.
1966	G. Hanway (E)–S. Crothers (NI)
1967	P. Morgan (E)–D. Anderson (NI)
1968	A. Higgins (NI)–G. Hanway (E)
1969	D. Anderson (NI)–D. Daley (E)
1970	J. Clint (NI)–D. Sheehan (E)
1971	D. Sheehan (E)–S. Crothers (NI)
1972-73	No contests
1974	P. Donnelly (NI)–P. Burke (E)
1975-78	No contests
1979	E. Hughes (E)–R. Burke (NI)
1980	D. Sheehan (E)–S. Clarke (NI)

BILLIARDS CHAMPIONSHIP

Year	Result
1933	J. Ayres–S. Fenning
1934	S. Fenning–n.r.
1935	S. Fenning–n.r.
1936	S. Fenning–n.r.
1937	T. O'Brien–n.r.
1938-47	No contests
1948	W. Brown–n.r.
1949	S. Fenning–n.r.
1950-51	No contests
1952	M. Nolan–T. McCucker
1953	D. Turley–M. Nolan
1954	M. Nolan–D. Barry
1955	M. Nolan–D. Barry
1956	M. Nolan–S. Fenning
1957	M. Nolan–E. Morrissey
1958	W. Dennison–K. Smith
1959-60	No contests
1961	K. Smyth–J. Hanlon
1962	K. Smyth–F. Murphy
1963	J. Bates–P. Fenelon
1964	J. Bates–L. Codd
1965	L. Codd–J. Shortt
1966	L. Codd–G. Connell
1967	P. Morgan–L. Codd
1968	P. Morgan–T. Doyle

REPUBLIC OF IRELAND

Year	Result
1969	J. Rogers–L. Codd
1970	L. Drennan–T. Doyle
1971	L. Codd–P. Fenelon
1972	L. Codd–n.r.
1973	T. Martin–n.r.
1974	T. Doyle–A. Roche
1975	P. Fenelon–T. Martin
1976	J. Rogers–P. Fenelon
1977	E. Hughes–T. Martin
1978	E. Hughes–R. Brennan
1979	n.r.
1980	P. Burke–n.r.
1981	P. Burke–n.r.

SNOOKER CHAMPIONSHIP

Year	Result
1933	S. Fenning–J. Ayres
1935	S. Fenning–n.r.
1937	P. J. O'Connor–n.r.
1940	P. Merrigan–S. Fenning
1947	C. Downey–P. Merrigan
1948	P. Merrigan–n.r.
1949	S. Fenning–n.r.
1952	W. Brown–S. Fenning
1953	S. Brooks–W. Brown
1954	S. Fenning–J. Redmond
1955	S. Fenning–W. Brown
1956	W. Brown–S. Fenning
1957	J. Connolly–G. Gibson
1958	G. Gibson–F. Murphy
1959-60	No official contests
1961	W. Brown–F. Murphy
1962	J. Weber–G. Buffini
1963	J. Rogers–G. Hanway
1964	J. Rogers–G. Buffini
1965	W. Fields–J. Grace
1966	G. Hanway–J. Rogers
1967	P. Morgan–J. Rogers
1968	G. Hanway–T. G. Hearty
1969	D. Dally–J. Rogers
1970	D. Sheehan–P. Thornton
1971	D. Sheehan–J. Weber
1972	J. Rogers–D. Sheehan
1973	F. Murphy–J. Bannister
1974	P. Burke–P. Miley
1975	F. Nathan–J. Weber
1976	P. Burke–L. Watson
1977	J. Clusker–F. Murphy
1978	E. Hughes–N. Lowth
1979	E. Hughes–D. Sheehan
1980	D. Sheehan–E. Hughes
1981	A. Kearney–P. Miley

three times the Championship runner-up.

Seamus Fenning, whom Joe Davis rated one of the best amateurs he had ever seen, dominated the early Eire Championships and represented Irish Free State in the 1935 Empire Championship in London. Amazingly, Southern Ireland has never since been represented in international amateur billiards, surely one of the reasons its standards have remained modest.

Its 1947 amateur snooker champion, Charles Downey, a master of the slow drag shot, moved to London and proved in 1952 an English amateur champion of outstanding quality.

In more recent times, another London based Dubliner, Patsy Fagan, now a professional, reached the English Amateur final at his first attempt in 1974.

The Republic of Ireland's first international snooker representative was Paddy Morgan, a Belfast man who chose to play much of his snooker across the border, winning the billiards title in 1967 and 1968 and the snooker in 1967. Morgan, now a professional in Australia, reached the semi-final of the 1968 World Amateur snooker in Sydney.

Jack Rogers, who won three national snooker and two billiards titles, sensationally defeated Jonathan Barron, the Cornishman who went on to win the title, in the 1970 World Amateur snooker in Edinburgh and also beat the Welshman Des May, who finished second in the group, but could himself finish only fifth in this seven man section.

Pascal Burke earned a semi-final place in the 1974 World Amateur in Dublin but Eugene Hughes, winner of the British Junior Championship at both games in 1975, just failed to reach the quarter-finals both in 1978 in Malta and 1980 in Launceston, though his break of 127 in the latter event was a championship record.

SCOTLAND

W. M. Green is the earliest recorded professional champion though he is described as having won it from a Glaswegian J. Meaney. J. G. Sala deprived Green of the title in 1888 and retained it unchallenged until his death in 1901.

Tom Aiken beat Tom Rae for the vacant title in 1902 and remained undefeated champion until 1904 during which period he scored many wins on both sides of the border against top English professionals, most of whom forced unwanted starts upon him to guard their reputations. He beat both Inman and Fred Lindrum in fortnight's matches on level terms and in 1911-12 won the Burroughes and Watts tournament in London, twice scoring his allotted sessional points of 600 in two visits without his opponent scoring. He beat both Diggle and Newman in 1912 but turned down an offer from John Roberts Jnr to be taken under the great man's wing. Aiken remained freelance and in obscurity while Newman, whom Roberts subsequently offered a contract, prospered under his protection.

A redoubtable Scot, Major Fleming – no one seemed to have the temerity to accord him an initial, much less a first name – won the Amateur Championship in 1909 and was runner-up in the next three, his defeat by a mere seven points in 1912 still being the closest final in the history of the event. Fleming also won the rival amateur championship organised by the Billiards Control Club in 1914.

Scotland opted out of the BA & CC organised Amateur Championship in favour of organising their own national championship in 1925.

Malcolm Smith, who represented Scotland in the Empire Championships of 1926, 1927 and 1933, was the best Scottish player of the period before Joe

McGhie took Scotland into second place in 1935.

After the war, Walter Ramage, a superb red ball player if limited in other departments, won fourteen Scottish amateur billiards titles between 1948 and 1967, a period in which he twice performed with distinction in the World Amateur Championship.

In London in 1951, Ramage finished fourth of seven competitors, recording a win over the talented if then inexperienced Indian, Wilson Jones, who was later to win the title. Ramage also defeated Jones in finishing fourth of the six competitors in Calcutta in 1952. He compiled his highest championship break, 283, in finishing fifth out of eight in Edinburgh in 1960.

An Irishman, Jack Bates, briefly lived in Scotland and won the billiards title twice but when he returned home and Ramage retired, Scottish billiards standards declined, all the more so through not competing in World Amateur Championships. Having had such little experience against quality opposition, David Sneddon did extremely will to reach the 1975 world semi-final in Auckland.

The Scottish Amateur Snooker Championship, founded as recently as 1946, provided a 16-year-old winner in David Edmond in 1954, though he surprisingly did not continue to play competitively.

Bert Demarco, who won three Scottish amateur titles, became his country's first world amateur snooker competitor in 1966. Generous and outgoing, he developed friendships in all snooker playing countries and became Scotland's best known figure on the international scene.

Walter Donaldson (see p. 63) has been Scotland's only snooker professional to reach world class but the outstanding Scottish amateur snooker player, Eddie Sinclair, British Junior champion in 1956, seven times Scottish Amateur champion between 1960 and 1976, and semi-finalist in the 1974 World Amateur Championship turned professional in 1979 and beat an Anglo-Scot, Chris Ross, for the revived Scottish Professional Championship later that year.

Six more Scots turned professional in 1981, thus

Eddie Sinclair

SCOTLAND

BILLIARDS CHAMPIONSHIP						
1933	A. Ramage–n.r.	1965	W. Ramage–A. Kennedy	1955	L. U. Demarco–P. Spence
1934	N. Canney–n.r.	1966	W. Ramage–L. U. Demarco	1956	W. Barrie–R. McKendrick
1935	H. King–n.r.	1967	W. Ramage–A. Kennedy	1957	T. Paul–H. D. Thompson
1936	N. Canney–R. Pollock	1968	A. Kennedy–L. U. Demarco	1958	J. Phillips–J. Ferguson
1937	J. McGhee–J. S. Patterson	1969	A. Kennedy–R. Eprile	1959	J. Phillips–E. Sinclair
1938	J. McGhee–n.r.	1970	D. Sneddon–L. U. Demarco	1960	E. Sinclair–A. Kennedy
1939-45	No contests	1971	D. Sneddon–R. Eprile	1961	J. Phillips–L. U. Demarco
1946	J. Levey–R. McKendrick	1972	L. U. Demarco–D. Sneddon	1962	A. Kennedy–L. U. Demarco
1947	A. Ramage–G. Aitken	1973	D. Sneddon–L. U. Demarco	1963	E. Sinclair–D. Miller
1948	W. Ramage–A. Ramage	1974	D. Sneddon–R. McCurley	1964	J. Phillips–E. Sinclair
1949	W. Ramage–A. Ramage	1975	D. Sneddon–A. Sutherland	1965	L. U. Demarco–P. Spence
1950	A. Ramage–W. Ramage	1976	D. Sneddon–J. Craig	1966	L. U. Demarco–P. Spence
1951	W. Ramage–G. Jardine	1977	J. Nugent–L. U. Demarco	1967	E. Sinclair–L. U. Demarco
1952	J. Murray–R. Gillon	1978	n.r.	1968	E. Sinclair–J. Zonfrillo
1953	J. Bates–W. Ramage	1979	H. Nimmo–A. Sutherland	1969	A. Kennedy–L. U. Demarco
1954	J. Bates–J. Murray	1980	D. Sneddon–H. Nimmo	1970	D. Sneddon–M. McLeod
1955	W. Ramage–A. Ramage	1981	D. Sneddon–J. Nugent	1971	J. Phillips–D. Miller
1956	W. Ramage–A. Ramage	**SNOOKER CHAMPIONSHIP**		1972	D. Sneddon–L. U. Demarco
1957	W. Ramage–M. Morrin	1946	J. Levey–N. McGowan	1973	E. Sinclair–J. Zonfrillo
1958	W. Ramage–P. Spence	1947	J. Levey–T. Gray	1974	D. Sneddon–E. Sinclair
1959	W. Ramage–W. Taylor	1948	I. Wexelstein–R. Walls	1975	E. Sinclair–J. Phillips
1960	A. Ramage–C. Spence	1949	W. Ramage–P. Spence	1976	E. Sinclair–D. Sneddon
1961	P. Spence–W. Ramage	1950	W. Ramage–R. McKendrick	1977	R. Miller–E. McLaughlin
1962	W. Ramage–A. Kennedy	1951	A. Wilson–A. Wishart	1978	J. Donnelly–E. McLaughlin
1963	W. Ramage–A. Kennedy	1952	D. Emerson–P. Spence	1979	S. Nivison–I. Wallace
1964	W. Ramage–A. Kennedy	1953	P. Spence–H. Thompson	1980	M. Gibson–R. Miller
		1954	D. Edmond–P. Spence	1981	R. Lane–J. Rea

enabling an eight man Scottish professional championship to be held. One of the newcomers, Ian Black, won the title by beating Matt Gibson 11-7 in the final.

WALES

Wales has always possessed world class players but only in the seventies did it begin to play its rightful part in the world game. In the days before Sports Council grants were even dreamt of, finance was usually an insuperable problem. It required an immense effort to compete in the English Amateur Championship in London and competing further afield, with rare exceptions, was out of the question.

As long as the BA & CC (later B & SCC) remained, simultaneously and incompatibly, the English and world amateur governing bodies, its near neighbours, like Wales, inevitably remained poor relations. England, through the BA & CC, exerted a dictatorial control over the game and monopolised status, influence and resources while associations like that of Wales, who reckoned their assets only in petty cash, struggled to stay afloat.

What has made South Wales and the valleys in particular such fruitful nurseries of snooker talent has been the way in which their closely knit communities, often revolving round a local club or billiard hall, have transmitted from generation to generation the skills and tactical know-how of their local heroes. In this way, snooker and, to a regrettably declining extent, billiards, can be seen as being among the last genuinely folk sports.

As young Welsh players have always had the opportunity of learning good snooker habits from their local stars, the Welsh snooker tradition has become so deeply ingrained that at club level the average general standard is probably the highest in the world.

The origins of the national association and the national championships have defied research. It appears that the earliest billiards championship was that of 1920 which, like the next four, was won by Horace Coles, who subsequently represented both Wales and (because of his performances in the English Amateur Championship) England in the Empire Championship, the forerunner of the World Amateur Championship. It was in England's colours that Coles won that title in 1935.

Joe Tregoning, whose first and last titles were separated by 36 years, was another oustanding billiards exponent whose finest feat was reaching three consecutive English finals between 1949 and 1951.

Tom Jones, who with John Ford shares the distinction of having won the Welsh title at both games, took Wales into second place in the 1933 Empire Championship, the principality's best Empire/world amateur billiards placing.

In the last two decades Welsh billiards has been dominated by Roy Oriel (14 times champion) and Clive Everton (five). Oriel, an extremely fast scorer for a player specialising in the in-off game, set the Welsh championship break record of 345 in the 1971 quarter-final, in which he also set a two hour session record of 1384. He competed only once in the World Amateur Championship, finishing seventh out of eleven in London in 1969, while Everton, who also reached the final of the English Championship five times without winning it, reached two world semi-finals, in Auckland in 1975 and Melbourne in 1977, before he turned professional in 1981.

Although there was a match for the Welsh Professional Snooker Championship in 1922—J. S. Nicholls beating W. Davies 1032-777 over the aggregate score of 18 frames—the best Welsh players tended to flourish in the atmosphere of money matches rather than tournament play. George Hargest, manager of the local billiard hall at Blackwood, Monmouthshire, made a total clearance of 112 in 1915 but appears never to have played competitively.

Snooker flourished in South Wales as it did in any area where unemployment was high and where the local billiard hall or institute became not only a refuge from the weather but a focus for activity which provided diversion and the hope of a few extra shillings. Bill Withers was one of the few Welshmen to gain even a precarious foothold in the professional tournament world, beating Fred Davis 17-14 on his world championship debut in 1937 before Fred's elder brother Joe, full of wrath at this blot on the family escutcheon, hammered him 30-1 in the next round.

Times were still hard when Ray Reardon and Cliff Wilson fought their great battles in the early fifties when, as a 1979 BBC Wales documentary clearly

Roy Oriel

WALES

BILLIARDS CHAMPIONSHIP

Year	Result	Year	Result
1920	H. F. E. Coles–n.r.	1956	A. J. Ford–A. Davies
1921	H. F. E. Coles–n.r.	1957	R. Smith–A. J. Ford
1922	H. F. E. Coles–n.r.	1958	R. W. Oriel–A. J. Ford
1923	H. F. E. Coles–n.r.	1959	A. J. Ford–E. Marks
1924	H. F. E. Coles–n.r.	1960	C. Everton–P. J. Morris
1925	n.r.	1961	R. W. Oriel–P. J. Morris
1926	n.r.	1962	R. W. Oriel–E. Marks
1927	n.r.	1963	R. W. Oriel–P. J. Morris
1928	G. Moore–n.r.	1964	R. W. Oriel–D. E. Edwards
1929	J. Tregoning–n.r.	1965	R. W. Oriel–N. Jaynes
1930	n.r.	1966	R. W. Oriel–A. Davies
1931	L. Prosser–n.r.	1967	R. W. Oriel–C. Jenkins
1932	T. Jones–n.r.	1968	D. E. Edwards–R. W. Oriel
1933	T. Jones–n.r.	1969	R. W. Oriel–T. J. Entwistle
1934	n.r.	1970	R. W. Oriel–D. E. Edwards
1935	I. Edwards–n.r.	1971	R. W. Oriel–C. Everton
1936	J. Tregoning–n.r.	1972	C. Everton–R. W. Oriel
1937	B. Gravenor–n.r.	1973	C. Everton–J. Terry
1938	J. Tregoning–n.r.	1974	R. W. Oriel–C. Everton
1939-45	No contests	1975	R. W. Oriel–C. Everton
1946	T. G. Rees–n.r.	1976	C. Everton–R. W. Oriel
1947	T. C. Morse–R. Smith	1977	C. Everton–R. W. Oriel
1948	J. Tregoning–I. Edwards	1978	R. W. Oriel–C. Everton
1949	I. Edwards–T. Jones	1979	R. W. Oriel–D. E. Edwards
1950	W. Pierce–W. T. Jones	1980	No contest
1951	W. Pierce–n.r.	1981	No contest
1952	J. Tregoning–L. Davis		
1953	B. Sainsbury–W. Pierce		
1954	R. Smith–R. Keats		
1955	J. Tregoning–R. W. Oriel		

SNOOKER CHAMPIONSHIP

Year	Result	Year	Result
1947	T. Jones–R. Smith	1951	R. Reardon–n.r.
1948	R. Smith–A. J. Ford	1952	R. Reardon–A. J. Ford
1949	A. J. Ford–C. Coles	1953	R. Reardon–A. Kemp
1950	R. Reardon–A. J. Ford	1954	R. Reardon–A. J. Ford
		1955	R. Reardon–A. J. Ford
		1956	C. Wilson–V. Wilkins
		1957	R. D. Meredith–N. Williams
		1958	A. Kemp–R. D. Meredith
		1959	J. R. Price–M. L. Berni
		1960	L. Luker–A. Kemp
		1961	T. Parsons–J. R. Price
		1962	A. J. Ford–M. L. Berni
		1963	R. D. Meredith–J. R. Price
		1964	M. L. Berni–A. J. Ford
		1965	T. Parsons–A. J. Ford
		1966	L. L. O'Neill–D. Mountjoy
		1967	L. L. O'Neill–K. Weed
		1968	D. Mountjoy–J. Terry
		1969	T. Parsons–J. T. Prosser
		1970	D. T. May–G. Thomas
		1971	D. T. May–R. W. Oriel
		1972	G. Thomas–T. Griffiths
		1973	A. Lloyd–G. Thomas
		1974	A. Lloyd–G. Thomas
		1975	T. Griffiths–G. Thomas
		1976	D. Mountjoy–A. Lloyd
		1977	C. Wilson–D. Thomas
		1978	A. Lloyd–S. Newbury
		1979	C. Wilson–G. Thomas
		1980	S. Newbury–A. Lloyd
		1981	C. Roscoe–E. Richards

recalled, Tredegar was a town divided into two camps. Reardon won six consecutive Welsh titles, the first when he was only 17, between 1950 and 1955 but Wilson enjoyed his share of success when they met in the English Championship and in the money matches in which the whole town seemed to have an interest. Wilson, three times Welsh amateur champion, also won the World Amateur title in 1978, keeping in Welsh hands the trophy Doug Mountjoy had won in 1976.

Reardon and Wilson, though very much part of the current scene, were essentially products of snooker's hungry fifties. Mountjoy and Terry Griffiths, world professional champion at his first attempt in 1979 after a very successful amateur career, are products of the seventies when government grants helped make it possible for leading Welsh amateurs to enjoy the experience of amateur internationals and overseas competition. Quicker roads and the removal of restrictions on the award of prize money in amateur tournaments also encouraged Welsh amateurs to venture further afield in search of competitive experience.

It was through a Welsh initiative that amateur international matches started in 1969 and Wales is the only country apart from England to have won the Home International Amateur Championship which grew from that initial contest.

Of the many first class Welsh amateurs who have not turned professional, Alwyn Lloyd, with three Welsh titles and quarter-final places in the 1974, 1978 and 1980 World Amateur Championships to his credit, possesses the most distinguished record though Geoff Thomas gave Wales an interest in the 1974 World Amateur final, the best Welsh performance in the event until Mountjoy outclassed the rest of the field in Johannesburg in 1976.

Several century breaks have been made in the Welsh Amateur Snooker Championship with 123 by Tony Chappell in 1980 as the highest.

Alwyn Lloyd

AUSTRALIA

The father of billiards in Australia was Henry Upton Alcock, a Dubliner who learnt the billiard table trade in London and emigrated to Australia in 1852. Soon, he was manufacturing some 150 tables a year, not only for clubs and private homes but for out of the way places like gold diggings for which the slates were made in eight or ten pieces so that they could be transported by packhorse.

Alcock brought British professionals over to tour, notably John Roberts Snr in 1864 and later William Cook and John Roberts Jnr. It was almost certainly Roberts Jnr, who had been introduced to snooker on a tour of India in 1885, who brought snooker to the attention of Frank Smith Snr who is generally credited with introducing the game to Australia in 1887.

Early billiards championships were run on a challenge basis. Joseph Byrne (Victoria) beat J. James (New South Wales) 1000-878 to win the first contest for the Australian Championship on 8 September 1881 at Perkin's Exchange Hotel, Sydney. Byrne made a 66 break by all round play and a 59 which included 18 spots as he took the £100 side stake in front of a crowd of about 200 who had paid ten shillings each.

Harry Evans, an expatriate Englishman, dominated the championship from 1882 to 1892, keeping at bay, among others, Fred Lindrum, father of Walter, and Harry Gray, father of George. Lindrum beat Gray for the 'native born' Australian Championship in 1887.

Charles Memmott beat Evans to become champion in 1892, making a break of 1238, largely through the spot stroke. As occurred in Britain, the game then diverged into two codes with Memmott supreme at all in and Fred Weiss at spot barred.

From 1900-10 the top Australians were Fred Lindrum Jnr (born 1888), who took the title from Memmott, and George Gray (born 1892), who was only 14 when he made a 513 break entirely by in-off reds. Lindrum, an excellent top of the table player, certainly had the better all-round game but himself concentrated much more on the red ball after Gray had once beaten him with the aid of an 836 break which included 831 off the red.

Fred Lindrum Jnr, who had beaten Memmott in 1908 for the Australian title, was never challenged for it either by Gray or his younger brother Walter but eventually lost it in 1934 to his nephew, Horace Lindrum (neé Morell). Walter Lindrum's career is profiled on page 40.

Horace, a player of outstanding natural gifts, first came to Britain for the World Professional Snooker Championship in 1936, leading Joe Davis 27-24 in the final before losing 31-27. With his fluent, attractive style he was much in demand as an exhibition player but his relish for the cut and thrust of matchplay, never great, diminished with the years. He reached the world professional final of 1946 but the world championship which he won in 1950 was a travesty, recognised as such by the public since only he and Clark McConachy, who was not a front rank snooker player, remained loyal to the event conducted by the Billiards Association and Control Council while all the other professionals supported the rival championship organised by the professionals' own association.

Although he never beat Joe Davis on level terms, Horace was several times successful in weeks matches when receiving 7 points start in each frame. In one of these encounters, he made breaks of 141 and 135 which were not ratified as records and in another, at Thurston's, one of 135 which was.

Urged on, particularly early in his career, by his aggressive, domineering mother, he found 'the Lindrum name' an increasingly heavy burden in his mature years.

He retained unchallenged until his retirement from competition in 1957 both the Australian professional snooker title he won from Frank Smith Jnr in 1931 and the Australian professional billiards title he won with the aid of a break of 1431 from his uncle Fred in 1933. He made a 147 snooker maximum in an exhibition at Penrith School of Arts, New South Wales in 1941. He died in 1974.

Norman Squire, who was New Zealand-born, and Warren Simpson were the two other outstanding snooker players on the Australian scene until the emergence of Eddie Charlton, who won the Australian professional title every year except one since 1964. Charlton's career is profiled on page 67.

Squire, who made over 2000 centuries, including one maximum, was no one's inferior in touch and close positional control. His long game was not of comparable standard and limited his success against players of similar ability to his own and he was at his best conceding huge starts for money to poor players, mostly in City Tattersalls Club, Sydney where Simpson was also a regular.

Simpson, also a great money player, enjoyed some notable successes in competition, winning the inaugural Australian Amateur Championship in 1953 and again in 1957, the Australian Open titles in 1954 and 1957 and the Australian Professional Championship in 1963 and 1968. He played the game of his life to beat Charlton 27-22 in the 1970 World Professional Championship semi-final but, partly through the diabetes which he suffered, partly through his easygoing nature, rarely recaptured this standard in match play.

Apart from Simpson, Charlton's toughest opposition came from two expatriates, Gary Owen, born in Llanelli but twice winner of the World Amateur

Horace Lindrum with Fred Davis, 1950.

Bob Marshall

Championship in England's colours when he was a Birmingham fireman, and Paddy Morgan, born in Belfast, who reached the semi-final of the 1968 World Amateur Championship in Sydney.

Australia produced surprisingly few amateur snooker players of top quality. Frank Harris was runner-up to Owen in the 1963 World Amateur but their most consistent performer was Max Williams, who won eight national titles and came within one frame of beating England's David Taylor in the 1968 World Amateur final.

In recent years, Ron Atkins made good the handicap of having his right leg amputated above the knee after a teenage shooting accident to the extent of winning three national titles and reaching the final of the 1980 World Amateur in his native Launceston. Kevin Burles won the 1978 Australian Amateur title 18 years after the second of his other two successes and died suddenly in the course of the 1979 event.

Australia did, though, produce two of the finest amateur billiards players of all time, Bob Marshall and Tom Cleary. Between 1936 and 1970, Marshall won 19 titles, Cleary five and, as they passed their peak, Jim Long the other five.

Marshall, who first won his national title in 1936 went on to win four world amateur titles (two when the event was known as the Empire Championship) while Cleary, who first became Australian champion

in 1950, won the world amateur title in 1954. Their rivalry inspired record upon record, Marshall, the harder man, relentlessly piling up points with deadly repetitive sequences of 'postman's knock', Cleary only marginally less prolific with the more varied and artistic version of top of the table, 'floating white'.

After his first world amateur title in Johannesburg in 1936, Marshall successfully defended in Melbourne in 1938 when, averaging 49, he hammered Kingsley Kennerley, an outstanding English champion 6639-4705 in the deciding match, Kennerley's match average of 35 being nearly six points higher than the English record he had just set.

In the second of the six sessions of the match Marshall made two triple centuries and three doubles in setting a new amateur session average record of 115. Twice during the event he made seven centuries in a session and set a two hour session aggregate record of 1864 which stood until he himself broke it with 1876 in the 1959 Australian amateur.

Cleary held the Australian break record with 435 in 1947 but Marshall beat it with 500 and 540 in 1948. Cleary set a four hour aggregate record of 3185 in 1950.

Marshall retained the World Amateur Championship, held for the first time since 1938, at Burroughes and Watts, London in 1951. The superfine super fast cloth was foreign to his style and the usual run of Australian tables but he was still much too good both

127

for Cleary and Frank Edwards, the English champion, who was then at the peak of his form.

Shortly before coming to London, Marshall made a 589 unfinished in the Australian Championship plus 498, 418 and nine more over 300. Unexpectedly, he lost to the Indian no. 2, Chandra Hirjee in the 1952 World Amateur in Calcutta and failed to beat England's Leslie Driffield in the last match to force a play off.

He trailed Cleary by 400 with less than an hour to go in the 1953 Australian final, but, starting with a fluke from a double baulk, all but played out time with a new world amateur record break of 702 to win the title.

Cleary's compensation was a victory over Marshall in the 1954 World Amateur in Sydney. With this vital success behind him, Cleary made a new championship record of 682 and went on to win the title.

Marshall's supremacy was only briefly interrupted. In the 1957 Australian Championship he set a new world four hour aggregate record of 3364 and in the course of the event made a 596, three 400s and eight 300s. He did not defend in 1958 when Cleary equalled his record of seven centuries in a session and made two breaks of 446 but won again in 1959 with a new world session aggregate record of 1876, a new four hour record of 3391, a new session average record of 115 which he increased to 118·7 on a tour of India in 1961.

Long, who never beat Marshall, beat Cleary in the Victoria Championship in both 1956 and 1960 and with Marshall not entering on either occasion won his first two Australian Championships. It was the latter

success which saw him invited to represent Australia in the 1960 World Amateur in Edinburgh.

In 1962, in his home city of Perth, Marshall was a strong favourite for the World Amateur but seemed to have lost his chance when he was beaten by 168 points by the Indian Wilson Jones. Cleary lost to the other Indian, Samir Banerjee, but then beat Jones to take the championship into a play-off between Marshall and Jones.

Jones made a 489 break in the first session but in a fabulous third session Marshall outpointed him by 1200 in setting a new session average record of 128·4. After this, his fourth and last world title, he retired with no intention of playing again but made a brief comeback as a much reduced force to win his national title in 1969 and 1970 and compete, albeit with scant success, in the 1969 World Amateur.

Cleary's standard gradually faded away as, slightly later, did Long's. Philip Tarrant won two Australian titles and finished fourth in the 1973 World Amateur in Bombay before turning professional. George Ganim Jnr won his national title at his first attempt in 1976 and retained it, albeit with the general standard declining, until 1980.

The official Australian break records are – Billiards: R. Marshall 702 (1953) (two pots); J. Long 472 (1967) (15 pots); P. Tarrant 388 (1973) (five pots); G. Ganim Jnr 423 (1979) (three pots). Snooker: M. Williams (1973), J. Campbell (1980) 101 (national championships); M. Williams (1965) 118 (state championship). Two Australian amateurs, Leon Heywood and Ray Launder, both made witnessed breaks of 147 in practice frames in 1979.

AUSTRALIA BILLIARDS CHAMPIONSHIP				AUSTRALIA SNOOKER CHAMPIONSHIP	
1913	G. B. Shailer	1951	R. Marshall	1953	W. Simpson
1914-19	No contests	1952	R. Marshall	1954	W. Simpson
1920	J. R. Hooper	1953	R. Marshall	1955	E. Pickett
1921	G. B. Shailer	1954	R. Marshall	1956	R. Marshall
1922	G. B. Shailer	1955	R. Marshall	1957	W. Simpson
1923	G. B. Shailer	1956	J. Long	1958	F. Harris
1924	E. Eccles	1957	R. Marshall	1959	K. Burles
1925	G. B. Shailer	1958	T. Cleary	1960	K. Burles
1926	L. W. Hayes	1959	R. Marshall	1961	M. Williams
1927	L. W. Hayes	1960	J. Long	1962	W. Barrie
1928	L. W. Hayes	1961	R. Marshall	1963	F. Harris
1929	A. H. Hearndon	1962	R. Marshall	1964	W. Barrie
1930	S. Ryan	1963	R. Marshall	1965	W. Barrie
1931	H. L. Goldsmith	1964	J. Long	1966	M. Williams
1932	A. Sakzewski	1965	T. Cleary	1967	M. Williams
1933	L. W. Hayes	1966	T. Cleary	1968	M. Williams
1934	L. W. Hayes	1967	J. Long	1969	W. Barrie
1935	L. W. Hayes	1968	J. Long	1970	M. Williams
1936	R. Marshall	1969	R. Marshall	1971	M. Williams
1937	R. Marshall	1970	R. Marshall	1972	M. Williams
1938	R. Marshall	1971	M. Williams	1973	M. Williams
1939	R. Marshall	1972	P. Tarrant	1974	L. Condo
1940-45	No contests	1973	P. Tarrant	1975	R. Atkins
1946	R. Marshall	1974	J. Reece	1976	R. Atkins
1947	T. Cleary	1975	J. Long	1977	R. Atkins
1948	R. Marshall	1976	G. Ganim Jnr	1978	K. Burles
1949	R. Marshall	1977	G. Ganim Jnr	1979	J. Campbell
1950	T. Cleary	1978	G. Ganim Jnr	1980	W. King
		1979	G. Ganim Jnr		
		1980	G. Ganim Jnr		

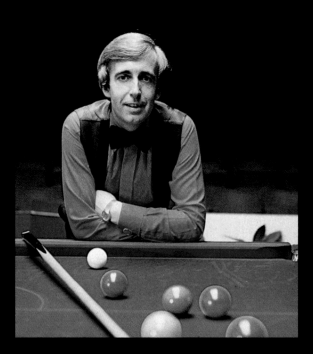

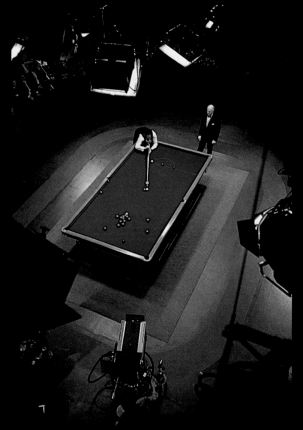

Above: Terry Griffiths. *Top right:* An early Pot Black recording with ''Old Style'' television lighting. *Below left:* John Roberts Snr. *Below right:* John Roberts Jnr.

LE TYRAN D'ESTAMINET.

Above: Steve Davis in play as Terry Griffiths sits out.

Below: John Spencer

CANADA

Until the late seventies, when the game began to acquire a genuine tournament structure, snooker in Canada was sustained almost exclusively as a gambling and leisure activity. A number of clubs did possess tables but essentially the game was based in public saloons.

Championships were promoted from time to time but with no national governing body or affiliation to world governing bodies to lend them any kind of official status, such events were subject to the whims of promoters and a maelstrom of personal squabbles.

Though the billiard players of old toured Canada as they toured all countries where there was substantial British influence, billiards never became popular enough to produce a first class Canadian player. Snooker, with its wider scope for gambling, struck a much more responsive chord.

In January 1923, Con Stanbury potted the last 14 reds, 14 blacks, yellow and green in a break of 125 at the Palace Billiard Hall, Winnipeg. When he became Canada's first World Professional Snooker Championship entrant in 1935, his style was greeted with amazement. Unlike the British players, who, having received their grounding in the gentler game of billiards tended to avoid power shots for aesthetic reasons, Stanbury revelled in them.

Failure at a simple middle pocket pink cost Stanbury a 13-12 defeat to Willie Smith, who went on to reach the final quite comfortably, and despite many subsequent efforts and near misses the Canadian could never quite achieve a major breakthrough. Stanbury spent the last 40 years of his life in London, chiefly as a coach, until his death in 1975.

Clare O'Donnell, who hit even harder than Stanbury and eccentrically kept his chalk under his bridge hand when striking, entered the championship in 1936. A third Canadian, Jimmy Reed, arrived in London shortly after the start of the war but by then there were no tournaments to play in.

The first Canadian of genuine world class was George Chenier, who lost honourably to Joe Davis

George Chenier (*left*) and Joe Davis at Leicester Square Hall, 1950.

41-30 in a week's match in Bermuda and was thence invited to Britain for the 1949-50 season. During this visit Chenier brought home to British professionals the possibilities of plants and sets, these combination shots being much used in pool, snooker's American sister game played on smaller tables with larger pockets, at which Chenier was a player of high standard.

Disappointingly, Chenier finished last in the *News of the World* tournament but beat the South African champion Peter Mans 37-34 in the world quarter-final before losing 43-28 to Fred Davis in the semi. He also made a world record break of 144 at Leicester Square Hall though this stood for only five weeks before Joe Davis eclipsed it with 146.

Back in Canada, Chenier retained his Canadian and North American titles against a variety of opponents though he was beaten by Fred Davis in Vancouver in 1957 in a match enthusiastically billed by the promoter as being for the World Championship.

In 1963, Chenier trounced the former world champion Irving Crane 150-0 in the World 14·1 Pool Championship. He was still recognised as Canadian snooker champion when he died in 1970.

As snooker in Canada was played on tables with generous pockets and with Vitalite balls which were much livelier than Crystalate or even the later Super Crystalate, century breaks were common-place. In these flattering conditions, there was even a sprinkling of 147s, the first by Leo Levitt at Windsor Billiards and Bowling Club, Montreal on 24 November 1948.

Other Canadians who had joined the 147 club by 1 February 1981 include Cliff Thorburn (20), Bernie Mikkelsen (10), Vic Kireluk (8), Bill Werbeniuk (6), Mario Morra (4), Eddie Agha (3), Tom Regina (3), Jim Wych, John Sharp, John Bear, Robert Paquette (two each) and Kirk Stevens, Jim Jones, Ken Shea, Tony LeMay, Kevin Robitaille, Bill Ganne, Tom Gauthier, Don Gooch, Peter Kippie, Gino Rigitano, Cecil Dacey, John Jorgenson, Frank Jonik and Joe Big Plume (one each).

The visits of Fred Davis and Rex Williams and John Spencer, then reigning world champion, in 1971 were a vague general stimulus but more crucially introduced Thorburn to the authentic international circuit. The tournament performances of Thorburn (who first entered the World Professional Championship in 1973) and Werbeniuk (who first did so in 1974) stimulated interest in Canada and kindled a demand that Canada itself should stage international tournaments.

The Canadian Open Championship was first staged during the annual Canadian National Exhibition in Toronto in August 1974 and has been repeated each year since. The tournament has brought young Canadians like Kirk Stevens, Jim Wych and Mikkelsen to

CANADA SNOOKER CHAMPIONSHIP	
1979	J. Wych
1980	Jim Bear

international attention for the first time.

Canada's first competitor in the World Amateur Snooker Championship was John Sklazeski in 1974. As a degree of organisation began to be imposed on the amateur game, the Canadian challenge grew stronger. Neither Paquette nor Mikkelsen reached the 1976 World Amateur quarter-finals but two years later, in Malta, Paquette reached the quarter-finals and Stevens the semis. In 1980, in Launceston, Paquette narrowly missed a quarter-final place.

Billiards, which had been virtually extinct, trembled into life. Ed Fisher represented Canada in the 1979 World Amateur Billiards Championship in Colombo, a billiards event was run annually in conjunction with the Canadian Open Snooker Championship and Norman Dagley, the twelve times English Amateur champion, made a billiards tour in May 1980.

INDIA

When the Indian Billiards and Snooker Association (later Indian Billiards and Snooker Federation) was founded in 1930, M. M. Begg was one of its joint honorary secretaries. Begg won the inaugural billiards championship but it was as an administrator that he made his outstanding contribution. It was, for instance, due to his persistence that the World Amateur Snooker Championship came into being. The BA & CC had delayed from 1952 until Begg donated a cup and concluded arrangements for a tournament in Calcutta in 1963 to which the BA & CC and other interested nations agreed.

It was not until after the war that India produced a player of genuine world class in Wilson Jones, whose wealthy patron R. K. Vissanji arranged a not too onerous job for him which allowed him to practise several hours a day in Vissanji's own beautifully appointed billiard room. Vissanji, a great enthusiast and fine administrator, became chairman of the International Billiards and Snooker Federation in 1978-79.

Visits by leading overseas amateurs also provided a stimulus for the game and several were invited to compete in the Indian championships, thus explaining why there are several non-Indians in the championship rolls.

Jones started as a snooker player, winning the Indian title in 1948, but a tour that year by Kingsley Kennerley interested him in top of the table play. Bob Marshall's 1949 tour, in which he made an Indian all comers record break of 405 and an aggregate of 1379 in two hours, also furthered his billiards education.

Beaten by T. A. Selvaraj a redoubtable red ball player, Jones won his national title in 1950 by beating another tourist, Frank Edwards, by 67 in the semi-final before beating Selvaraj to earn a trip to the 1951 World Amateur Championship in London.

Partly through inexperience, Jones could not settle to the conditions and won only one of his six matches, a dismal showing he repeated in the 1952 World Amateur in Calcutta where his great domestic rival Chandra Hirjee gave India something to shout about by beating Marshall by 105 in the Australian's second match. Hirjee also led Leslie Driffield, who was to go on to win the title, by 43 with 20 minutes to go before the Yorkshireman got home with a late spurt. Hirjee then ran out of steam and finished third.

Jones restored some of his confidence by beating Hirjee by 61 in 1954 for the fourth of the 12 Indian billiards titles he was to win—Hirjee winning four—but again cut no ice in the 1954 World Amateur in Sydney.

It was four years before the event was held again and Jones, by now at his peak, won it in Calcutta in 1958 in spectacular fashion.

Aided by a 501 break, Jones beat Tom Cleary, the holder, by 1069 and was undefeated when he tackled Driffield, his penultimate opponent. Driffield led by 660 with only 90 minutes to play before Jones came to life with 170 and 232 to narrow the gap to 262. Driffield made 124 but Jones, with 113 and 117, got to within 170 and, with 147 and 106 went 68 in front. He held on to win by 136 and, starting with three double centuries and three single centuries in the first session, overwhelmed his last opponent, Hirjee, by 1768 to become champion.

Hirjee retired shortly afterwards with a mysterious skin complaint to leave Jones in a class of his own domestically. He compiled a world record eight cen-

turies in a session in the Bombay State Championship in 1959 but Collins Music Hall, Edinburgh, was not the most promising of settings for Jones to defend his world title in 1960.

Accustomed to warmth and large, excited crowds, Jones could not reproduce his best and the English red ball specialist Herbert Beetham defeated him by 138. A second defeat by the Australian Jim Long put him down to third place.

A win over Marshall by 168 gave Jones a flying start in the 1962 World Amateur in Perth but Jones then lost to Cleary, who had previously lost to India's no. 2, Samir Banerjee. Marshall also beat Cleary to force a play-off with Jones and beat him by 732 for the title.

Jones, determined to add a world title on foreign soil to the one he had won in Calcutta, achieved his ambition in the small New Zealand country town of Pukekohe in 1964 when he went through the ten man round robin undefeated.

His closest match—a winning margin of 144—was against his young compatriot, Michael Ferreira, who in due course was to take over his position as India's no. 1. This, though, did not become undisputed until Satish Mohan had won five of the six domestic championships between 1968 and 1973. Ferreira, meanwhile, achieved third place in the World Amateur of 1964, fourth in 1967 in Colombo and second equal in London in 1969, a tournament in which his break of 629 set a world amateur record under the five pot rule.

Mohan, who had finished third in the 1971 World Amateur, was favourite for the 1973 championship in Bombay but pressure of home expectation took its toll. In finishing second, he displayed disturbing signs of the instability of temperament which led him into heavy drinking and a swift disappearance from the competitive scene, a tragic fate for one of the quickest and most exciting players in modern billiards.

Ferreira, who finished third, amassed four world records against the Scot Bert Demarco: a four hour aggregate of 3202, a two hour aggregate of 1688, ten centuries in a session and 16 in a four hour match. Further world records fell to his skill and fluency in his 1975 national championship: a 128·4 average for a two hour session and 69·7 for a four hour match but,

Wilson Jones, 1951

throughout his career, his best tended to elude him when it was most urgently required.

This was certainly the case in the 1975 World Amateur final against Norman Dagley and it was to be the case in the 1979 World Amateur semi-final against Paul Mifsud. In the interim, he won the 1977 World Amateur title in Melbourne, albeit with a mediocre performance in the final against the Englishman Bob Close, whose mental resources appeared spent after his surprise semi-final win over Dagley. Ferreira's form was much more impressive in winning the unofficial 'World Open' in Christchurch which immediately followed, setting a new session average record of 189·8 in the final.

Ferreira reached new heights in the 1978 Indian Championship when he seized the world amateur break record with 1149 (superseding Dagley's 862 earlier that year). He compiled a 995 for good measure and raised the four hour and two hour average records to 158·0 and 243·6 respectively. His 1949 session aggregate in the latter was also a record.

With the rules changed from 'five pots' to 'three', Ferreira claimed a world record under the revised

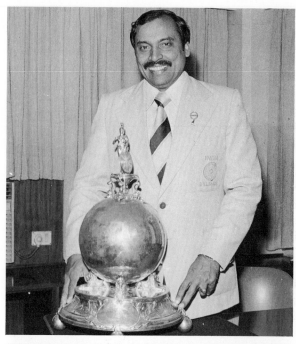

Michael Ferreira with the World Amateur Billiards Championship trophy he won in 1977.

INDIA
BILLIARDS CHAMPIONSHIP

1931	M. M. Begg	**1957**	W. Jones
1932	P. K. Deb	**1958**	C. Hirjee
1933	Major Meade	**1959**	T. Cleary (Aust)
1934	Mg Ba Sin	**1960**	W. Jones
1935	P. K. Deb	**1961**	W. Jones
1936	P. K. Deb	**1962**	R. Marshall (Aust)
1937	M. M. Begg	**1963**	W. Jones
1938	P. K. Deb	**1964**	W. Jones
1939	P. K. Deb	**1965**	W. Jones
1940	S. H. Lyth	**1966**	W. Jones
1941	V. R. Freer	**1967**	A. Savur
1942	V. R. Freer	**1968**	S. Mohan
1943-45	No contests	**1969**	M. Ferreira
1946	C. Hirjee	**1970**	S. Mohan
1947	C. Hirjee	**1971**	S. Mohan
1948	V. R. Freer	**1972**	S. Mohan
1949	T. A. Selvaraj	**1973**	S. Mohan
1950	W. Jones	**1974**	M. Ferreira
1951	W. Jones	**1975**	G. C. Parikh
1952	W. Jones	**1976**	M. Ferreira
1953	L. Driffield (Eng)	**1977**	M. J. M. Lafir (Sri L)
1954	W. Jones	**1978**	M. Ferreira
1955	W. Jones	**1979**	M. Ferreira
1956	C. Hirjee	**1980**	M. Ferreira

SNOOKER CHAMPIONSHIP

1939	P. K. Deb	**1961**	M. J. M. Lafir (Sri L)
1940	P. K. Deb	**1962**	R. Marshall (Aust)
1941	V. R. Freer	**1963**	M. J. M. Lafir (Sri L)
1942	P. K. Deb	**1964**	S. Shroff
1943-45	No contests	**1965**	S. Shroff
1946	T. A. Selvaraj	**1966**	T. Monteiro
1947	T. Sadler	**1967**	S. Shroff
1948	W. Jones	**1968**	S. Mohan
1949	T. A. Selvaraj	**1969**	S. Shroff
1950	F. Edwards (Eng)	**1970**	S. Shroff
1951	T. A. Selvaraj	**1971**	T. Monteiro
1952	W. Jones	**1972**	S. Shroff
1953	A. L. Driffield (Eng)	**1973**	S. Shroff
1954	W. Jones	**1974**	M. J. M. Lafir (Sri L)
1955	T. A. Selvaraj	**1975**	M. J. M. Lafir (Sri L)
1956	M. J. M. Lafir (Sri L)	**1976**	A. Savur
1957	M. J. M. Lafir (Sri L)	**1977**	M. J. M. Lafir (Sri L)
1958	W. Jones	**1978**	A. Savur
1959	M. J. M. Lafir (Sri L)	**1979**	A. Savur
1960	W. Jones	**1980**	J. White (Eng)

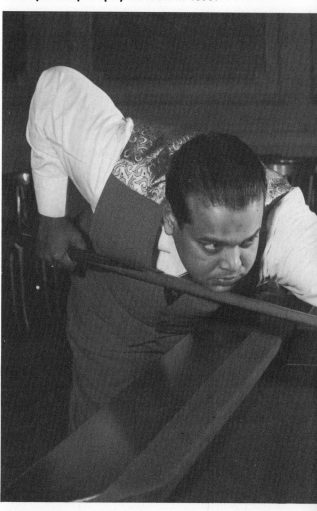

Arvind Savur

rules with a break of 566 in the Islam Gymkhana Open in 1979, superseding Dagley's 506 in the 1980 English Amateur final. His 3046 four hour aggregate in the 1980 Indian Championship was also claimed as a world record under revised rules.

Arvind Savur, also a very useful billiards player, emerged as India's finest ever snooker exponent with three national titles and semi-final places in the 1972 and 1980 World Amateur Championships.

India also held the world amateur break record through the 122 by Ratan Bader in the West Bengal State Championship in 1964. Bader's previous best had been 82 in practice and 50 in a match and he never again made a century, but his 122, a total clearance but for pink and black, remained the record until 1977.

Snooker, as it has in other countries, has overtaken billiards in popularity but India has continued to produce first class billiards players in greater numbers than can be found elsewhere. One important reason for this is that clubs employ markers to field out and, in effect, referee. The drudgery of fielding out, the bane of billiards, is thus removed.

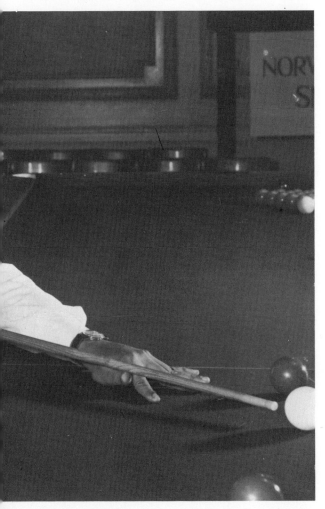

MALTA

The games became popular on the island in the days when it was a key British base in the Mediterranean. National championships were instituted in 1947.

The outstanding early champions were Wilfred Asciak (six snooker titles and 18 billiards between 1950 and 1972) and Alfred Borg (13 snooker and one billiards between 1952 and 1974).

Asciak was Malta's first competitor in the World Amateur Billiards Championship, finishing last but one in Calcutta in 1958 and last but two in Edinburgh in 1960 when he made a break of 194. Perhaps his best Championship performance, though, was a narrow loss 1230-1160 to Norman Dagley when the Englishman went on to win the 1971 event at the Malta Hilton, the first world championship to be staged on the island.

Far and away the most successful Maltese in international competition has been Paul Mifsud, world amateur billiards champion in 1979 and runner-up in the world amateur snooker in 1976.

Mifsud competed with only modest success in the World Amateur Billiards Championships of 1969 and 1971 but came to prominence in the 1970 World Amateur Snooker in Edinburgh, beating England's no. 2 in that event, Sid Hood, 4-0 and finishing second in his group. But for a 4-3 loss to Mohammed Lafir (Sri Lanka) in his last match, Mifsud would have forced a play-off with Hood for a place in the final.

In the 1972 championship, Mifsud beat Ray Edmonds, the ultimate winner, 4-2 in the preliminary round robin but after finishing last in his four man semi-final group was rushed to hospital with a collapsed lung.

With Borg representing Malta as her national champion in the 1974 world amateur Mifsud did not compete again until 1976 when he reached the final in Johannesburg, heading his group and then beating the defending champion, Ray Edmonds, 5-1 in the quarter-final and the South African Jimmy van Rensburg 8-4 in the semi before being outclassed 11-1 by the Welshman Doug Mountjoy.

On home territory in 1978, in Malta's National Sports Pavilion, Mifsud found the burden of national expectation too heavy and was beaten by the Canadian Kirk Stevens in the quarter-finals but made unexpected amends by carrying off the world amateur billiards title in Colombo in 1979.

Mifsud, who had not competed in the world amateur billiards since 1973, when he had finished seventh of ten competitors, arrived only ten hours before his first match after being delayed 24 hours in Paris and 26 in Bombay. The physical reserves which had enabled him to withstand such an energy sapping journey also helped him cope better than the other players who were not from the continent of India with the sauna like heat.

Qualifying in second place in his group, Mifsud overturned arrears of 618 halfway through his six hour semi-final against the Indian Michael Ferreira, the defending champion, to win by 633.

Having turned this match with a break of 338, Mifsud crucially played out time with 359 (completed next day to 361) to reach the halfway mark of his final against Dagley with a lead of 823 on which the Englishman never looked like making any impression.

Though he practised billiards much less than snooker, Mifsud had probably benefited from having to rise to the domestic threat posed by Joe Grech, who made breaks of 567 and 510 in winning the Malta Championship in 1978. Mifsud won his eighth Malta billiards title the following year.

Grech, like Mifsud a quarter-finalist in the World Amateur Snooker in 1978, firmly established himself as Malta's no. 2 at both games while Mifsud came within striking distance of completing a unique world amateur billiards /snooker double.

Undefeated in his group of the 1980 World Amateur Snooker in Launceston, Mifsud beat the Australian John Campbell 5-3 in the quarter-final and led the eventual champion, Jimmy White, 3-0, 5-3, and 6-4 in the semi-final before losing 8-6.

Joe Grech holds the national championship break record with 567, and Borg the snooker record with 108.

MALTA
BILLIARDS CHAMPIONSHIP

Year	Champion	Year	Champion
1947	V. Micallef	1964	W. Asciak
1948	No contest	1965	W. Asciak
1949	E. Bartolo	1966	W. Asciak
1950	W. Asciak	1967	W. Asciak
1951	W. Asciak	1968	W. Asciak
1952	W. Asciak	1969	P. Mifsud
1953	W. Asciak	1970	W. Asciak
1954	W. Asciak	1971	P. Mifsud
1955	W. Asciak	1972	W. Asciak
1956	W. Asciak	1973	P. Mifsud
1957	W. Asciak	1974	P. Mifsud
1958	W. Asciak	1975	P. Mifsud
1959	W. Asciak	1976	P. Mifsud
1960	W. Asciak	1977	P. Mifsud
1961	A. Borg	1978	J. Grech
1962	J. Bartolo	1979	P. Mifsud
1963	J. Bartolo	1980	J. Grech

SNOOKER CHAMPIONSHIP

Year	Champion	Year	Champion
1947	L. Galea	1964	A. Borg
1948	T. B. Oliver	1965	A. Borg
1949	L. Galea	1966	A. Borg
1950	W. Asciak	1967	A. Borg
1951	W. Asciak	1968	P. Mifsud
1952	A. Borg	1969	P. Mifsud
1953	A. Borg	1970	P. Mifsud
1954	W. Asciak	1971	P. Mifsud
1955	A. Borg	1972	P. Mifsud
1956	W. Asciak	1973	A. Borg
1957	W. Asciak	1974	A. Borg
1958	W. Asciak	1975	P. Mifsud
1959	A. Borg	1976	P. Mifsud
1960	A. Borg	1977	A. Borg
1961	A. Borg	1978	P. Mifsud
1962	A. Borg	1979	P. Mifsud
1963	M. Tonna	1980	J. Grech

Paul Mifsud

NEW ZEALAND

Although the New Zealand Amateur Billiards Championship has taken place, except for 1909, annually since 1908, the New Zealand Billiards and Snooker Association was formed only in 1935 when competitors and delegates from four provinces, Auckland, Wellington, Canterbury and Otago, met at the Commercial Travellers Club, Auckland. There are now 16 associations affiliated to the parent national body and the New Zealand Amateur Snooker Championship has taken place annually since 1945.

Far and away the outstanding cueist New Zealand has produced is Clark McConachy MBE, whose career is fully detailed on p. 44. Two other professionals, Norman Squire and Murt O'Donoghue, who spent most of their careers in Australia, were also New Zealand born.

In the amateur game New Zealand was first represented internationally by Billy Hackett, who was over 60 when he won his one and only New Zealand billiards title in 1930 before competing in the Empire Championship the following year. Arthur Albertson, who won the title four times between 1933 and 1961, and Sam Moses, who won four billiards titles between 1936 and 1944 and the inaugural snooker title in 1945, were New Zealand's representatives in 1938 in Melbourne but not until Bill Harcourt was sent to Perth in 1962 was New Zealand again represented.

This interim period nevertheless produced New Zealand's best amateur thus far, Rupert Carrick, who won seven titles between 1939 and 1950. Five of these wins were in a six year period from 1946 to 1951. In 1947, Carrick fell to a veteran 'Pod' Smith, whose break of 180 was then a New Zealand record, and the title went to Charlie Peek.

Carrick turned to contract bridge so what could have been a great rivalry with Alan Twohill never developed. As it was, Twohill won five titles in succession from 1953 to 1957 and nine in all. His break of 204 in 1956 was the first double century in the New Zealand Championship. A year later, he made a break of 222 but it was not until 1966 that he improved the record to 238 unfinished, a timely effort as he was then trailing Herbie Robinson, who has himself won four titles, by 60 points with 20 minutes to play. His two hour session aggregate of 933 earlier in this competition remains a New Zealand record.

Twohill's break record was eclipsed by Robinson with 280 in 1970 but no New Zealander has yet made much headway in the World Amateur Championship even if Brian Kirkness, three times national champion, has at times threatened to do so.

With a good grasp of top of the table technique and an insatiable appetite for practice, Kirkness extended the national championship break record to 301 in 1978 and had a run of 326 in another competition. He

\begin{array}{l}\text{NEW ZEALAND}\\\text{BILLIARDS CHAMPIONSHIP}\end{array}			
1908	J. Ryan	1944	S. Moses
1909	No contest	1945	J. Shepherd
1910	F. Lovelock	1946	R. Carrick
1911	F. Lovelock	1947	C. Peek
1912	H. Valentine	1948	R. Carrick
1913	H. Valentine	1949	R. Carrick
1914	N. Lynch	1950	R. Carrick
1915	W. E. Warren	1951	R. Carrick
1916	H. Siedeberg	1952	L. Stout
1917	H. Siedeberg	1953	A. Twohill
1918	W. E. Warren	1954	A. Twohill
1918	W. E. Warren	1955	A. Twohill
1919	H. Siedeberg	1956	A. Twohill
1920	W. E. Warren	1957	A. Twohill
1921	H. Siedeberg	1958	A. Albertson
1922	E. V. Roberts	1959	A. Twohill
1923	E. V. Roberts	1960	W. Harcourt
1924	R. Fredotovich	1961	A. Albertson
1925	C. Mason	1962	W. Harcourt
1926	E. V. Roberts	1963	H. C. Robinson
1927	E. V. Roberts	1964	T. Yesberg
1928	A. Bowie	1965	L. Napper
1929	L. Stout	1966	A. Twohill
1930	W. E. Hackett	1967	A. Twohill
1931	A. Duncan	1968	A. Twohill
1932	C. Mason	1969	E. Simmons
1933	A. Albertson	1970	L. Napper
1934	H. McLean	1971	W. Harcourt
1935	L. Holdsworth	1972	B. Kirkness
1936	S. Moses	1973	H. C. Robinson
1937	S. Moses	1974	H. C. Robinson
1938	L. Holdsworth	1975	T. Yesberg
1939	R. Carrick	1976	H. C. Robinson
1940	S. Moses	1977	B. Kirkness
1941	R. Carrick	1978	B. Kirkness
1942	R. Carrick	1979	R. Adams
1943	A. Albertson	1980	D. Meredith
SNOOKER CHAMPIONSHIP			
1945	S. Moses	1963	W. Harcourt
1946	J. Munro	1964	T. Yesberg
1947	W. Thompson	1965	L. Napper
1948	L. Stout	1966	L. Napper
1949	L. Stout	1967	R. Flutey
1950	L. Stout	1968	L. Napper
1951	N. Lewis	1969	L. Glozier
1952	L. Stout	1970	K. Tristram
1953	L. Stout	1971	B. J. Bennett
1954	R. Franks	1972	N. Stockman
1955	L. Stout	1973	W. Hill
1956	L. Stout	1974	K. Tristram
1957	W. Harcourt	1975	K. Tristram
1958	W. Harcourt	1976	D. Kwok
1959	W. Thomas	1977	D. Meredith
1960	T. Yesberg	1978	D. Meredith
1961	F. Franks	1979	D. Meredith
1962	K. Murphy	1980	D. O'Kane

also made a break of 304 in the unofficial world open in Christchurch in 1977 in which wins over Michael Ferreira and John Barrie helped him finish sixth in a high quality 12 man round robin.

In the subsidiary snooker event, Kirkness made a break of 128 which remained the official world amateur record for almost a year but New Zealand snooker standards, in international terms, generally remained modest until the late seventies produced two young champions, Dale Kwok (1976) and Dave Meredith (1977, 1978, 1979), capable of considerable further improvement if exposed regularly to top class international competition. The first New Zealand champion of the eighties was their youngest ever, Dene O'Kane, a 17-year-old of professional potential.

A break of 85 in 1957 by Harcourt remained New Zealand's championship record until it was equalled by Meredith in 1976 and superseded by Grant Hayward with 103 in 1978.

One curiosity of the 1976 New Zealand billiards final was that it is the only national final on record in which a father, Herbie Robinson, defeated his son, Russell Robinson.

Two administrators, Frank Holz and Brien Bennett, have made outstanding contributions not only to their domestic organisation but the international game.

Holz, who received the MBE for services to charity – to which virtually all his promotional enterprises were directed – in 1977, brought the 1964 World Amateur Billiards Championship to Pukekohe, a small South Auckland country town, and made it a resounding success.

He organised two unofficial World Open Billiards Championships in Pukekohe in 1972 and Christchurch in 1977 and his organisational abilities were so highly rated that he was brought in to organise the 1970 World Professional Snooker Championship in Australia. Other ventures included the match between McConachy and Rex Williams for the World Professional Billiards Championship in Auckland in 1968, the first time the event had been contested for 17 years, and extensive exhibition tours, too numerous to mention, by leading professionals. Less spectacularly but no less valuably Holz worked indefatiguably in the areas of coaching and refereeing.

Bennett, a useful player who won the New Zealand snooker title in 1971, maintained as president of the New Zealand Association the high standard of domestic administration he inherited from Holz and made a major contribution at international level in the difficult early years of the International Billiards and Snooker Federation, of which he was elected chairman in 1980.

SOUTH AFRICA

The South African Billiards and Snooker Association, founded in 1915, has organised a national amateur billiards championship since 1920 and a snooker championship since 1937.

In 1920, Arthur Walker, a millionaire South African, proposed an Empire championship which the BA & CC in London rejected as impracticable. However, it was approved in principle in 1922 and was held for the first time in 1926 at Thurston's with Walker's trophy, still in circulation for the World Amateur Championship, at stake.

Percy Rutledge, later a professional, won only one of his four matches but Allan Prior, a 6 ft 5 in policeman won the 1927 event, also at Thurston's, beating both Horace Coles (Wales) and Laurie Steeples (Eng-

Mannie Francisco

land).

This gave South Africa the right under the championship conditions then pertaining, to stage the event. They did so at the Carlton Hotel, Johannesburg in 1929 when Prior, despite setting a South African record break of 226, was beaten into second place by an Australian, Les Hayes.

Prior, who won seven South African titles at billiards and two at snooker, was third in London in 1933 and second to the great Australian Bob Marshall in Johannesburg in 1936. Prior, indeed, held Marshall until half an hour from time.

An expatriate Welshman, Glyn Rees won four billiards and three snooker titles between 1949 and 1953 and Gerry Povall, though he won only one billiards title, set a world amateur snooker break record of 106 in the 1956 South African Championship in which event the previous record had been 72 by Jimmy van Rensburg in 1952. Ken O'Kennedy made a break of 122 on a standard table in a non-championship match in 1955.

The year after Mannie Francisco won the first of his twelve South African billiards titles, and the first of his six snooker titles, this talented all rounder finished fourth of eight competitors in the 1960 World Amateur Billiards Championship in Edinburgh.

In 1964 World Amateur Billiards in Pukekohe, making liberal use of the infamous 15 pot rule, Francisco set a new South African amateur record of 518 in finishing fourth again; in 1965, he set a South African championship record of 433 which still stands; and in 1967 in Colombo he led Leslie Driffield by 500 with an hour to play before the Englishman recovered to win by 162 and go on to take his second world amateur billiards title. Francisco, who also lost to Mohammed Lafir (Sri Lanka), was third.

In 1969, in London, Francisco was again well in the running. When he played the Englishman, Jack Karnehm, both players had one defeat. Francisco led by

Jimmy van Rensburg

152 with 17 minutes remaining but the fatal inhibitions which seemed to assail him throughout his career on the brink of important victories proved his undoing once more. He missed an in-off at the top of the table and Karnehm played out time to win by 9.

Though well beaten by England's Norman Dagley in the concluding four man round robin, Francisco followed his joint second place in London in 1969 with an outright second place in Malta in 1971.

He did not thereafter compete in a World Amateur Billiards Championship. As it gathered strength, the anti-apartheid movement increasingly limited South African involvement in international sport though the country was represented in the World Amateur Snooker Championships of 1972, their first participation, and 1976 when they hosted the event lavishly in the President Hotel, Johannesburg.

In Cardiff, in 1972, Francisco demonstrated his determination when faced with defeat, when, after a series of nerve wracking group matches, he trailed the Indian Arvind Savur 0-4 in the semi-final before winning on the final black 8-7. He led Ray Edmonds (England) 6-0 and 7-2 in the final only to lose 11-10, a tribute to the Englishman's fighting qualities but also clinching evidence of Francisco's fatally flawed temperament.

Francisco won his group in the 1976 World Amateur but suffered his first competitive defeat to his younger brother Silvino in the quarter-finals. Silvino, with three South African snooker titles and three billiards, and Jimmy van Rensburg, a world amateur semi-finalist in 1976 who also won 11 South African snooker and one billiards title, were the other outstanding postwar South African amateurs.

Victims of their government's unrelenting apartheid policies in that reaction to them caused their isolation from international amateur competition, the two Franciscos, van Rensburg, Derek Mienie and Roy Amdor all turned professional in 1978 though probably too late in their careers to make much impact on the professional game.

Far and away South Africa's most successful professional has been Perrie Mans, only 20 when he won his national amateur title at his first and only attempt in 1960 and his country's first ever world professional finalist in 1978.

His father, Peter Mans, South Africa's first professional snooker champion, competed with fair success in the *News of the World* tournament in London in 1949-50, in which season he also reached the quarter-final of the World Professional Championship. Mans, who won his national professional title from Freddie van Rensburg, relinquished it in van Rensburg's favour in 1950. In turn, van Rensburg held the title until defeated 13-11 by Perrie Mans in 1965. Mans retained the title until sensationally defeated by

Mienie in 1979 but regained it the following year.

Van Rensburg, who has also held the South African professional billiards title unchallenged since 1956, was a player of little cue-power but considerable touch. He gave Fred Davis his closest match, 5-4, in the 'World' Open in Australia in 1960 but was past his best when, on the challenge system then in operation, he lost a week's match 39-12 to John Pulman for the world professional title in 1965.

This match followed a 47 match series which Pulman and Rex Williams played for the world professional title throughout South Africa, the first time the event had been held abroad. It was during this series that Williams set a world championship record of 142, superseding his own 141 against Fred Davis at Birmingham in 1966. After the series Williams made a 147 maximum against Mannie Francisco which was recognised as a joint world record.

Professional tours to South Africa have been common since the days of John Roberts, Billy Matchell, H. W. Stevenson and Cecil Harverson, who settled in South Africa and whose son, Ronny, became a professional there. Frank Ferraro, who played with a 12 oz cue, was for some years in the inter-war period recog-

nised as South African professional champion. Walter Lindrum, Joe Davis and Horace Lindrum each made several tours, as have Ray Reardon and Rex Williams in modern times.

It was Sid Gillett, a director of Thurston's, London, until he settled in South Africa as managing director of Thurston's (South Africa), who in 1952 asked the BA & CC to consider a world amateur snooker championship. The request was deferred but it at least started this particular ball rolling. Another trade personality, Ken Shaw of Union Billiards, has been South Africa's most persistent promoter.

When South Africa was barred from competing in the first two world amateur snooker championships in Calcutta in 1963 and Karachi in 1966 and anxious not to be left behind, the South African Association invited Ray Reardon and Jonathan Barron (representing England), for a Test Series against Mannie Francisco and Jimmy van Rensburg, representing South Africa.

In the course of the series, won 2-1 by England, Shaw offered to organise a South African tour for Reardon should he decide to turn professional. It was this tour which enabled Reardon's professional career

George Chenier (*left*) and Peter Mans, past professional champions of Canada and South Africa respectively.

SOUTH AFRICA BILLIARDS CHAMPIONSHIP

Year	Winner	Year	Winner
1920	Sgt. Bruyns	1956	G. Povall
1921	A. Prior	1957	F. Walker
1922	A. Prior	1958	F. Walker
1923	No contest	1959	M. Francisco
1924	A. Prior	1960	R. Walker
1925	P. Rutledge	1961	M. Francisco
1926	A. Prior	1962	M. Francisco
1927	A. Percival	1963	M. Francisco
1928	P. Rutledge	1964	M. Francisco
1929-30	No contests	1965	M. Francisco
1931	A. Prior	1966	M. Francisco
1932-36	No contests	1967	J. van Rensburg
1937	A. M. Burke	1968	M. Francisco
1938	A. Prior	1969	M. Francisco
1939	A. Prior	1970	M. Francisco
1940-45	No contests	1971	M. Francisco
1946	P. G. Kempen	1972	S. Francisco
1947	No contest	1973	S. Francisco
1948	P. G. Kempen	1974	M. Francisco
1949	T. G. Rees	1975	S. Francisco
1950	T. G. Rees	1976	No contest
1951	I. Drapin	1977	M. Francisco
1952	T. G. Rees	1978	C. van Dijk
1953	T. G. Rees	1979	C. van Dijk
1954	F. Walker	1980	C. van Dijk
1955	F. Walker		

SNOOKER CHAMPIONSHIP

Year	Winner	Year	Winner
1937	A. Prior	1962	J. van Rensburg
1938	A. H. Ashby	1963	J. van Rensburg
1939	A. Prior	1964	M. Francisco
1940-45	No contests	1965	M. Francisco
1946	F. Walker	1966	M. Francisco
1947	No contest	1967	J. van Rensburg
1948	F. Walker	1968	S. Francisco
1949	E. Kerr	1969	S. Francisco
1950	T. G. Rees	1970	J. van Rensburg
1951	T. G. Rees	1971	M. Francisco
1952	T. G. Rees	1972	J. van Rensburg
1953	J. van Rensburg	1973	J. van Rensburg
1954	J. van Rensburg	1974	S. Francisco
1955	J. van Rensburg	1975	M. Francisco
1956	F. Walker	1976	No contest
1957	J. van Rensburg	1977	S. Francisco
1958	R. Walker	1978	J. van Niekerk
1959	M. Francisco	1979	F. Ellis
1960	P. Mans Jnr	1980	F. Ellis
1961	J. van Rensburg		

On the professional front, its players have been free to compete as individuals and a number of professional tournaments have been organised with an international flavour within South Africa.

SRI LANKA

The Billiards Association and Control Council of Ceylon, the precursor of the Sri Lanka Billiards and Snooker Association was founded only in 1948 though the games of billiards and snooker had been popular in the clubs of the island for many years. Its small population, isolated situation and for the most part poor playing conditions are all against producing large numbers of high quality players.

It was thus all the more remarkable that Mohammed Lafir, who learnt to play on an improvised table in which a sarong acted as the cloth and a bicycle tyre for the cushions, should become his country's first ever sporting world champion when he captured the World Amateur Billiards Championship in Bombay in 1973.

Having soon outclassed all his domestic rivals, both at billiards and snooker, Lafir developed his game by competing in the Indian and World Amateur Championships and learning from the players he encoun-

to get under way in December 1967. In 1974, Reardon made a four month tour in which he made no less than 65 snooker centuries in public. Two English amateur champions, Ray Edmonds and Chris Ross, made tours and in 1975 Edmonds and the Welshman Alwyn Lloyd constituted the British amateur team which won one and drew two of three Tests in which South Africa was variously represented by the Francisco brothers and van Rensburg.

South Africa's unprecedented offer to pay air fares for one competitor and one delegate from each affiliated country to the 1976 World Amateur Snooker Championships in Johannesburg enabled some of the more impoverished national associations to be represented and others who would have been refused a grant by their governments to be represented at no cost to themselves. The championship was conspicuously well staged but international governments were not impressed. South Africa has not since been allowed to participate in international amateur competition.

tered. In 1967, he was runner-up in the World Amateur Billiards Championship when it was staged before his own countrymen at the Samudra Hotel, Colombo; in 1973, after setting a new national championship break record of 500 unfinished, he won the title at the Cricket Club of India, Bombay in the course of which he set a new world amateur break record of 859.

His new status as an authentic national hero created a burden of expectation which he was nervous of being unable to fulfil. He did not compete either in 1975 or 1977 and, though he reached the semi-finals, looked only a shadow of his Bombay self in the World Amateur Billiards of 1979 in Colombo, when he was clearly unhappy with the factional splits in his own national association.

He rarely played to his full potential out of the tropics and his snooker was not quite of the standard of his billiards but he nevertheless reached the quarter-finals of the 1974 World Amateur Snooker in Dublin and also did well in Sydney in 1968, Edinburgh in 1970 and Malta in 1978. He died in 1981 at the age of 53.

SRI LANKA
BILLIARDS CHAMPIONSHIP

Year	Winner	Year	Winner
1948	A. C. Cambal	1963	M. H. M. Mujahid
1949	M. J. M. Lafir	1964	M. J. M. Lafir
1950	M. J. M. Lafir	1965	n.r.
1951	M. J. M. Lafir	1966	M. J. M. Lafir
1952	M. J. M. Lafir	1967	J. K. Bakshani
1953	M. J. M. Lafir	1968	n.r.
1954	A. C. Cambal	1969	M. J. M. Lafir
1955	T. A. Selvaraj	1970	M. J. M. Lafir
1956	T. A. Selvaraj	1971	n.r.
1957	M. J. M. Lafir	1972	M. J. M. Lafir
1958	n.r.	1973	M. J. M. Lafir
1959	M. J. M. Lafir	1974	S. Shaharwardi
1960	M. J. M. Lafir	1975	M. S. U. Mohideen
1961	M. J. M. Lafir	1976	W. Weerasinghe
1962	M. J. M. Lafir	1977-80	Results not known

SNOOKER CHAMPIONSHIP

Year	Winner	Year	Winner
1948	M. J. M. Lafir	1963	M. J. M. Izzath
1949	M. M. Faiz	1964	M. J. M. Lafir
1950	M. J. M. Lafir	1965	M. J. M. Lafir
1951	M. S. A. Hassan	1966	M. J. M. Lafir
1952	M. J. M. Lafir	1967	N. J. Rahim
1953	M. J. M. Lafir	1968	No contest
1954	M. J. M. Lafir	1969	M. J. M. Lafir
1955	M. J. M. Lafir	1970	N. J. Rahim
1956	M. J. M. Lafir	1971	No contest
1957	M. J. M. Lafir	1972	N. J. Rahim
1958	M. J. M. Lafir	1973	M. J. M. Lafir
1959	M. J. M. Lafir	1974	Abandoned
1960	M. J. M. Lafir	1975	N. A. Rahim
1961	M. J. M. Lafir	1976	M. S. U. Mohideen
1962	M. J. M. Lafir	1977-80	Results not known

Mohammed Lafir

WORLD AMATEUR CHAMPIONSHIPS

In September 1922 the BA & CC approved in principle a British Empire championship though it was not until 1926 that the first event took place at Thurston's, London. Arthur Walker, a South African millionaire, whose conception the event had been, presented the trophy which is still in circulation although the title of the event was changed to World Amateur Billiards Championship in 1951.

Sid Gillett, a director of Thurston's until he settled in South Africa as managing director of Thurston's (South Africa), asked the BA & CC in 1952 to consider a World Amateur snooker championship and Australia made a similar request shortly afterwards only to have it 'deferred until some improvement in

WORLD AMATEUR BILLIARDS CHAMPIONSHIPS

	Won	Pts.	Av.	Highest break	No. of centuries
1926: *London*					
J. Earlham (Eng)	4	8 000	25·6	282	18
G. Shailer (Aust)	3	7 394	16·8	203	13
M. Smith (Sco)	2	6 569	12·7	130	4
P. Rutledge (S A)	1	5 902	12·5	142	2
T. McCluney (N Ire)	0	5 617	11·9	144	4
1927: *London*					
A. Prior (S A)	3	6 000	16·6	184	9
H. F. Coles (Wal)	2	5 533	12·2	164	2
L. Steeples (Eng)	1	5 506	14·8	236	9
M. Smith (Sco)	0	4 499	12·6	158	1
1929: *Johannesburg*					
L. Hayes (Aust)	3	6 000	15·5	136	6
A. Prior (S A)	2	5 512	16·0	226	7
H. F. Coles (Eng)	1	5 592	14·7	170	7
P. Rutledge (S A)	0	2 882	10·9	164	1
1931: *Sydney*					
L. Steeples (Eng)	4	8 000	37·3	461	24
S. Lee (Eng)	3	7 126	22·1	433	18
L. Hayes (Aust)	2	6 113	15·3	167	6
H. Goldsmith (Aust)	1	4 995	13·0	179	4
W. Hackett (N Z)	0	3 549	7·7	97	0
1933: *London*					
S. Lee (Eng)	4	12 402	28·0	394	31
T. Jones (Wal)	3	9 883	18·7	144	8
A. Prior (S A)	2	9 113	18·3	235	13
M. Smith (Sco)	1	8 292	17·5	166	5
J. Blackburn (N Ire)	0	6 362	12·5	94	0
1935: *London*					
H. F. Coles (Eng)	4	13 665	28·4	267	33
J. McGhie (Sco)	3	9 359	19·4	207	11
I. Edwards (Wal)	2	9 814	18·1	196	11
S. Fenning (Irish Free State)	1	9 068	17·4	161	6
P. Deb (Ind)	0	7 461	13·1	123	5
1936: *Johannesburg*					
R. Marshall (Aust)	3	8 526	22·0	248	24
A. Prior (S A)	2	7 014	17·7	197	11
J. Thompson (Eng)	1	7 705	21·2	245	15
A. Bowlly (S A)	0	4 548	9·0	93	0
Three 2½ hour sessions					
1938: *Melbourne*					
R. Marshall (Aust)	6	17 626	39·0	427	59
K. Kennerley (Eng)	5	14 528	30·1	472	45
T. Cleary (Aust)	4	8 535	19·7	322	17
S. Moses (N Z)	2	6 727	13·1	129	4
M. M. Begg (Ind)	2	6 685	13·4	111	2
A. Burke (S A)	1	5 993	12·0	119	1
A. Albertson (N Z)	1	5 805	12·4	107	1
1951: *London*					
R. Marshall (Aust)	6	14 735	38·1	423	42
F. Edwards (Eng)	5	13 459	26·7	345	36
T. Cleary (Aust)	4	12 373	25·5	330	31
W. Ramage (Sco)	3	7 638	19·1	151	8
W. Pierce (Wal)	2	6 029	13·6	225	3
W. Jones (Ind)	1	7 202	16·6	138	10
E. Haslem (N Ire)	0	5 896	14·1	125	3

the BA & CC's finances takes place'. In 1958, the BA & CC announced its intention of inaugurating the event in London the following year but both India and Australia felt that London should not be the venue and persuaded two other countries likewise, so the event fell through until M. M. Begg, chairman of the BA & CC of India, donated a cup and concluded arrangements for the inaugural tournament in Calcutta in 1963 to which the BA & CC and other interested nations agreed.

The championships are held biennially with the billiards taking place in the odd years and snooker the even. A rota of venues is agreed several years in advance by the International Billiards & Snooker Federation. Each affiliated country is allowed to nominate two players for each event.

	Won	Pts.	Av.	Highest break	No. of centuries
1952: *Calcutta*					
L. Driffield (Eng)	5	8 529	34·5	278	31
R. Marshall (Aust)	3	9 237	37·3	351	27
C. Hirjee (Ind)	3	7 701	22·7	230	14
W. Ramage (Sco)	3	6 525	20·8	211	10
W. Jones (Ind)	1	6 731	23·3	253	6
A Yunoos (Burma)	0	3 768	11·0	79	0
1954: *Sydney*					
T. Cleary (Aust)	4	11 496	33·5	682	35
R. Marshall (Aust)	3	11 488	36·0	407	35
F. Edwards (Eng)	2	9 053	24·7	328	26
W. Jones (Ind)	1	8 523	20·5	209	17
T. G. Rees (S A)	0	6 271	16·9	207	6
1958: *Calcutta*					
W. Jones (Ind)	5	16 493		501	56
L. Driffield (Eng)	4	14 370		499	48
T. Cleary (Aust)	3	13 626		431	52
C. Hirjee (Ind)	2	12 853		226	38
W. Asciak (Malta)	1	6 329		154	7
M. Hman (Burma)	0	5 633		215	8
1960: *Edinburgh*					
J. H. Beetham (Eng)	7	9 351		277	29
J. Long (Aust)	6	10 634		353	26
W. Jones (Ind)	5	12 397		589	30
M. Francisco (S A)	4	7 773		148	11
W. Ramage (Sco)	3	7 938		283	12
W. Asciak (Malta)	2	8 408		194	11
W. Dennison (N Ire)	1	6 231		155	4
A. Ramage (Sco)	0	5 706		101	2
1962: *Perth*					
R. Marshall (Aust)	5	12 367	35·6	348	57
W. Jones (Ind)	5	10 805	26·9	489	34
T. Cleary (Aust)	4	9 808	27·0	315	27
J. H. Beetham (Eng)	3	7 626	22·9	283	18
S. Benajee (Ind)	3	8 332	17·2	219	9
R. A. Karim (Pak)	1	5 657	11·9	130	3
W. Harcourt (N Z)	0	5 623	14·3	123	5
Play-off: Marshall beat Jones 3623-2891					
1964: *Pukekohe*					
W. Jones (Ind)	9	16 628	24·5	294	49
J. Karnehm (Eng)	8	12 953	21·8	390	28
M. Ferreira (Ind)	7	13 345	19·0	182	29
M. Francisco (S A)	6	12 957	22·0	518	38
A. Nolan (Eng)	5	12 126	19·9	259	26
T. Cleary (Aust)	4	10 781	13·9	241	19
H. Robinson (N Z)	3	7 643	10·5	85	0
T. Yesberg (N Z)	2	7 528	10·4	80	0
M. Mavalwala (Pak)	1	8 404	11·3	174	1
A. E. Redmond (S A)	0	6 914	9·0	107	1
1967: *Colombo*					
L. Driffield (Eng)	8	13 556	30·5	421	53
M. J. M. Lafir (Sri Lanka)	7	12 562	18·4	218	31
M. Francisco (S A)	6	12 477	20·4	301	32
M. Ferreira (Ind)	5	11 140	19·5	507	22
J. Long (Aust)	4	11 068	17·5	261	27
T. Cleary (Aust)	3	9 252	11·6	322	15
N. J. Rahim (Ceylon)	2	6 895	8·8	116	3
M. S. M. Marzuq (Ceylon)	1	7 153	7·9	88	0
F. Holz (N Z)	0	5 350	7·1	68	0

	Won	Pts.	Av.	Highest break	No. of centuries
1969: *London*					
J. Karnehm (Eng)	9	12 902		232	27
M. Ferreira (Ind)	7	14 115		629	34
M. Francisco (S A)	7	13 760		335	35
M. J. M. Lafir (Ceylon)	7	12 934		296	28
R. Marshall (Aust)	6	13 033		216	33
M. Wildman (Eng)	6	11 739		274	22
R. Oriel (Wal)	5	13 306		297	30
S. Mohan (Ind)	5	13 407		219	24
P. Mifsud (Malta)	2	10 410		173	8
A. Twohill (N Z)	1	10 016		146	12
F. Holz (N Z)	0	6 061		65	0
1971: *Malta*					
Group A					
M. Francisco (S A)	4	6 450		321	15
M. J. M. Lafir (Sri Lanka)	3	4 757		233	4
P. Mifsud (Malta)	2	4 142		134	2
D. Sneddon (Sco)	1	3 160		121	2
L. Napper (N Z)	0	3 798		87	0
Group B					
S. Mohan (Ind)	4	5 839		188	11
N. Dagley (Eng)	3	5 454		330	11
M. Ferreira (Ind)	2	4 423		227	4
C. Everton (Wal)	1	3 893		205	5
W. Asciak (Malta)	0	4 511		188	7
Play-offs:					
Dagley	3	6 041		348	17
Francisco	2	3 981		353	11
Mohan	1	3 822		327	11
Lafir	0	2 514		211	5
1973: *Bombay*					
M. J. M. Lafir (Sri Lanka)	9	16 956	34·1	859	43
S. Mohan (Ind)	7	17 016	30·8	468	53
M. Ferreira (Ind)	7	15 639	25·4	421	41
P. Tarrant (Aust)	6	13 200	24·4	373	36
C. Everton (Wal)	5	9 921	18·2	240	17
A. Nolan (Eng)	4	12 709	20·8	265	31
P. Mifsud (Malta)	4	12 253	18·8	203	23
E. Simons (N Z)	2	8 521	12·4	94	0
B. Kirkness (N Z)	1	8 464	13·5	195	7
L. U. Demarco (Sco)	0	7 488	10·4	87	0
1975: *Auckland*					
Group A					
N. Dagley (Eng)	5	9 257		477	24
D. Sneddon (Sco)	4	6 272		124	4
G. Parikh (Ind)	3	6 471		197	16
J. Reece (Aust)	2	4 058		125	4
H. Robinson (N Z)	1	4 529		123	2
M. Shaharwardi (Sri Lanka)	0	4 032		121	1

Right: **Alex Higgins**

Above: Fred Davis

Left: Bill Werbeniuk

Below: Ray Reardon

	Won	Pts.	Av.	Highest break	No. of centuries
Group B					
M. Ferreira (Ind)	5	9 022		411	26
C. Everton (Wal)	4	6 043		272	13
R. Close (Eng)	3	5 449		164	10
T. Yesberg (N Z)	2	4 373		131	3
J. Long (Aust)	1	4 598		157	5
B. Bennett (N Z)	0	3 684		95	0

Play-offs
Semi-finals: Dagley beat Everton 1293-755; Ferreira beat Sneddon 2470-681
Final: Dagley beat Ferreira 3385-2268

1977: *Melbourne*

Group A	Won	Pts.	Av.	Highest break	No. of centuries
N. Dagley (Eng)	5	7 546		272	16
C. Everton (Wal)	4	4 962		170	7
S. Aleem (Ind)	3	7 028		263	11
G. Ganim Snr (Aust)	2	6 322		231	6
H. Robinson (N Z)	1	4 133		93	0
J. Nugent (Sco)	0	4 131		68	0

Group B					
M. Ferreira (Ind)	5	12 554		519	33
R. Close (Eng)	4	7 252		207	15
G. Ganim Jnr (Aust)	3	6 424		192	9
T. Yesberg (N Z)	2	4 349		109	1
W. Weerasinghe (Sri Lanka)	1	4 364		97	0
D. Pratt (Sco)	0	4 316		108	1

Play-offs
Semi-finals: Ferreira beat Everton 2155-1310; Close beat Dagley 1912-1781
Final: Ferreira beat Close 2683-2564

1979: *Colombo*

Group A	Won	Pts.	Av.	Highest break	No. of centuries
M. Ferreira (Ind)	7	14 695		467	40
M. J. M. Lafir (Sri Lanka)	5	12 456		370	30
K. Shirley (Eng)	5	10 656		195	13
W. Barrie (Aust)	4	8 255		128	2
B. Kirkness (N Z)	4	7 283		214	8
H. Nimmo (Sco)	2	7 022		105	2
M. S. U. Mohideen (Sri Lanka)	1	6 408		76	0
R. Lim Sin Foo (Singapore)	0	6 433		97	0

Group B					
N. Dagley (Eng)	6	12 539		466	39
P. Mifsud (Malta)	6	12 193		325	31
S. Agrawal (Ind)	6	11 924		355	30
G. Ganim Jnr (Aust)	3	8 486		267	15
C. Everton (Wal)	3	6 905		211	11
W. A. J. Weerasinghe (Sri Lanka)	3	7 883		202	7
B. Bennett (N Z)	1	6 083		101	1
E. Fisher (Can)	0	4 198		88	0

Play-offs
Semi-finals: Mifsud beat Ferreira 2489-1856; Dagley beat Lafir 2694-1692
Final: Mifsud beat Dagley 2943-2152

WORLD AMATEUR SNOOKER CHAMPIONSHIPS

	Wins	For	Agnst	Highest break
1963: *Calcutta*				
G. Owen (Eng)	4	23	7	71
F. Harris (Aust)	3	21	17	52
M. J. M. Lafir (Ceylon)	2	19	18	67
T. Monteiro (Ind)	1	14	19	56
W. Jones (Ind)	0	7	24	36
1966: *Karachi*				
G. Owen (Eng)	5	30	7	118
J. Spencer (Eng)	4	26	14	101
W. Barrie (Aust)	3	23	22	73
M. J. M. Lafir (Ceylon)	2	22	20	45
L. U. Demarco (Sco)	1	14	28	36
H. Karim (Pak)	0	6	30	60
1968: *Sydney*				
Group A				
D. Taylor (Eng)	4	24	13	96
J. van Rensburg (S A)	3	22	14	
H. Andrews (Aust)	2	17	16	
T. Monteiro (Ind)	1	17	22	
L. Napper (N Z)	0	9	24	
Group B				
M. Williams (Aust)	3	22	14	
P. Morgan (Ire)	3	19	14	88
M. J. M. Lafir (Ceylon)	2	19	16	
S. Shroff (Ind)	2	20	19	
R. Flutey (N Z)	0	7	24	

Play-offs
Semi-finals: Williams beat van Rensburg 8-7; Taylor beat Morgan 8-3
Final: Taylor beat Williams 8-7

	Wins	For	Agnst	Highest break
1970: *Edinburgh*				
Group A				
S. Hood (Eng)	5	20	9	50
P. Mifsud (Malta)	4	22	11	61
M. J. M. Lafir (Sri Lanka)	4	20	16	50
J. Phillips (Sco)	4	19	18	62
D. Sneddon (Sco)	2	17	17	38
L. Glozier (N Z)	2	10	21	34
J. Clint (N Ire)	0	8	24	46
Group B				
J. Barron (Eng)	5	21	13	51
D. May (Wal)	4	22	18	64
S. Shroff (Ind)	3	18	14	47
E. Sinclair (Sco)	3	16	16	49
J. Rogers (Ire)	3	16	19	65
L. U. Demarco (Sco)	2	15	19	32
H. Andrews (Aust)	1	13	22	35

Final: Barron beat Hood 11-7

	Wins	For	Agnst	Highest break
1972: *Cardiff*				
Group A				
J. van Rensburg (S A)	3	12	6	45
K. Tristram (N Z)	1	8	8	50
G. Thomas (Wal)	1	6	8	32
L. U. Demarco (Sco)	1	6	10	41
Group B				
M. Francisco (S A)	3	15	5	47
J. Barron (Eng)	3	15	10	50
A. Borg (Malta)	2	12	11	59
A. Lloyd (Wal)	2	11	14	41
T. Monteiro (Ind)	0	3	16	46

	Wins	For	Agnst	Highest break
Group C				
P. Mifsud (Malta)	4	16	5	61
R. Edmonds (Eng)	3	14	7	101
J. Rogers (Ire)	2	8	8	36
M. Berni (Wal)	1	7	12	47
B. Bennett (N Z)	0	3	16	30
Group D				
A. Savur (Ind)	2	10	6	38
M. Williams (Aust)	2	9	7	48
D. Sneddon (Sco)	2	9	9	34
D. May (Wal)	0	6	12	42
Semi-final groups				
Group A				
Barron	3	12	4	35
Savur	2	10	8	68
Tristram	1	6	8	29
Mifsud	0	6	12	50
Group B				
Francisco	2	11	9	70
Edmonds	2	11	9	39
Van Rensburg	1	8	10	51
Williams	1	9	11	78

Semi-finals: Edmonds beat Barron 8-6; Francisco beat Savur 8-7 (51, 72)
Final: Edmonds beat Francisco 11(40)-10

1974: *Dublin*				
Group A				
R. Edmonds (Eng)	7	31	11	66
M. J. M. Lafir (Sri Lanka)	6	30	19	77
E. Sinclair (Sco)	6	28	21	67
G. Thomas (Wal)	4	24	22	43
D. Sheehan (Ire)	4	25	24	43
P. Donnelly (N Ire)	3	21	28	42
S. Shroff (Ind)	3	16	26	44
N. Stockman (N Z)	2	18	29	51
J. Sklazeski (Can)	1	18	31	79
Group B				
A. Lloyd (Wal)	8	32	14	104
W. Hill (N Z)	5	26	21	58
P. Burke (Ire)	4	26	20	71
L. Condo (Aust)	4	26	21	53
A. Borg (Malta)	4	27	23	37
D. Sneddon (Sco)	4	23	21	54
A. Savur (Ind)	4	24	23	50
R. Cowley (Isle of Man)	3	16	27	50
N. J. Rahim (Sri Lanka)	0	2	32	25

Quarter-finals: Edmonds beat Condo 4(60)-3; Sinclair beat Hill 4-2; Burke beat Lafir 4-3; Thomas beat Lloyd 4-2
Semi-finals: Edmonds beat Sinclair 8(54)-4(79); Thomas beat Burke 8-2
Final: Edmonds beat Thomas 11-9

1976: *Johannesburg*				
Group A				
D. Mountjoy (Wal)	7	28	9	107
J. van Rensburg (S A)	5	24	16	72
R. Edmonds (Eng)	4	20	18	77
N. Stockman (N Z)	4	21	19	45
E. Sinclair (Sco)	4	21	21	51
P. Burke (Ire)	2	17	25	48
J. van Niekerk (S A)	1	17	27	35
P. Reynolds (Isle of Man)	1	14	27	46

	Wins	For	Agnst	Highest break
Group B				
P. Mifsud (Malta)	6	25	9	47
S. Francisco (S A)	6	27	12	68
T. Griffiths (Wal)	5	23	14	69
C. Ross (Eng)	4	19	17	58
R. Paquette (Can)	4	22	22	72
E. Swaffield (N Ire)	1	16	26	59
L. Heywood (Aust)	1	13	27	46
L. Watson (Ire)	1	9	27	45
Group C				
M. Francisco (S A)	6	27	12	62
R. Atkins (Aust)	6	25	12	45
R. Andrewartha (Eng)	5	25	14	100
J. Clint (N Ire)	4	17	18	33
L. U. Demarco (Sco)	3	21	21	75
B. Mikkelsen (Can)	3	19	22	60
K. Tristram (N Z)	1	9	27	46
R. Cowley (Isle of Man)	0	11	28	41

Elimination match: Griffiths beat Andrewartha 4(51)-0
Quarter-finals: Mountjoy beat Atkins 5(80)-1; van Rensburg beat Griffiths 5-3(52); S. Francisco beat M. Francisco 5-1; Mifsud beat Edmonds 5-1
Semi-finals: Mountjoy beat S. Francisco 8(51)-2; Mifsud beat van Rensburg 8(50)-4
Final: Mountjoy beat Mifsud 11(62, 79)-1

1978: *Malta*

	Wins	For	Agnst	Highest break
Group A				
K. Burles (Aust)	6	26	10	69
P. Mifsud (Malta)	6	26	10	62
J. Johnson (Eng)	5	23	9	101
J. Donnelly (Sco)	5	20	13	78
D. McVeigh (N Ire)	2	15	20	56
P. Reynolds (Isle of Man)	2	10	22	45
V. Cremona (Malta)	2	9	25	–
M. Mohideen (Sri Lanka)	0	8	28	–
Group B				
A. Lloyd (Wal)	6	26	12	65
K. Stevens (Can)	5	23	16	94
J. Grech (Malta)	4	23	16	63
E. Hughes (Ire)	4	23	21	56
M. J. M. Lafir (Sri Lanka)	3	19	20	50
D. Meredith (N Z)	3	18	20	81
S. Shroff (Ind)	2	14	23	39
L. McCann (N Ire)	1	10	27	40
Group C				
C. Wilson (Wal)	8	32	10	66
R. Paquette (Can)	5	24	14	81
D. Kwok (N Z)	5	23	20	49
A. Savur (Ind)	5	26	22	56
I. Williamson (Eng)	3	22	24	52
R. Atkins (Aust)	3	21	24	49
R. Miller (Sco)	3	18	24	48
A. Borg (Malta)	2	15	27	44
C. Cooper (Isle of Man)	2	13	29	33

Elimination match: Grech beat Kwok 4-0(35)
Quarter-finals: Burles beat Paquette 5(46)-4(47); Stevens beat Mifsud 5(36)-0; Johnson beat Lloyd 5(72)-0; Wilson beat Grech 5(49)-4
Semi-finals: Johnson beat Burles 8(85)-4(47); Wilson beat Stevens 8(64)-2(81)
Final: Wilson beat Johnson 11(87)-5(66)

1980: *Launceston*

	Wins	For	Agnst	Highest break
Group A				
J. White (Eng)	6	24	9	99
A. Savur (Ind)	4	20	11	67
E. Hughes (Ire)	4	21	13	127

	Wins	For	Agnst	Highest break
J. Grech (Malta)	3	19	18	80
L. Adams (N Z)	3	15	18	54
Loo Yap Long (Singapore)	1	6	23	57
R. Burke (N Ire)	0	11	24	50
Group B				
J. Giannaros (Aust)	6	24	11	54
S. Newbury (Wal)	4	20	14	100
R. Paquette (Can)	4	20	15	90
D. Meredith (N Z)	4	20	16	67
G. Parikh (Ind)	2	17	18	46
S. Clarke (N Ire)	1	10	22	44
Lau Weng Yew (Singapore)	0	8	24	36
Group C				
P. Mifsud (Malta)	6	24	3	77
R. Atkins (Aust)	4	19	15	67
J. Bonner (Aust)	4	17	17	53
W. King (Aust)	3	19	15	57
E. McLaughlin (Sco)	3	16	16	67
J. O'Boye (Eng)	1	14	21	98
S. Padayachi (Fiji)	0	2	24	40
Group D				
A. Lloyd (Wal)	6	24	4	47
J. Campbell (Aust)	5	22	8	84
D. Sheehan (Ire)	4	17	14	69
M. Gibson (Sco)	3	16	20	80
H. Boteju (Sri Lanka)	2	16	20	45
P. Reynolds (Isle of Man)	1	11	23	35
W. Barrie (Aust)	0	7	24	39

Quarter-finals: Savur beat Lloyd 5(54)-3; Atkins beat Giannaros 5(53)-3(82); Mifsud beat Campbell 5(63)-3; White beat Newbury 5(44)-4(70)
Semi-finals: Atkins beat Savur 8(46)-6; White beat Mifsud 8(100)-6(83)
Final: White beat Atkins 11(80, 101)-2(60)

WORLD AMATEUR CHAMPIONSHIP RECORDS

Billiards

T. Cleary (Aust)	682 (2 pots)	1954	M. Ferreira (Ind)	467 (3 pots)	1979
M. J. M. Lafir (Sri Lanka)	859 (5 pots)	1973	**Snooker**		
			E. Hughes (Ire)	127	1980

THE WOMEN'S GAME

The Women's Billiards Association (later Billiards and Snooker Association) founded in 1931, has been responsible for the Women's Amateur Billiards Championship since 1931 and Snooker Championship since 1933.

The association fell on hard times in the late sixties and early seventies but was spectacularly revived by Wally West, a well known London amateur, who became secretary in 1978. Given a free hand, he employed his entrepreneurial talents to secure a variety of sponsors for the tournament circuit he built up, culminating in the Women's World Open, first sponsored by Guinness in 1980.

Women's standards have been and to some extent still are affected by restricted opportunities. In the game's early days, it was socially unthinkable for a woman to play in a public saloon and most clubs were likewise implacably male bastions though in the kind of socially privileged homes spacious enough to accommodate a billiard room, a degree of cuemanship was regarded as an acceptable feminine social grace.

A few women nevertheless did play in public. Ruby Roberts, a niece of the Australian Charles Memmott, could make century breaks and John Roberts Jnr toured at one time with Madam Strebor, a less curiously named lady if one discerns that, backwards, it spells 'Roberts'. Eva Collins, daughter of the 19th-century professional George Collins and sister of Frank, who refereed at Burroughes and Watts, Soho Square until well into his eighties, was a well known coach.

The Women's Professional Billiards Championship, instituted in 1930, was won seven times by Joyce Gardner, once by Ruth Harrison and on the four occasions it was last staged by Thelma Carpenter. It has not been contested since 1950. With the abolition of any distinction between amateurs and professionals within the women's game it seems unlikely that it will ever be contested again.

Miss Gardner, born in Gloucester but a Londoner

Thelma Carpenter (in play) and Ruth Harrison, the two outstanding pre-war lady professionals.

by adoption, made a break of 96 in the 1930 championship which was the first certificated women's record. It was superseded by Margaret Lennan, a Scot, with 176 in 1931 and Miss Harrison, a Tynesider, with 197 in the 1937 women's championship, still the women's world record.

Miss Gardner, a gifted auctioneer and commere, fulfilled exhibition engagements in her youth with Tom Reece and Tom Newman and toured extensively for charity until the late seventies, playing at one time or another with all the leading male professionals. Her lifetime best breaks in public were 318 at billiards and 82 at snooker.

Miss Carpenter, whose father kept the Solent Cliffs Hotel, Bournemouth, a favourite haunt of professionals, retired after her marriage, having also won the Women's Professional Snooker Championship in 1950, the last time it was held, though Miss Harrison, with eight title successes, was by far the most successful exponent of the 22 ball game in her day.

The 1949 winner, Agnes Morris, learnt to play in the one table billiard hall started by her father in Ammanford with his miner's disability pension. She retired from the game for almost 30 years but returned as Mrs Davies to win the women's title (amateur/professional distinctions having been abolished in the interim) in 1978. She scored other notable successes on the expanding women's circuit of the late seventies and was losing finalist in the Guinness Women's World Open in May 1980.

Among the outstanding women's champions, Maureen Baynton (née Barrett) won eight snooker titles between 1954 and 1968 and seven billiards titles between 1955 and 1980. She would have assuredly won more if she had not retired from competitive play for several years.

Vera Selby, who captains a men's team in the Gateshead League, won eight billiards and five snooker titles and also the Embassy Women's World Open Snooker Championship at Middlesbrough in 1976 which was run in conjunction with the men's World Professional Championship. Though that sponsorship, which included a £500 first prize, was not repeated, it broke new ground in bringing together an international field in the women's game for the first time with Australian, Canadian and Irish as well as British competitors. The event also broached the need to differentiate between British women's champions and world champions who had hitherto, in default of any other arrangements, been regarded as synonymous. Mrs Selby regained the

Women's World Open Championship in 1981.

Two recent British champions, Ann Johnson and Susan Foster, came through fields growing both in quality and numbers while standards also improved strikingly in both Australia, where a national championship involving all state champions was inaugurated in 1976, and Canada, where women were encouraged to play in public halls.

The Australian Championship was dominated by

Lesley McIlrath, Guinness Women's World Open Snooker champion 1980.

Vera Selby (*left*), champion, and Mandy Fisher, runner-up, in the Guinness Women's World Open Snooker Championship, 1981.

first ever half century by a woman in competition, in winning her sixth Canadian Women's title.

Quarter-finals: Sue Foster (Eng) beat Lesley McIlrath (Aust) 3-2; Mandy Fisher (Eng) beat Ann Johnson (Eng) 3-1; Fran Lovis (Aust) beat Natalie Stelmach (Can) 3-1; Vera Selby (Eng) beat Mary Ann McConnell (Can) 3-0; *Semi-finals*: Fisher beat Lovis 3-1; Selby beat Foster 3-0; *Final*: Selby beat Fisher 3-0.

Mrs Selby took £2000, a new record prize for the women's game, and Miss Fisher £1000.

Fran Lovis, champion from 1976 to 1980 and Lesley McIlrath and the Canadian scene by Natalie Stelmach, who won the women's section of the Canadian Open from 1977 to 1979. In a practice frame Miss Stelmach recorded a century break, far above standards reached in the competition and in winning her fifth Canadian title in 1981 a break of 56, the first ever half century by a woman in competition.

In an entry of 46 for the inaugural Guinness World Open at Warners Sinah Warren Holiday Camp, Hayling Island, in May 1980 there were three English, one Welsh, two Australian and two Canadian quarter-finalists.

The latter stages of the event resulted thus: *Quarter finals*: Ann Johnson (Eng) beat Vera Selby (Eng) 3-2; Lesley McIlrath (Aust) beat Mary Ann McConnell (Can) 3-1; Agnes Davies (Wal) beat Fran Lovis (Aust) 3-2; Natalie Stelmach (Can) beat Susan Foster (Eng) 3-2; *Semi-finals*: McIlrath beat Johnson 3-1; Davies beat Stelmach 3-0; *Final*: McIlrath beat Davies 4-2.

Miss McIlrath's £700 first prize was a record for the women's game. Mrs Davies took £350 as runner-up.

The 1981 Guinness Women's World Open at Thorness Bay, Isle of Wight saw Mrs Selby's cool temperament, sure grasp of tactics and safety play overcome technically more gifted players as she went through the championship without losing a frame. Mandy Fisher, 19, impressed with her crisp, stylish game in reaching the final.

Miss Stelmach, who again lost in the quarter finals, had a few weeks previously made a break of 56, the

WOMEN'S PROFESSIONAL BILLIARDS CHAMPIONSHIP

Year	Champion	Year	Champion
1931	Joyce Gardner	1938	Joyce Gardner
1932	Joyce Gardner	1939	Ruth Harrison
1933	Joyce Gardner	1940	Thelma Carpenter
1934	Ruth Harrison	1941-48	No contests
1935	Joyce Gardner	1949	Thelma Carpenter
1936	Joyce Gardner	1950	Thelma Carpenter
1937	Joyce Gardner		

WOMEN'S PROFESSIONAL SNOOKER CHAMPIONSHIP

Year	Champion	Year	Champion
1934	Ruth Harrison	1939	Ruth Harrison
1935	Ruth Harrison	1940	Ruth Harrison
1936	Ruth Harrison	1948	Ruth Harrison
1937	Ruth Harrison	1949	Agnes Morris
1938	Ruth Harrison	1950	Thelma Carpenter

WOMEN'S AMATEUR BILLIARDS CHAMPIONSHIP

Year	Champion	Year	Champion
1931	R. Harrison	1959	M. Hazeldine
1932	T. Carpenter	1960	M. Barrett
1933	T. Carpenter	1961	No contest
1934	T. Carpenter	1962	T. Hindmarch
1935	V. Seals	1963	S. Isaacs
1936	V. Seals	1964	M. Baynton (née Barrett)
1937	G. Phillips	1965	V. Youle
1938	V. McDougall	1966	M. Baynton
1939	V. McDougall	1967	T. Hindmarch
1940-46	No contests	1968	M. Baynton
1947	S. Isaacs	1969	T. Hindmarch
1948	E. Morland Smith	1970	V. Selby
1949	M. Keeton	1971	V. Selby
1950	H. Futo	1972	V. Selby
1951	No contest	1973	V. Selby
1952	E. Morland Smith	1974	V. Selby
1953	E. Morland Smith	1975	No contest
1954	H. Futo	1976	V. Selby
1955	M. Barrett	1977	V. Selby
1956	M. Barrett	1978	V. Selby
1957	No contest	1979	M. Baynton
1958	No contest	1980	No contest

WOMEN'S AMATEUR SNOOKER CHAMPIONSHIP

Year	Champion	Year	Champion
1933	M. Quinn	1961	M. Barrett
1934	E. Morris	1962	M. Baynton
1935	M. Hill		(née Barrett)
1936	V. Seals	1963	R. Holmes
1937	E. Morland Smith	1964	M. Baynton
1938	E. Morris	1965	S. Jeffries
1939	A. Morris	1966	M. Baynton
1940-46	No contests	1967	H. Futo
1947	M. Knight	1968	M. Baynton
1948	J. Adcock	1969	R. Craven
1949	R. Davies	1970	M. Hazeldine
1950	P. Holden	1971	M. Hazeldine
1951	R. Davies	1972	V. Selby
1952	R. Davies	1973	V. Selby
1953	R. Holmes	1974	V. Selby
1954	M. Barrett	1975	V. Selby
1955	M. Barrett	1976	A. Johnson
1956	M. Barrett	1977	A. Johnson
1957	R. Holmes	1978	A. Davies
1958	R. Holmes		(née Morris)
1959	D. Thompson	1979	V. Selby
1960	M. Hazeldine	1980	S. Foster

WOMEN'S WORLD OPEN SNOOKER CHAMPIONSHIP

Year	Champion	Year	Champion
1976	V. Selby	1980	L. McIlrath
1977-79	No contests	1981	V. Selby

INDEX

159

WORLD RECORDS

BILLIARDS

There have been so many changes in billiards that any list of records requires a note stating the precise variant of the rules under which each break, aggregate or average was made. In broad terms, the stricter the limitation incorporated in the rules, the more control and skill is required to make a large break.

WORLD

Professional:	Walter Lindrum (Aust) (two pots, 15 hazards, 200 baulk line, 35 direct cannons)	4137	1932
Amateur:	M. Ferreira (India) (five pots, 15 hazards, 75 cannons)	1149	1978
	M. Ferreira (India) (three pots, 15 hazards, 75 cannons)	566	1979

NATIONAL CHAMPIONSHIPS (AMATEUR)

England	N. Dagley	862	(5 pots)
	N. Dagley	506	(3 pots)
Northern Ireland	R. Taylor	278	(2 pots)

Republic of Ireland	J. Bates	370	(2 pots)
Scotland	J. Bates	323	(2 pots)
Wales	R. Oriel	345	(5 pots)
Australia	R. Marshall	702	(2 pots)
India	M. Ferreira	1149	(5 pots)
	A. Savur	556	(3 pots)
Malta	J. Grech	567	(5 pots)
New Zealand	B. Kirkness	326	(5 pots)
South Africa	M. Francisco	433	(15 pots)
Sri Lanka	M. J. M. Lafir	500	(5 pots)

In all the above breaks, the 15 hazard rule applied. There were some variations in the cannon limitations but since none of these breaks were made with the aid of lengthy cannon sequences this had no effect on the size of the breaks.

Ferreira's 566 break was made in the Islam Gymkhana Open in 1979.

SNOOKER

WORLD

Professional:	Joe Davis (Eng)	147	1955
	Rex Williams (Eng)	147	1965
Amateur:	J. Johnson (Eng)	140	1978

NATIONAL (AMATEUR)

England	B. Harris	123
Northern Ireland	N. Gill	87
Republic of Ireland	P. Morgan	89
Scotland	E. Sinclair	91
Wales	A. Chappell	123
Australia	M. Williams, J. Campbell	101
India	S. Shroff	98
Malta	A. Borg	108
New Zealand	G. Hayward	103
South Africa	G. Povall	106

Note: Joe Johnson's world amateur record of 140 was made in the Tyne Tees television tournament of 1978. There have been many breaks in excess of national championship records recorded in non-championship events.

To be accepted for world record purposes a break must have been made (a) on a standard size table on which the pocket openings conform to the approved templates; (b) in a match to which members of the public are admitted; and (c) with a qualified referee officiating.

PHOTOGRAPH ACKNOWLEDGEMENTS

All Sport/Don Morley: 130 (bottom), 148 (centre left). Central Press: 27, 36-7, 38, 39, 42-3, 45, 55, 112, 126, 131, 133. Norman Clare: 141. *Evening Mail,* Birmingham: 74-5. Hulton Picture Library: 12, 13, 24, 40-41, 47, 64, 110 (inset), 111, 154. Chris Marks: 77, 82-3. Marshall's Sport Service: 105, 156. Mary Evans Picture Library: 11, 24-5, 129 (bottom left and right). Dave Muscroft: 9, 62, 65, 66, 68, 69, 70, 72-3, 74, 76 (top), 79, 80, 81, 83, 84, 85, 86-7, 88, 115 (bottom), 122, 129 (top left), 130 (top), 147, 148 (top and bottom). *Snooker Scene*: 76 (bottom), 78, 106, 113 (top), 115 (top), 123, 124, 127, 134, 134-35, 136-37, 139, 140, 142-43. Neil Wigley: 14-21, 26, 33, 35, 71.